# ENERGY AND ENVIRONMENT:
## A COLLISION OF CRISES

# ENERGY AND ENVIRONMENT: A COLLISION OF CRISES

Introduction by Russell E. Train
Edited by Irwin Goodwin

The Washington Journalism Center
CRITICAL ISSUES SERIES

WJC

## PUBLISHING SCIENCES GROUP, INC.
### ACTON, MASSACHUSETTS

*We travel together, passengers on a little space ship; dependent on its vulnerable reserve of air and soil; all committed for our safety to its security and peace; preserved from annihilation only by the care, the work, and the love we give our craft.*

— Adlai Stevenson

**About the Editor:** While serving as a correspondent and editor for *Newsweek,* Irwin Goodwin gained a firsthand knowledge of the interrelationship between energy and environment. He was among the first to sound the warnings of Nobel Laureate Hermann J. Muller against the potential hazards of nuclear radiation. He reported the "spontaneous" overheating of Windscale No. 1, the nuclear power station that spewed radioactivity over Britain in 1957. He witnessed the breaking up in 1967 of the *Torrey Canyon,* the tanker that dumped 119,000 tons of crude oil onto the beaches of England and France. A life member of the American Association for the Advancement of Science, he has also worked for Science Research Associates in Chicago and the Smithsonian Institution in Washington, D.C.

Printed in the United States of America.

International Standard Book Number: 0-88416-001-7

Library of Congress Catalog Card Number 73-84166

# FOREWORD

■ For many Americans the first warning came suddenly and chillingly. As night fell on November 9, 1965, and the surge of electrical voltage increased to meet "peak load," power fizzled and lights blinked out from Ontario, Canada, through the villages of New England, across metropolitan New York, and into Pennsylvania and Ohio. During the next thirteen hours of the Big Blackout, some 30 million inhabitants of eight northeastern states received a classic lesson in America's dependence on energy. It was the Great Energy Awakening.

A little more than three years later came the Great Ecological Awakening. On January 28, 1969, a massive outpouring of natural gas and oil roiled up in the Santa Barbara Channel where riggers were changing a bit to drill 700 feet down. In the next eleven days, the offshore well spouted more than 400,000 gallons of crude oil, defiling 40 miles of some of California's most exclusive and expensive beaches, decimating sea life and shore birds by the thousands, and destroying rookeries of the sea elephant, the Guadalupe fur seal, and the rare sea otter.

The two events dramatized an inevitable conflict between the nation's insatiable demand for power and its insistence on a clean environment. In the years since, with the country's sources of energy dwindling and its environment still under assault, that conflict has become, truly, a collision of crises.

It is a collision that no American can ignore — not if he expects his children and grandchildren to enjoy the conveniences of "modern" living on a viable planet. As Ali B. Cambel of Detroit's Wayne State University has observed, energy is the Dr. Faustus of the age. At the beginning of the Industrial Revolution, man unconsciously but decisively struck a Faustian bargain, trading off an elemental Arcadian environment for a technological Golden Age.

The United States, which only yesterday thought itself so rich in energy resources that it could afford the luxury of limiting oil imports and encouraging lavish use of power, is waking up to the grim reality of shortages, higher prices, and fuel imports that adversely affect our balance of payments.

Incredible as it seems, the United States, with less than 6% of the world's population, consumes 34% of the world's energy. Per capita consumption, increasing roughly five times as fast as population growth, is now nearly 400 million Btu's a year, doubling in the past thirty years and doubling again, experts predict, in the next thirty years.

It is understandable that energy policy has become the focus of congressional hearings, scientific conferences and special studies like that of the Ford Foundation's Energy Policy Project. In numerous speeches, articles, and books, frightening scenarios of economic collapse and environmental catastrophe have been advanced — if the United States limits the production of energy or ignores the preservation of nature. President Nixon, in a three-month period of 1973, delivered to Congress two special messages in which he identified energy as "one of the most critical problems on America's agenda" and proposed that $10 billion of federal funds be spent on research and development in the next five years to provide clean new energy sources. The priority given this problem recalls World War II's prodigious Manhattan Project which, for about $2 billion, produced the first atomic bombs.

In his messages (see Appendixes, page 247), Mr. Nixon, in effect, declared that the "joyride" was over, that Americans would have to learn to conserve energy, while increasing their imports of relatively clean oil and natural gas from abroad, until science and technology can come up with something better — a nuclear breeder reactor, solar energy, fusion, or some more exotic source of power. To help coordinate research and development activities, now fragmented and often conflicting, President Nixon named Colorado Governor John A. Love to head a new White House Energy Policy Office, proposed an Energy Research and Development Council to provide technical advice and direction to energy programs, and urged creation of a cabinet-level Department of Energy and Natural Resources. The new department would gather together components from thirty-four separate departments and agencies, including the Atomic Energy Commission.

Senator Henry M. Jackson, chairman of the Senate Interior Committee, criticized Mr. Nixon's program for putting too little emphasis on conservation. "The Administration appears to be taking the 'quick-fix' approach to energy conservation," he said, "emphasizing short-term voluntary measures to reduce shortages rather than serious Federal efforts to change the basic patterns of energy use. For a nation that is consuming one-third of the world's energy supplies, that is not good enough."

To assay whether America's efforts in the energy-environment field are "good enough," the Washington Journalism Center assembled eighteen of the nation's leading experts and twenty-two seasoned journalists in April 1973 for a four-day conference on "The Energy Crisis—and the Environment." Their discussions, which follow in edited form, provide a thorough and thoughtful examination of these interwoven problems and their implications for such vital national concerns as foreign policy, trade balances, industrial development, and public health—the very quality of life in the United States.

Such in-depth discussions, as an aid to better reporting, are what the late Willard M. Kiplinger had in mind when he established the Washington Journalism Center in 1965. In the past two years, the Center has held thirteen conferences on such critical issues as health care, welfare, crime, tax reform, and foreign policy.

The publication of these proceedings was generously assisted by a grant from The Johnson Foundation of Racine, Wisconsin.

Alexandria, Va., July 30, 1973                                    Irwin Goodwin

# List of Figures

1   U.S. Energy Consumption, *page 10*
2   Growth Rate of Electrical Consumption, *page 11*
3   Per Capita Income and Energy Consumption, 1968, *page 14*
4   Air Pollutant Emissions, 1970, *page 32*
5   Gaseous Air Pollutant Levels, Selected Cities, 1968, *page 32*
6   Sources of Radiation, *page 35*
7   World Primary Energy Consumption, *page 50*
8   Primary Energy Consumption, 1950–1972, *page 51*
9   World Oil Consumption, *page 52*
10  Petroleum's Share of Energy Consumption, *page 52*
11  World Oil Production, *page 53*
12  Total Discovered Oil, *page 53*
13  Oil Imports and Exports, 1962 and 1972, *page 55*
14  Energy Used in Transportation, *page 69*
15  Energy and Price Data for Passenger Transport, *page 69*
16  Major Components of U.S. Energy Consumption, *page 70*
17  World "Published Proved" Oil Reserves at End of 1972, *page 110*
18  If Domestic Sources Were Fully Developed, *page 122*
19  Phases in Achieving LMFBR Program Objectives, *page 179*
20  Steps in the Supply of Atomic Fuel—Light Water Cycle, *page 180*
21  U.S. Total Energy Requirements, *page 181*
22  Size Trend of U.S. Steam Electric Power Units, *page 184*
23  U.S. Central Station Nuclear Power Plants, *page 185*
24  Four Major Types of Reactors in U.S., *pages 190–191*
25  Constituents of Nuclear Facility Safety, Economics, and Reliability, *page 192*
26  Safety—Order of Approach, *page 196*
27  Federal Funds for Pollution Control and Abatement, *page 222*

# Contents

INTRODUCTION 1
Russell E. Train

PART ONE

**THE POWER SHOCK**

1 The Energy Crisis: Is It Real? 9
S. David Freeman

2 The Environment: When Is Doomsday? 31
Dean E. Abrahamson

3 The Global Energy-Environment Problem 49
Charles A. Zraket

4 How Much Energy Do We Waste? 67
Harry Perry

5 A Consumer's Slant on the Energy Crisis 79
Lee C. White

PART TWO

**THE SECURITY FACTOR**

6 The Oil Industry and the Energy Environment Problem 93
Frank N. Ikard

7 Cartels and the Threat of Monopoly 105
Morris A. Adelman

8 Energy and Foreign Policy: How Dependent Must We Be? 117
Lawrence Rocks and Richard P. Runyon

PART THREE      THE CONSERVATION POTENTIAL

  9  Can Fossil Fuels Be Cleaned Up?  129
      George R. Hill

10  Are Antipollution Laws Working?  141
      William F. Pedersen, Jr.

11  Are Antipollution Laws Widening the Energy Gap?  155
      Bruce C. Netschert

12  Can Resources From Public Lands Be Developed in
      Environmentally Acceptable Ways?  167
      Stephen A. Wakefield


PART FOUR      THE SURVIVAL STRATEGY

13  Is Atomic Power the Answer?  177
      Milton Shaw

14  Fuels for the Future  201
      Richard E. Balzhiser

15  Who Should Pay for Clean Energy Research?  215
      Stephen J. Gage

16  Reconciling Our Energy and Environmental Demands  229
      Charles J. DiBona

17  Is a National Energy-Environment Policy Possible?  237
      Henry M. Jackson


     APPENDIX A, The President's Energy Message
to Congress  247

     APPENDIX B, The President's Energy Statement  265

# INTRODUCTION
## Russell E. Train

*A lawyer by education and experience,
Russell E. Train has the distinction of
having held the two top environmental
jobs in the Nixon administration. From
1970 to 1973, he was the first chairman of
the Council on Environmental Quality and
then, in July 1973, he was named administrator of the Environmental Protection
Agency. Before turning to conservation
work, Mr. Train served as an attorney on
the staff of the Joint Congressional Committee on Internal Revenue Taxation, as
head of the Treasury's legal staff, and as a
judge on the United States Tax Court. He
has also served as undersecretary of the
Department of the Interior, as president of
the Conservation Foundation and African
Wildlife Foundation, and as vice president
of the World Wildlife Fund.*

■ We face a wide variety of energy problems. There are short-term problems of adequate gasoline and fuel oil supplies and electrical generating capacity. There are long-term problems of securing supplies of crude oil and achieving major technological advances such as the breeder reactor and coal gasification. There are also a variety of environmental problems associated with the exploitation of energy resources and the conversion of those resources to useful forms of power.

Both sets of problems are serious and real. Neither set of problems will go away simply by wishing or ignoring. Those who call for "more energy now, damn the environment" ill serve the country, their companies, and con-stituents. Those who try to stop or delay every energy project in their own backyard ill serve the interests of our common possession, the environment.

We need balance and restraint—by both environmentalists and industrialists—as we pursue both objectives as matters of high priority national interest. Confrontation can only lead to polarization and irrational responses from all sides. We need to keep the problems in proper perspective. Above all, we need full disclosure of all the facts and the broadest possible public understanding of the issues.

We must reconcile the often diverging goals of adequate energy and a cleaner environment. The industrialist or engineer who plans a new energy development or builds a new plant should know what the total impact of that action will be on the human environment. The biologist or lawyer who intervenes in that project should know how it fits into the region's energy supply patterns and whether there are really acceptable alternatives. Innovative solutions can be found for the toughest problems, I believe, if all the dimensions of the problems are adequately understood. As Coleridge wrote, "Imagination reveals itself in the balance or reconciliation of opposite or discordant qualities."

The Council on Environmental Quality is deeply concerned about the impact of the total energy system on the quality of life. It is axiomatic that the exploitation of any energy resource inevitably leads to some environmental damages. However, in reaching our decisions on the use of energy or the development of energy resources, we have not reflected a keen understanding of the specific environmental penalties that each decision forces us to incur. For example, the construction of a power plant which will use coal, oil, natural gas, or nuclear energy usually reflects consideration for the environmental impacts at the power plant site but rarely reflects concern for the environmental impacts of obtaining the fuel.

Generally, we have failed to look systematically at the totality of environmental impacts caused by a single decision. We have considered only the direct environmental implications of each decision. The council finds that this myopic approach is not good enough and has undertaken an extensive effort to determine the environmental consequences of energy systems—from extraction to consumption.

As a first step, CEQ recently issued a report that quantifies the specific environmental impacts derived from the production and use of electricity—not just at the power plant, but at the mine, the oil well, the pipeline, the tanker, the refinery, and the transmission line. The report quantifies the environmental effects of electric energy systems with today's minimal or presently prevailing environmental controls and looks at the economic costs and environmental gains that result from the use of controls that are now, or soon will be, available. However, the report is concerned not only with the costs and effects of sulfur oxide and with particulate and thermal discharge controls at the power plant but also with the results of improved strip-mine reclamation, better controlled refineries, and cleaner tankers.

By looking at the entire electric energy system—from the point of energy extraction to the delivery of electricity to the consumer—we will be able to assess more effectively the environmental implications of specific electric energy decisions. Further, as we broaden our studies, we will be able to extend our assessments to other energy systems as well. Through the knowledge and experience gained in this and numerous other efforts, the council is in an excellent position to sort out the facts from the myths in dealing with the trade-offs between energy and environmental concerns.

I would like to present several short case studies to illustrate my point on the need for accommodation between energy and environmental goals. These examples will more than amply demonstrate that neither side possesses the whole truth. Strong interest, somewhat resembling a new "gold rush," is now focused on the potential of the West's low-sulfur coal reserves to satisfy power plant needs. Part of the reason for this interest is the stringent air quality control regulations which will be required in order to meet the standards of the Clean Air Act in many heavily industrialized cities of the Midwest. Another reason is that this coal, located primarily in Wyoming and Montana, is found in seams 75 to 100 feet thick as opposed to the typical 3- to 4-foot seam in Appalachia; also, it is relatively inexpensive to extract by strip mining.

The council, in fulfilling its responsibilities to help coordinate programs and actions of federal agencies which affect, protect, or improve environmental quality, has been investigating the implications of these developments. The situation is a classic equation for balancing the social benefit and environmental protection for one region against the economic reward and environmental damage to another region. Put epigrammatically, the equation could read: Strip mining in Colorado equals air conditioning in Chicago.

The use of western low-sulfur coal in midwestern power plants will reduce sulfur oxide emissions and, if precipitators can be modified to handle ash and dust, will not significantly increase particulate emissions. While the additional land disturbed in the western coal fields would be significant, it would be much smaller in area than the amount of midwest land which would otherwise have to be mined to provide the same amount of coal.

The potential impact on the western lands might, however, be much more severe. Although revegetation is not inherently difficult in most parts of Appalachia and in the central coal region—both have adequate rainfall and sufficient topsoil—there are unanswered questions about the extent to which lands can be revegetated in the Far West, where there is little rainfall and often poor topsoil. In some areas, little or no vegetation may exist under normal circumstances. The largest stripable coal reserves lie in the Fort Union formation of Montana and Wyoming, where the rainfall is fourteen to sixteen inches per year compared with an average annual rainfall of forty to forty-five inches in Appalachia.

In the Southwest region, embracing New Mexico, Arizona, Utah, Nevada, and Colorado, conditions are arid, with less than five inches of rain, and the surface soil is usually alkaline. Experimental reclamation projects in these arid regions are meeting with mixed results and none of the projects has been conducted for an adequate time to demonstrate whether or not revegetation will be successful.

A second case study is the Alaska pipeline. While the pipeline may not have been a tidy example of the judicial process, it has been an excellent example of where the National Environmental Protection Act (NEPA) and the courts have forced the reconciliation of environmental concerns, with sound engineering practices, on a major energy project. To some, any delay in the completion of the pipeline is considered unreasonable. Still, as it happens, much of the delay has been beneficial. The problems of constructing a hot oil pipeline across permafrost in one of the most seismically active and remote areas of the world are very real. These and other significant complications simply were not adequately faced when the initial proposal was presented to the Department of the Interior in 1969. If the pipeline had been constructed using the original design specifications, it would very likely have resulted in not only very serious environmental damage but also serious operational problems. The physical integrity of the pipeline was at stake.

The case of the trans-Alaska pipeline has not been simply one of aesthetics or of concern over wildlife and wilderness disturbance or of worries over water pollution, important as all of these are. It has been a clear example emphasizing where and when sound environmental analysis is essential to sound engineering and siting. It involved a learning process for both industry and government. Industry seriously underestimated the technical difficulties of the task and failed to appreciate fully—particularly at the outset—the new conditions for decision-making in matters that substantially affect the environment. For its part, government was ill-equipped both institutionally and informationally for dealing with the complex problems of the pipeline. Few would now contend that the first response of the Department of the Interior to NEPA on the right-of-way application for the pipeline was really adequate.

While another case, the eight-month legal delay in the department's offshore oil leasing program in the Gulf of Mexico, is often cited as an example of unreasonable obstructionism on the part of environmentalists, it was actually the result of Interior's initial refusal to acknowledge its full responsibilities under NEPA. For NEPA requires an agency to identify and analyze the available alternatives to its proposed course of action. In this case, however, despite strong advice from the CEQ and others to the contrary, the Department of the Interior addressed this statutory obligation in its environmental impact statement by simply listing in one sentence, without discussion, all conceivable alternative energy sources ranging from imported oil to solar energy—hardly the kind of analysis of alternatives contemplated by the statute. This situation has since been corrected. Subsequently, leasings have been accompanied by impact statements which respond to the hard questions required under NEPA.

There are exceptions. I would be less than candid not to point out that there have been long delays in the issuance of final impact statements on two energy programs of considerable interest in the West—the leasing of geothermal and oil shale lands. While the draft statement on geothermal leasing was issued in September 1971 and the statement on oil shale in September 1972, neither has been issued in final form by the Department of the Interior. The delays, moreover, are not attributable to obstruction by environmentalists. Nor should the Department of the Interior be singled out for criticism. The Federal Power Commission's NEPA procedures were declared inadequate last October in a legal action *(Greene County Planning Board* v. *FPC)*. The Atomic Energy Commission has decided not to appeal a court decision on the liquid-metal fast-breeder reactor (LMFBR) program and, instead, will prepare an impact statement on it.

In doing its part to balance energy and environmental needs, the council is continuing to flag emerging issues, particularly in the energy field. Illustrative of these are studies on supertanker ports, oil and gas development on the Outer Continental Shelf of the Atlantic Ocean and Gulf of Alaska, and energy conservation. The nation's growing demand for energy requires significant increases in oil imports, production from the shelf, and vigorous attempts to conserve resources by reducing demand.

The council's efforts to assess the environmental implications of supertankers and superports have already had implications for national policy. Our preliminary results served as the basis for the administration's recent bill to require the licensing of deepwater ports on the Outer Continental Shelf. The study revealed that the use of properly regulated supertankers and superports could result in 90% less oil spillage than the use of smaller tankers. These findings certainly have important implications for the transportation of oil from Alaska to West Coast ports as well as from the Persian Gulf to our East and Gulf coasts.

The council is using many of the same techniques developed for the superport study in the environmental assessment of oil and gas production in the Atlantic and Gulf of Alaska, as requested by the president. In addition to the questions of oil transportation and shoreside development related to production in the Outer Continental Shelf, the study will examine the environmental hazards associated with well drilling, operating, and accidents.

Equally significant, the council has worked for an awareness throughout the federal government of the need for energy conservation and has sponsored federal initiatives to reduce energy consumption everywhere. As a result, home insulation standards have been strengthened, an energy efficiency labeling program has been established, and energy conservation is being designed into federal buildings.

But there is more to be done. Energy conservation will require the personal commitment of individual Americans. Foregoing the relatively greater luxury of a large automobile in favor of a compact car gives personal meaning to the "energy crisis." There is, in fact, no better way for the average American to make his contribution to reducing the nation's voracious appetite for gasoline. As the weight of a car is reduced from 4,000 pounds to 3,000 pounds, the gas mileage can increase from 11.2 to 16.2 miles per gallon—an improvement of 45%.

There are many other steps we can take: requiring homes and offices to conserve energy, buying appliances which are more efficient, joining car pools, or using public transportation.

The reconciliation between meeting our national energy needs and achieving our environmental goals must be sought not only at each governmental level but also at the personal level. We must, in short, reorient our thinking about energy and its role in the environment. Even as we look for much needed energy supplies today, we must shift our efforts to learning how to use energy to meet our many needs in ways which are more in harmony with the environment.

# PART ONE

# THE POWER SHOCK

# The Authors

### S. David Freeman
*The Energy Crisis: Is It Real?*

Mr. Freeman is director of the Ford Foundation's $3.5 million Energy Policy Project. Before this, from 1967 to 1971, he headed the Energy Policy Staff in the Office of Science and Technology for Presidents Johnson and Nixon. As a civil engineer, he designed hydroelectric stations and conventional electric power plants at TVA and later served as a TVA attorney. From 1961 to 1965, Mr. Freeman was also assistant to the chairman of the Federal Power Commission.

### Dean E. Abrahamson
*The Environment: When Is Doomsday?*

Both a physicist and a physician, Dr. Abrahamson is director of the Center-for Studies of the Physical Environment at the University of Minnesota's Institute of Technology and is chairman of the All-University Council of Environmental Quality. He took a leading role in the environmental battle that forced the Northern States Power Co. and the AEC to reduce the radiation emissions for the nuclear power station on the upper Mississippi River and in 1971 challenged the AEC's entire breeder reactor program.

### Charles A. Zraket
*The Global Energy-Environment Problem*

Senior vice president of The Mitre Corporation, Mr. Zraket directs the company's systems engineering and research work for the federal government in such areas as energy and resources, environmental monitoring and controls, health care and transportation. Before joining Mitre he worked at M.I.T.'s Lincoln Laboratory in computer research and was a consultant to President Nixon's Scientific Advisory Committee.

### Harry Perry
*How Much Energy Do We Waste?*

Mr. Perry, now a consultant to Resources for the Future, was for many years one of the federal government's principal experts on energy and environment matters. He spent most of his career with the Bureau of Mines, where he was director of Coal Research. He also has been an energy specialist with the Organization for Economic Cooperation and Development (OECD) in Paris and with the Library of Congress.

### Lee C. White
*A Consumer's Slant on the Energy Crisis*

Recently named chairman of an Energy Policy Task Force established by the Consumer Federation of America, Mr. White, who holds degrees in law and electrical engineering, worked as a lawyer at TVA until he joined the staff of then Senator John F. Kennedy as a legislative aide. Mr. White has served as assistant special counsel to President Kennedy and special counsel to President Johnson, who named him chairman of the Federal Power Commission, a post he held from 1966 to 1969.

# Chapter 1
S. David Freeman

# The Energy Crisis: Is It Real?

In the early 1960s, I helped write the Federal Power Commission's *National Power Survey,* which was an attempt to promote a practical energy policy for the United States. It advocated an enormous expansion of electric power as a way of achieving the "good life." By common agreement between private utilities and public authorities, the growth and development of the power industry was considered inseparable from the growth and development of the American economy. "One nourishes the other," we stated with absolute confidence in the FPC report. (See Figures 1 and 2.)

That was 1964. Since then my view has changed considerably, because the situation has changed considerably. As we learn more about power production and its environmental effects, I think we Americans are reassessing our basic beliefs, traditional habits, and even life-styles. By the late 1960s, the energy industry, which had done so much to expand technology and production, came under assault, and it, in turn, started to respond to the increasing outrage. Realistically and simplistically, *Americans are using up too much, consuming it too fast, and putting back little or nothing.* In short, there is not, never will be, and possibly never was anything like a free lunch in America.

It is interesting how quickly we Americans are able to pin the label of "crisis" on a plethora of problems that we don't fully understand and cannot seem to patch up, paint over, or parry aside. Only six years ago, well after the 1965 cascade failure that plunged New York City and much of New England into darkness for up to eight hours, a report published by the now defunct White House Office of Science and Technology stated emphatically that no energy supply problems would exist for the rest of this century. In fact, the report went on to say rather cheerfully, there could well be reductions in production costs and consumer prices. Indeed, this was the prevailing opinion in government and industry at the time.

## Figure 1.
## U. S. Energy Consumption

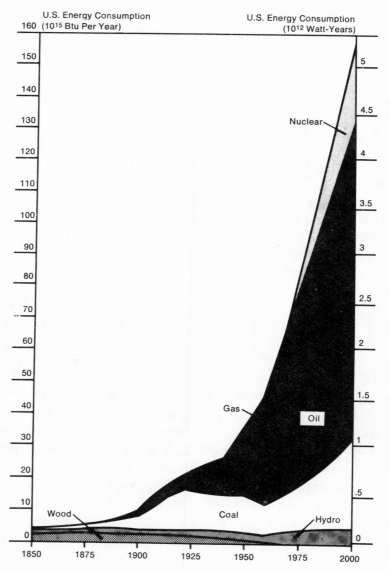

Source: Bureau of Mines, U. S. Department of the Interior.

Note: U. S. Energy Consumption: The use of energy has multiplied some thirty times since 1850, when wood provided more than 90% of all the energy consumed. By 1900 coal had superseded wood as the dominant fuel, accounting for 70% of the total. In 1950 the use of coal had dropped to 36.5%, and the use of oil and natural gas had taken precedent with 55.5% of the energy total. In 1972 oil accounted for 46% of all energy needs, natural gas 32%, coal 17%, hydropower 4% and nuclear power 1%.

Figure 2.
Growth Rate of Electrical Consumption

| Year | Population | Electrical Consumption (billion kwhrs) | Electrical Consumption Per Capita (billion kwhrs) | Average Annual Rate of Growth Per Capita |
|------|-----------|------|------|------|
| Historical | | | | |
| 1950 | 152.3 | 160 | 1,051 | |
| 1955 | 165.9 | 250 | 1,507 | 7.5 |
| 1960 | 180.7 | 370 | 2,048 | 6.3 |
| 1965 | 194.6 | 571 | 2,934 | 7.4 |
| 1970 | 204.8 | 879 | 4,292 | 7.9 |
| Forecast | | | | |
| 1975 | 216.2 | 1,242 | 5,745 | 6.0 |
| 1980 | 229.4 | 1,770 | 7,715 | 6.0 |
| 1985 | 243.3 | 2,286 | 9,395 | 4.0 |
| 2000 | 279.7 | 4,417 | 15,791 | 3.5 |

Source: U.S. Department of the Interior.

I recall going up to Capitol Hill in 1968, the last year of the Johnson administration, seeking $500,000 for a major study of our energy policy. The reaction was: "The budget is tight. This is obviously something that can wait. It is not an item of high priority." I don't think that energy was considered an important item to anyone in government outside of the Atomic Energy Commission back in 1968.

## THE PROBLEMS SURFACE

We had spent the 1960s believing that there was a virtually bottomless barrel of resources and that we would zoom through the 1970s and 1980s in overdrive. Then, in the late 1960s, the United States was hit by a double whammy. We found that the resource base that was available at prices anywhere near what we were accustomed to paying was either much smaller than we thought or not so quickly run through the production pipeline as we thought. We began to encounter some constraints in supply. At the same time, the words "pollution," "contamination," and "waste product" became part of the American vocabulary and the American ethic, and a series of environmental protection laws passed through Congress almost unanimously.

These measures were embraced by President Nixon in 1970 when he signed the Environmental Policy Act and delivered a statement beginning with "The time is now." The nation responded with laws to clean the environment and punish the polluters. Nearly all the states set up agencies, boards, and commissions to implement the federal standards or to establish their own. But we failed to give proper consideration to these laws and agencies, and, even when we did, we failed to carry out those thoughts through enforcement.

The Clean Air Act spoke of pure air, but air pollution is, with the exception perhaps of burning leaves, entirely a by-product of power consumption. We find as we try to implement the Clean Air Act that Detroit pleads, "One more year!" and the utilities cry, "We just can't do it!" So here we are, three years later, listening to scientific evidence that the quality of air we breathe is impairing our well-being.

The awful truth is that we don't possess the technology today to comply with the standards that we have set for ourselves; the awful effect is that the laws tend to constrain the production of energy we need to make the wheels turn. These constraints are superimposed upon the physical limitations of the most easily obtained fuels. We have skimmed — to mix the metaphor — the cream off our oil, gas, and coal reserves. The remaining reserves are more difficult, dangerous, and costly to obtain. Not very surprisingly, the Santa Barbara oil spill resulted in inhibiting the offering of new leases and the drilling of offshore wells. The air pollution law resulted in curtailing the supply of coal, not because it's not there but because we don't know how to mine it or burn it in ways compatible with our present environmental and social goals.

In effect, our national policy toward energy output right now is hesitant and at times stalled; it is proceeding apace with the New Deal programs of the 1930s to subsidize, promote, and even accelerate the uses of energy. We have depletion allowances and tax laws designed for many power companies to exclude the cost of government in the price of energy. We have pricing structures that call for paying less per kilowatt-hour the more kilowatts we burn, so that the biggest consumers, with the biggest discounts, have no incentive to conserve power.

It is anachronistic that the United States operates its big power machine today with one foot on the accelerator and the other on the brake. It is no wonder we encounter the fitful starts and stops, the stalls, and the scares. These are early warning signals that something is wrong with our power system.

## MULTIPLE IMPACT

We have, I think, reached a four-way intersection on what was, until a few years ago, a "joyride" to the "good life." The signposts are plain for all to read. One says price, another foreign policy, a third shortages, and the fourth environment. Price is bumpy with potholes. Until now we have enjoyed riding on low-priced energy because the price did not include the inherent costs to the physical environment, such as ravaged landscapes and fouled atmosphere. Prices will increase inexorably as the costs of reclaiming the strip mines and scrubbing the smoke fumes are included in the new rates for energy. Prices will go up further when the years of shameful neglect of research and development require us to search for additional and alternative sources of energy. There is little likelihood of increased power plant efficiency in the 1970s. The energy companies are going to bear the full brunt of inflation—something they haven't had to do in the past because of offsetting economies.

In the 1970s, therefore, energy prices will increase regardless of any efforts to hold the line. There will be sharp price rises—perhaps as steep as inflation itself, which, according to the view of academic economists, is not an increase in a real sense, but, as consumers view it, is a whopping increase compared with the rather stable energy rates of the past. As a consequence, consumers are certain to become more concerned with energy. Power boycotts may not appear as widespread as meat boycotts, but the potential of consumer resistance, rage, and perhaps backlash to yearly price increases has been grossly underestimated. I anticipate a fervid battleground at the regulatory commissions when the utilities and the consumers clash over energy rates.

We need to look at whether the regulatory process in this country is strong enough, viable enough, and responsive enough to the needs of the consumers and the industry to hold up under a period, a decade, say, of continuous price increases. I don't believe that the energy industry will go the way of the railroads—at least I hope they won't. It would be bad for the country if they did. We have yet to test this system of state commissions and cost-plus regulations, having very few incentives for efficiency and very little ability to respond to consumer concerns in a prolonged period of price increases. We have yet to realize what a very bad impact on the lower income groups massive increases in the price of energy can have. Energy represents a significant percentage of the cash budget of people at the lower end of the income scale. If we talk about major increases in the price of energy, we're talking about major hardships to one segment of our population at least. (See Figure 3.)

Foreign policy is another peril at the energy crossroads. We have succeeded so well in draining America first that we are now importing significant quantities of oil. We can foresee that in the next decade most of this country's fuel is likely to come from foreign sources. This is being decried as about

14

Figure 3.
1968 Per Capita Income and Energy Consumption

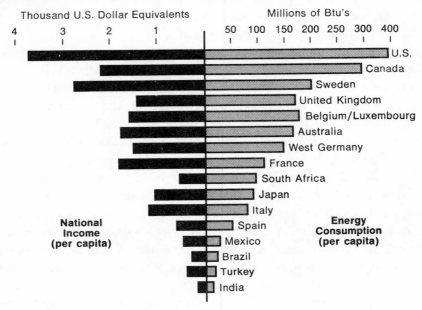

Source: U. N. Statistical Yearbook, 1970.

the worst of all news. It certainly doesn't seem to be good news. As it happens, the subject of energy policy and foreign policy is one for which we are lowest on the learning curve. I would think that there is an awful lot to be learned about both the problems and the opportunities involved in trading with other nations to obtain our energy supplies.

## PURSUING EVERY LEAD

One thing, though, is fairly clear: We can't adopt a relaxed and unrestricted policy on energy and assume that we can still ride around in large cars, burn more gasoline, travel more miles, and run more air conditioners and electric gadgets, all the while believing that there will be enough oil in the world to fuel an American future that is just a bigger version of an American past.

The growth in energy demand around the world is faster than in this country. Just as we find now that the oil fields of Texas can reach their productive limits, we will also find—in ten, fifteen, or twenty years—that the oil fields of the Middle East also have limits. The huge Middle East barrel has got a bottom. So the lead time for developing alternatives to our present consumption patterns has to be measured in decades. For that reason the future is now.

In sum, the logical conclusion is clear: *We are in the midst of an energy crisis all right.* To avoid epidemics of infectious disease, we ask our scientists to concoct a vaccine. To prevent floods, we ask our engineers to erect dams and levees and to redirect or rechannel rivers. To deal with the energy crisis, we have got to ask our scientists and engineers to provide providential solutions for clean, abundant, and cheap sources of power—to try to harness the sun, develop geothermal steam, persist in perfecting both fission and fusion processes, and invent other still unknown methods.

I do not think we can assume that there is just one option that appears so good and so clearly perfect that we can put all our eggs or money or talent in that basket. I am concerned that we seem to have only one option at the moment—the fast breeder nuclear reactor. We need a diversified research and development effort, pursuing every project that looks promising, as urgently as we know how, to the point of either failure or fruition.

But we also need to ask ourselves: How are we consuming all this energy? What is it doing for us? How efficient is the consumption process? What changes can we make in our pattern of consumption that will enable us to keep warm in the winter and reasonably comfortable in the summer, to get to work on time, to keep the factories humming with much less energy than we use today?

It is my view that our largest load today is waste. If we can eliminate that load, we can buy enough time to perfect the technologies that scientists and engineers have on paper—if we use that time wisely.

# Discussion

**We hear a lot of comments about the need for developing a national energy policy. What would it look like if we had one?**

*Well, if you took all those people who are proposing a national energy policy and put them in the same room, you would have as many policies as you have people. National energy policy is a good catchphrase when you feel that there is something wrong with the current policy and you want it straightened out. When environmentalists say, "We need a national energy policy," they seem to be suggesting that we ought to have a policy of energy conservation and strict enforcement of environmental laws. When industrialists speak of a national energy policy, they mean, "Let's get the environmentalists off our backs, raise prices, and get on with the show." When scientists say it, they mean we should be putting money into research and development. When consumer advocates argue for it, they want to know why power resources are not better regulated and prices prevented from going up.*

*I think that the cry for a national energy policy suggests that every group looking at the problem is interested in reform and change. It is instructive, though, that five or six years ago any suggestions that we needed a national energy policy would have been greeted by industry leaders with shouts of alarm, fears of more governmental intervention, and, perhaps, nightmares of socialism.*

*Now that the problems seem severe enough, a lot of people, including industrialists, would settle for perhaps more government planning and more government programs if these were meaningful. An oil industry executive once said to me that we can live with any damn fool government policy, but what we can't live with is a question mark. Maybe that sums up the desire for a rational national policy. But today we probably have only question marks.*

**Do you think we need a national energy policy?**

*I think we need to reform a lot of our laws and their administrative enforcement. My feeling is that we're going to be struggling with this issue the rest of our lives and making progress in bits and pieces. The idea of a national energy policy chiseled into two or three stone tablets as abiding commandments strikes me as overly simplistic.*

*We have in this mix of problems some really fundamental values of society, and they're probably not going to be resolved other than through the political process over a period of time. What this finally comes down to, I think, is the deliberate determination of the kind of America we are going to have in the decades ahead. Are we going to continue the growth patterns of the past? Do we want a society that will be somewhat less energy intensive? Will the development of land have more rhyme and reason to it than the helter-skelter growth of the past? Should we be dedicated to an ever-increasing gross national product or to an ever-improving quality of national life?*

*Energy policy is inextricably interrelated to our consumption pattern. When we, at long last, construct a national energy policy, we will have to deal with some of the problems and predicaments in our country.*

*Consider transportation, for example. We are going to have a shortage of gasoline this summer due, in large part, to many people who are prisoners of their personal automobiles. Many live far from their jobs in areas inadequately served by public transportation. If we think about how cities have expanded in the last two decades in the shape of irregular donuts around the old central cities, the resemblance is to concentric rings that are natural to trees but wasteful for human life. In this pattern, cars are necessary, in the absence of adequate urban transit, to move people in and out of the inner cities. We have neglected railways both above and below street levels in favor of road transportation by motorized vehicles. It takes four times as much energy per ton mile to move freight by truck as by train. It takes about eight or nine times as much energy to reach New York City from Washington, D.C. by an airline as by express train. The outlook is even worse to contemplate because we are developing transportation modes requiring more and more energy.*

*This is true of building construction as well. Architects fell in love with glass after the Second World War under the influence of the International School that was concerned with function and esthetics, not energy. As so often happens, these architectural forms are distorted so that, in some buildings with curtain walls of glass that cannot open to the outdoors, heating and cooling systems often work simultaneously, and only qualified engineers can alter the automatic mechanism regulating the systems.*

*In industry, managers have been less than frugal in using energy because it's a relatively unimportant overhead item in the overall budget. In homes, we are all power wastrels, dependent on automatic dishwashers, electric can openers, central heating and cooling, and other power-hungry devices that exemplify our affluence and our addictions.*

You suggest that we cannot continue a pattern that has existed for a good many generations and that we should alter it dramatically. Isn't it accurate, then, to characterize our present circumstances as crisis?

*What I was trying to suggest is that we have been so addicted to the constant availability of energy for everybody that our country is really in a state of shock. Still, it's very difficult to label this a crisis. We're now living with 5% unemployment, and we don't write about the "unemployment crisis." At least I don't see the term in the press. Fewer than 1% of the population has been touched by the fuel shortages of the winter, yet we speak of an energy crisis.*

*I think the reason it's gotten so much attention is its shock effect. It's maddening to Americans to find their gas stations closed because the pumps are empty or the refrigerators off because of an electrical problem up the line. We become disturbed and disoriented, doubting our basic way of life. And yet I'm concerned about using the word crisis when these shortages may be bizarre flukes, temporary shortages, technical failures, or something like that. I think we're exaggerating the past and underestimating the future.*

*I would like to suggest that the problem is somehow rooted in our attitude toward the gas station and the refrigerator-freezer. It was both funny and true when Pogo said: "We have met the enemy and they are us." Our life-style is at risk if energy does not keep pace with our demands, which may be wasteful and frivolous at times.*

*It's too easy to become obsessed with the supply of energy and think of the problem as one in which the demand is given and the unknown is the source—that is, oil or gas or coal or uranium or some combination of natural resources. Demand can be a significant variable. The best thinking at the moment is that as much as 30% of our nation's present consumption could be squeezed out over time. Obviously, conservation measures cannot be achieved instantaneously. People are not going to insulate their houses overnight. Mass transit systems are not going to appear at the wave of a wand. Housewives will have to be taught to turn down the heat at night and the air conditioning during the day. It's much tougher to put conservation methods into effect when habits are deeply ingrained.*

*The growth rate of energy consumption might be cut by one-third if we did something about waste. Americans double their consumption of energy about every thirteen years. The rest of the world is using more energy all the time as countries strive to attain some degree of affluence. Most of the world now lives in a perpetual blackout, but they aspire to join the high-energy civilization in one way or another. So, energy production will have to increase to meet the insatiable demands of energy consumption.*

*In our own self-interest, to sustain us in the coming era of intense world competition for energy resources, we will have to develop alternative renewable sources. I happen to think that solar energy is one of the options we have most neglected. Also, we ought to encourage those parts of the world possessing geothermal steam to develop that resource, otherwise they will be trying to drink from those Middle East wells along with us.*

You spoke of the tax policy of utilities as encouraging the consumption of energy. How does the tax structure work?

*The price of electricity in the Tennessee Valley Authority and Pacific Northwest doesn't include very much in the way of taxes. You have a situation where the price is lower than what it would be if these electricity producers paid taxes on the same basis as corporations generally. We have had the depletion allowance and the expensing of intangibles for petroleum, with the idea of encouraging exploration and development. Perhaps these devices have been successful to that end. But one effect is that the prices of natural gas and oil are lower than they would be if these industries were paying 52%, or whatever the corporate tax rate is today. The price of energy is lower in the TVA area, where I grew up, and in the Pacific Northwest because there is no equivalent of federal income tax in the price of energy. Of course, tax policy could be used as a conservation device. In Western*

*Europe, gasoline costs the equivalent of 80 cents to 95 cents a gallon —only because the governments impose huge taxes on gasoline. Perhaps as a direct consequence, most of the automobiles in Europe are small and operate on less gasoline. There are other factors, too. The level of income in Western Europe is lower than ours, and big cars are expensive to buy and to run. My point is that tax policy can encourage frugality and conservation. What's more, the money obtained from these taxes could be used to fund the research and development of new energy sources.*

**Wouldn't higher prices have substantially the same effect on consumption?**

*Yes, but I think that people generally might be interested in the difference between money going to the federal treasury as opposed to the energy industries. Consumers are somewhat interested in the profit levels of the energy companies. These profits have to be high enough to attract capital and provide incentives. But, if prices are, in effect, the means for rationing energy, I think most people would believe that the companies are getting higher profits than they should have. Taxes have the double advantage of doing what higher prices would do, as well as providing money for research and development to help find answers to the energy problem.*

**Are you suggesting an energy tax?**

*No, I'm just discussing possibilities that are pretty obvious to anyone who thinks about the subject. It's one option to which we ought to give serious attention. If we're going to launch a major research and development effort, the money has to come from somewhere.*

**Do you challenge any of the current predictions about fuel shortages and fuel rationing?**

*I don't know any more about that than what I read in the newspapers and what I gather from experience. Refinery capacity is running at 85% to 90% or just about the same as last year—maybe about 2% greater—but the demand is up from last year. We have more cars on the road, with registrations up 4% or 5% and people are driving more miles. So the demand for gasoline this summer is probably going to be up 5% or 6% over last year. And the industry's sales departments are urging more consumption than the production departments can supply.*

This winter the oil industry said that it didn't produce fuel oil because it was so busy last year producing gasoline. Now it's producing fuel oil when it needs to produce gas.

> *Someone on my staff looked into this and told me that there is no evidence that the oil industry produced fuel oil any later into 1972 than the year before. It's primarily a function of the demand growing faster than the productive capacities of the refineries. The fact that there is not enough gasoline available to independent companies doesn't necessarily mean there is a shortage. I know that some legal eagles in the states and in Washington have claimed that the shortages of gasoline and fuel oil are probably phony and perhaps the result of collusion by the major companies. I have heard of one Florida official who argued: "There is no energy crisis. There is a competition crisis." It is obvious that the major producers are going to supply their own filling stations before they supply the independent competitors. There are antitrust implications that are being investigated, I understand, by the Justice Department and the Congress.*

Could you shed a little more light on refinery capacity? None have been built recently and none are on the drawing board. How much truth is there in the argument that environmentalists have stopped the expansion of refineries?

> *If you're trying to read the corporate mind, it's a futile exercise. What really motivates the management of a major oil company in its decisions? I'm not trying to duck the question, but all I know is what they say and what I read. I've had a major oil company president tell me that the main reason for not expanding refineries is that the prices are just not good enough. He couldn't justify an expansion because the marginal cost of that investment would not bring in a return that would pay for it. The price ceilings on all products were such, he said, that it would cost him more to expand than he would make out of the expansion. So the major reason seems to be economics. The companies can't in good conscience justify it to stockholders. Oil companies are not utilities. They don't have any public franchise or any public responsibility to make the investments. They have no guaranteed rate of return.*
>
> *That is one explanation. The other is environmental opposition—the uncertainty over how much lead should be in gasoline.*

*It could also be that they just underestimated the demand. The estimates of industry that I have seen over the years have not been better or worse than the estimates of government. As a matter of fact, most government estimates are based on the industry estimates.*

**Will Alaska's oil make any difference in the shortages confronting the nation?**

*It will make a difference of 2 million barrels a day—perhaps more when it really comes in. I don't think anybody suggests that the Alaskan oil wouldn't make some difference. The debate is over which route from Alaska is superior and how urgent it is to have the oil at some particular moment in history.*

**Which route do you think is superior?**

*I testified last year before Congress that I felt the trans-Canada route was superior to the Alaska route, not only on environmental grounds, but, more importantly, on energy grounds. If we build an oil line through Canada, we will be providing an energy highway to open up the Canadian North. Some geologists tell us that there is as much oil in the frontier area of Canada as there is in Alaska. By building a pipeline through the oil country, we will be providing incentives, encouragement, and transportation to not only bring Alaskan oil to the United States, but to develop the large reservoir of oil in Northern Canada.*

*The cost comparisons between the two routes are misleading. Obviously, the Alaskan pipeline would be shorter than a trans-Canada pipeline, but all those tankers have to be built and subsidized. The question to ask is where the oil is needed the most. The evidence suggests the Midwest more than the West Coast.*

**You say you favor a Canadian pipeline over an Alaskan one because of the environment. What is the difference between the Canadian and Alaskan environments? Also, isn't there a problem of security involved in the choice of an oil route?**

*I hope I'm not so provincial and parochial that I would say we should mess up Canada's tundra and not our own. The environmental problem that is most serious is the danger of oil spills in the North Pacific and along the western coast of Canada as these supertankers shuttle back and forth between Prudhoe Bay and Puget Sound. The*

*Canadians themselves prefer the trans-Canada route, which actually is partially through Alaska as well as Canada. Also, the Canadians are probably going to build a pipeline to bring down their own oil. But they don't have sufficient oil developed yet, and it will be years before they build their own pipeline. It has been suggested that a corridor would be built for oil and gas pipelines.*

*As far as national security is concerned, we did war with Canada in 1812. But it is a ridiculous argument that a pipeline across Canada presents a security risk any greater than one that goes across Alaska and poses the additional risk of tankers on the open sea. In World War II, we started constructing an oil pipeline across Canada to Alaska for national security purposes. German submarines were knocking off so many of our ships that, for national security, a pipeline was considered by the military to be safer than tankers. I really don't put any weight on a strict national security argument, and I haven't heard the administration trying to make that argument —though it sometimes uses the catchwords "national security" in a vague way.*

**It is possible that some future Canadian government could be much more hostile toward the United States.**

*Yes, it is possible. But the idea that Canada would cut off oil to us is just a bit far-fetched. The economies of the United States and Canada are so intermingled and interdependent that an official action against our pipeline would be only one part of a problem a good deal more fundamental than oil.*

**Do you have any idea, Mr. Freeman, what the impact of the Vietnam War in the past ten years has had on energy?**

*I really don't think that is a major problem. Military consumption of energy is appreciably less than 10% of our total use. After World War I, we were concerned about fuel for our Navy and set up huge oil reserves at Elk Hills and Teapot Dome—the focus of a scandal during Harding's administration. Since World War II, our national concern has been fuel for commerce and industry and for private comfort and recreation. Military needs have not caused any problem, and in wartime, as experience proved in World War II, Americans accepted fuel rationing.*

**Is the argument of national security fallacious?**

> *In military terms, yes. But it's usually not couched in military terms. The argument is based on our civilian economy that is so dependent on energy that we cannot afford to risk its interruption and on our foreign policy that could be held to ransom by foreign oil-producing countries. Energy is critical to our security, but not particularly for military purposes. As the Navy goes nuclear, it is less dependent on oil. As a matter of fact, oil from the Middle East went directly to Vietnam, without transshipment through our country.*

**Are environmental and energy demands necessarily incompatible?**

> *Energy demands and environmental goals are on a collision course. We have no sources of clean energy today. Paradise is lost in a sense. I don't believe, however, that it's incompatible to think of energy sources that we can live with in a healthful and enjoyable manner. But today we are in very serious trouble in our efforts to reconcile energy and environment. If there is a crisis, it is the failure of present energy sources to meet the perceived environmental safeguards.*

**In the short-term, at least, is there any doubt in your mind, Mr. Freeman, that environmental standards set in recent years are going to have to be relaxed?**

> *Oh, yes, there's considerable doubt. We can go one of two ways: Either back up on the environmental standards or go forward into the kinds of research and development efforts that have a rather short-term payoff— say, enabling the cleaner use of coal, which is a key element in our present energy problem. Research and development might mean implementing some conservation measures quickly. For example, busing is not a very popular topic because it's associated with the education crisis, but, if we're serious about cleaning up the air in our cities, busing might well be a solution for getting to work and back. I don't think that we have explored modern bus systems as a way of solving the crucial problem in the metropolitan centers. I'm no expert on transportation, but I know I would be attracted by the idea of going into town on a bus which used an express lane and ran on a fairly regular schedule, and maybe even provided a bar in back on the homeward journey; a lot of other people who spend a great deal of their time fighting traffic would probably be similarly at-*

*tracted. I think this would cut the consumption of gasoline and the noise and smoke pollution. Indeed, the Environmental Protection Agency is considering something like this for major metropolitan centers, and a group of EPA workers has chartered a bus for themselves operating between Falls Church, Virginia, and Washington, D.C. We can either adopt such ideas, implement the laws, and clean up, or we can throw up our hands, relax the laws, and give up.*

### You're saying it's really a political decision?

*All these matters require political decisions.*

### Would our present state of technology enable us to maintain a semblance of our present life-style?

*I cannot answer that flatly. In the case of the electric power industry, it is not seeking a year's delay before cleaning up, yet it does not now possess the technology for removing sulfur and other effluents from burning coal. Unfortunately, we are pursuing the research and development for clean energy technology perhaps not in a lackadaisical way but not with the sense of urgency that would be consistent with implementing our laws.*

*It may very well be that some slippage of the timetable is going to be needed, but I think it's a question of either implementing the laws on a timetable or continuing to drift. After all, it was 1967 when Congress passed the first Air Quality Act which ordered the sulfur out of the stack gases. I think it's going to be very difficult for most Americans to accept the fact that our electric power industry and our government, with all of the technological know-how of this country and, after six years of effort, just can't figure out how to burn coal in compliance with air quality laws — not only can't, but has no target date for doing it. I worked with this program for years, and I think it's a difficult task because the quantities of stack gases are enormous. Yet it's hard to conclude that we have given it the kind of old college try that we applied, for instance, in going to the moon or in developing atomic energy.*

*We have government programs with small budgets and few people with technical knowledge associated with the programs. The programs are oriented to the proposals that come in, and the work is in the hands of utility companies which have, in turn, little incentive to get the job done because, as soon as they learn how to perfect the technology, there is another big chemical unit they have to buy and add to their power plant. This complicates the problems of running a power plant. So the program has been in the hands of people, in part, who, in the first place, don't believe that the sulfur problem is that bad, and, in the second place, feel that this problem is just not urgent.*

**Would you say that when all is said and done there's got to be what we might call a technological breakthrough of new energy sources to survive?**

*Yes.*

**When do you see a breakthrough coming?**

*The reason we require new sources, is that we have not reckoned with the quantities of energy that we're going to consume. This exponential growth is a very real thing. We talk in terms of 3% growth per year or 4% per year. But it's 4% of the number that's twice as big as the number fourteen years ago. Perhaps you remember the French riddle that was used in the Club of Rome's report,* The Limits of Growth *(1972). Suppose your pond had a single water lily that doubles in size each day. If the lily were allowed to grow unchecked, it would completely cover the pond in thirty days, choking off all other life in the water. For a while the lily seems small and you forget about it. But then you notice that it covers half the pond. What day would that be? Why, the twenty-ninth day, of course. So you have only one day to save your pond.*

*This is a useful illustration of exponential growth. It gives us some notion of what we're confronting in the demands for fossil fuels. Oil and gas resources are going to peak out — if not run out — in a matter of decades. We have gone more and more to concentrated sources of energy. We started with wood, went to coal, then petroleum, and now nuclear power. But it is going to require a scientific and technological breakthrough to provide the huge quantities of energy dictated by exponential growth without turning upside down all of Colorado and Montana.*

*In our attempts to continue to meet the demands of this dynamic growth with the kinds of fuel resources we have, our impact on land use is enormous. We fail to appreciate how much land is going to have to be dedicated to the energy industries if we strip-mine for coal, for example. If we contemplate the world-wide growth of population around the world, there is going to have to be a breakthrough. We like to think that the nuclear breeder reactor is just such a breakthrough. But think of the lead time: With some twenty-five years of experience in nuclear reactors, we still await the first demonstration of a breeder in this country in 1982 or 1983, and the first commercial plant probably won't appear until 1990. It's a very complicated technology.*

*We haven't made even a promising beginning toward other options such as synthetic fuels and magnetohydrodynamics, and solar energy and fusion power, into which we have put some money, have yet to achieve even scientific feasibility. Only some great technological alternative will sustain a high-energy civilization in the next century.*

What about a national land use policy? Is the federal government doing anything about this?

*As far as I can tell, very little—though it was two years ago that the Nixon administration first proposed legislation for a national land use policy. It was a measure encouraging the states to establish their own regulations mainly preventing misuse of areas of "critical state concern," such as wetlands, or ensuring the proper placement of airports or power plants. But on their own, several states—with Florida, Virginia, Vermont, and Colorado among them—have enacted land use control laws.*

*Land use is a key element of the energy problem. In testimony at a Congressional hearing two years ago, Russell Train, the chairman of the Council on Environmental Quality, described land use as the "single most important . . . substantially unaddressed" environmental matter. I suspect that a new mood is developing in America against the old "growth at any price" philosophy. In the politics of energy, a lot of leaders, it seems to me, are underestimating the strength and breadth of the "slow down" movement among people both here and abroad in developed countries. The reception given the Club of Rome study is an indication.*

If the problem is basic to so many people here and elsewhere, how long can energy be left in the hands of private interests?

*That's an interesting question. This country is one of the remaining few where energy is predominantly controlled by private interests—*

*and our oil companies are multinational as well as national. I think energy can be left to the private interests as long as they are responsive to the needs of society. Until now energy has been one of the goodies in our way of life. Everybody was happy with the energy industry. Prices for electricity are lower now than in the 1920s. When I was at the FPC in the early 1960s, we could get hardly any attention from the communications media. There was no problem, hence no press. Today, by contrast, energy is one of the baddies, due mainly to shortages, real or feared, and to environmental degradation, real or feared.*

*I hope that the energy industry remains in private hands, because if there's anything worse to deal with than a private monopoly, it's a government monopoly. TVA in some respects is more difficult to deal with because it is a government agency and doesn't have the same fear of EPA as a private company. I'm not enthusiastic about the prospect of national or state power companies because I think they will be less responsive to environmental goals and consumer rights. The experience of Britain and France and other countries with nationalized energy industries seems to show that government bureaucrats left in charge act like—or are worse than—private businessmen.*

It's conceivable, I suppose, that government is going to make plans and decisions of the necessary magnitude in time, but it's also conceivable that in ten years our economy and our society will be faced with collapse, our living standards reduced, our life-style wrecked.

*I'm not an energy Doomsayer. I think the apocalyptic scenario is exaggerated. My own Pollyannish hunch is that the American people are going to be making decisions about energy conservation that will have an impact. I don't believe the arguments suggesting that consumption is going to be as excessive in the future as in the past. General Motors, Allied Chemical, Eastman Kodak—all those companies are organizing energy conservation task forces. Some cut back their energy use by 10% just by turning a few valves.*

*I think the waste is so outrageous that the architects and housewives and the businessmen and bureaucrats and the contractors and congressmen will come to understand the importance of energy conservation—that we can, all at the same time, save energy, save money, and save the environment, too. Slogans will not be enough without action. One slogan, however, may appeal to some people— "Save energy and save Israel," meaning that by curtailing the use of oil, therefore relying less on the Middle East sheikdoms, we may be preventing a war against Israel.*

*The record of the American people for adjustment and practicality is a good one. Look at the population issue. Without a lot of laws and without a lot of exhortation, there has been a revolution not only in attitude but in the birth rate. Awareness of the energy issue is beginning to take hold in America. The politicians and the press are deeply concerned, and that's the first step toward arousing the public. It will be hard to reach agreement on what to do. We will muddle along. We will not witness a miracle. But with hard thought, good sense, some inspiration, and much imagination, we are not going to experience Doomsday either. We do not have to give up on modern society.*

# Chapter 2

Dean E. Abrahamson

# The Environment:
# When Is Doomsday?

Headlines and titles are often discomforting to reporters, writers, and even professors who may think the choice of words are not quite apt. So it is that the word "Doomsday" in my title disturbs me. The thought of Doomsday frightens most people, which is precisely why the word is so engaging and evocative. For me it raises compelling questions: Can we discuss environmental Doomsday without considering our resources, technology, and economy, as well as our national priorities, policies, and practices—all of which are intricate, imperfect, and interrelated? Are we, in fact, *really talking about the death of the American Way?*

Some would have us think so. An arresting advertisement appeared last fall picturing a power plant and a tombstone and stating: "Here lies the United States economy, killed by the energy crisis." In a book called *The Energy Crisis* (1972), written by Lawrence Rocks and Richard Runyon, both of whom are taking part in this symposium, a lot of the blame is placed squarely on utopian environmentalists. The irony is that those in search of an Earthly Paradise may well bring about an infernal Abaddon.

Statistics for 1971 show that 96% of all the energy generated in the United States pollutes, contaminates, and otherwise damages our air, water, and aesthetics. (See Figures 4 and 5.) Oil and gas account for 77% of our energy, coal for another 18%, and nuclear fuel for only 1%. Hydropower provides some 4% of our primary energy consumption, and, although it is nonpolluting, dams are now recognized as possible ecological disasters. There is, in short, no way today of generating power without some environmental impact, insult, degradation, or disruption.

## DIMENSIONS OF SIZE AND SEVERITY

The effects can be local or global, reversible or irreversible. Strip mining of coal, for example, is a strictly local scourge, but hardly a harbinger

## Figure 4.
## Air Pollutant Emissions, 1970

| Source Category | Total | Carbon monoxide | Sulfur oxides | Hydrocarbons | Particulates | Nitrogen oxides |
|---|---|---|---|---|---|---|
| **Total quantity** | **260.4** | **148.6** | **29.2** | **34.9** | **25.5** | **22.2** |
| Transportation | 143.9 | 110.9 | 1.0 | 19.5 | 0.8 | 11.7 |
| Fuel combustion (stationary) | 38.3 | 0.8 | 21.5 | 0.6 | 6.0 | 9.4 |
| Industrial processes | 36.8 | 11.4 | 6.4 | 5.5 | 13.3 | 0.2 |
| Refuse disposal | 11.1 | 7.2 | 0.1 | 2.0 | 1.4 | 0.4 |
| Miscellaneous | 30.3 | 18.3 | 0.2 | 7.3 | 4.0 | 0.5 |
| **Percent of total, by source** | **100.0** | **100.0** | **100.0** | **100.0** | **100.0** | **100.0** |
| Transportation | 55.3 | 74.6 | 3.4 | 55.9 | 3.1 | 52.7 |
| Fuel combustion (stationary) | 14.7 | 0.5 | 73.6 | 1.7 | 23.5 | 42.3 |
| Industrial processes | 14.1 | 7.7 | 21.9 | 15.8 | 52.2 | 0.9 |
| Refuse disposal | 4.3 | 4.9 | 0.4 | 5.7 | 5.5 | 1.8 |
| Miscellaneous | 11.6 | 12.3 | 0.7 | 20.9 | 15.7 | 2.3 |
| **Percent of total, by pollutant** | **100.0** | **57.1** | **11.2** | **13.4** | **9.8** | **8.5** |
| Transportation | 100.0 | 77.0 | 0.7 | 13.6 | 0.6 | 8.1 |
| Fuel combustion (stationary) | 100.0 | 2.1 | 56.1 | 1.6 | 15.7 | 24.5 |
| Industrial processes | 100.0 | 31.0 | 17.4 | 15.0 | 36.1 | 0.5 |
| Refuse disposal | 100.0 | 64.9 | 0.9 | 18.0 | 12.6 | 3.6 |
| Miscellaneous | 100.0 | 60.4 | 0.7 | 24.1 | 13.2 | 1.6 |

Source: U.S. Environmental Protection Agency, unpublished data.

Note: Quantity in millions of tons per year. Estimates.

## Figure 5.
## Gaseous Air Pollutant Levels, Selected Cities, 1968.

| City | Maximum day | Minimum month | Maximum month | Yearly average | Maximum day | Minimum month | Maximum month | Yearly average | Maximum day | Minimum month | Maximum month | Yearly average |
|---|---|---|---|---|---|---|---|---|---|---|---|---|
| | Sulfur Dioxide | | | | Nitric Oxide | | | | Nitrogen Dioxide | | | |
| Chicago | 0.51 | 0.03 | 0.27 | 0.12 | 0.23 | 0.04 | 0.11 | 0.07 | 0.10 | 0.04 | 0.06 | 0.05 |
| Cincinnati | 0.08 | 0.01 | 0.03 | 0.02 | .... | .... | .... | .... | 0.10 | 0.02 | 0.05 | 0.03 |
| Philadelphia | 0.36 | 0.04 | 0.16 | 0.08 | 0.37 | 0.02 | 0.10 | 0.05 | 0.09 | 0.02 | 0.05 | 0.04 |
| Denver | 0.05 | 0.00 | 0.03 | 0.01 | 0.21 | 0.01 | 0.07 | 0.04 | 0.12 | 0.03 | 0.05 | 0.04 |
| St. Louis | 0.16 | 0.01 | 0.06 | 0.03 | 0.13 | 0.02 | 0.05 | 0.03 | 0.05 | 0.01 | 0.04 | 0.02 |
| Washington, D.C. | 0.18 | 0.00 | 0.10 | 0.04 | 0.31 | 0.02 | 0.08 | 0.04 | 0.08 | 0.04 | 0.05 | 0.05 |
| | Carbon Monoxide | | | | Total Oxidants | | | | Total Hydrocarbons | | | |
| Chicago | 16 | 4.9 | 7.1 | 6.2 | 0.11 | 0.01 | 0.04 | 0.02 | 5.4 | 2.4 | 3.4 | 2.9 |
| Cincinnati | 32 | 3.5 | 7.7 | 5.6 | .... | .... | .... | .... | 5.6 | 2.2 | 3.2 | 2.6 |
| Philadelphia | .... | .... | .... | .... | 0.08 | 0.02 | 0.03 | 0.02 | 4.8 | 1.8 | 2.5 | 2.2 |
| Denver | 21 | 4.3 | 7.3 | 5.4 | 0.08 | 0.02 | 0.04 | 0.03 | 6.4 | 2.1 | 4.2 | 2.9 |
| St. Louis | 9 | 3.8 | 5.6 | 4.6 | 0.05 | 0.02 | 0.03 | 0.02 | 9.8 | 2.1 | 4.8 | 3.4 |
| Washington, D.C. | 14 | 1.9 | 6.6 | 3.4 | 0.10 | 0.01 | 0.04 | 0.03 | 5.7 | 1.9 | 3.0 | 2.2 |

Source: U.S. Public Health Service, *Annual Data Tabulations, Continuous Air Monitoring Projects, 1969.*

Note: Concentration in parts per million. Concentrations of gaseous contaminants are continuously measured in the indicated cities in order to provide basic data on the nature and extent of urban area pollution.

of Doomsday. By contrast, the proliferation of nuclear power plants along estuaries, which seem to be favored sites, could cause ghastly effects on marine life nurseries there.

Global environmental problems are critical. One that comes to mind is a drastic change of climate resulting from heat releases that upset the thermal balance of the earth or that alter the present patterns. Consider the possible effects: melting ice caps, rising sea levels, shifting rainfall, expanding deserts, and other major permutations.

Then there is the "greenhouse effect." This is a rather frightening, but still theoretical, occurrence that could result when high concentrations of carbon dioxide, the residue of all fuels except nuclear ones, accumulate in the atmosphere and act like the glass roof of a greenhouse trapping heat below it and warming our climate. If this were to happen, it could have far-reaching and trouble-making effects.

Particulate material from burning fossil fuels may also upset the earth's heat balance by blocking the sun's rays. A large increase of sulfur oxides from stack gases of industrial and power plants could have implications for human health by causing respiratory diseases and for the physical environment by causing acid rainfall. Until Britain began cleaning up large amounts of sulfur and sulfuric acid that were being pumped into the air from coal fires, Scandanavian countries complained about these pollutants carried by the prevailing winds from abroad. Britain itself had a high incidence of respiratory diseases, particularly during and after heavy fogs which were laden with sulfur and sulfuric acid.

So, in short, there are possible physical effects to our biosphere. When fossil fuels are converted to energy, giving off thermal and chemical pollutants, both human and environmental health are at risk, though to what extent we are uncertain.

Besides the physical mechanisms, there are social and political mechanisms that could possibly cause serious disruptions. Consider the implications of many nations, including the world's most powerful, competing for a diminishing supply of fossil fuels. Another serious—some say alarming—prospect concerns the proliferation of nuclear reactors, nuclear material, and nuclear technology among many nations. Then, too, beyond the internal social and political consequences of energy, there are external consequences involving pollution controls, monetary policies, multinational corporations, trade programs, and so on.

In considering environmental matters alone, one must reckon on the severity—whether or not they are reversible—and the consequences of a technical correction—whether or not the remedy is worse than the problem or results in some additional complication. Some of the widespread and long-term dangers do not appear, in our present state of knowledge, to have any scientific or technological redress. It seems that we are not particularly skilled at dealing with problems for which we have no known fix.

Let's look more closely at this. First of all, local environmental effects can be managed. Strip mining, oil spills, thermal wastes at power plants and other points—all are serious and significant, but are the kinds of problems to which people can relate and respond.

Second, the global effects of large releases of heat, carbon dioxide, and particulates that can possibly cause climatic changes, while extremely bothersome, take place over a long period of time. Even though we don't understand the effects that raising temperatures by one or two degrees would have, by looking at the total heat release or the release of carbon dioxide or particulates, we can be reasonably assured that we don't have to take action immediately. The time scale is relatively long—though these problems have cumulative importance for the future.

Third, other global effects may be much more imminent. Massive oil spills, for one, or actions that endanger the sealife nurseries of estuaries require immediate action. Estuaries are frequently viewed as convenient sites for refineries, ports, power plants, and similar enterprises. They bear a disproportionately heavy burden of environmental impact, and I think this is something we need to worry about immediately.

## THE NUCLEAR ISSUE

The problems of radioactive waste from nuclear power, which conventional wisdom now heralds as the energy source of the future, are both immediate and long-term. It doesn't matter whether light-water or fast-breeder reactors are involved, the issue is the same: How to manage and treat radioactive waste, from the mining of minerals to the disposal of dregs? At the mining stage, there have been incidents of carelessness and ignorance that have led to lung cancer in miners, dumping uranium tailings into rivers, and using radioactive sludge as residential land fill. Such episodes are disgraceful and tell us something about the competence of the nuclear industry. At the reactor stage, the problems become difficult to confine. There is, for one, waste heat, which is not much worse than that from other types of power plants. There is also, however, radioactive waste, the routine release of radioactive poisons into the air and water during normal plant operation. The safety standards of nuclear power became subjects of vigorous debate in the sixties, beginning in Minnesota and engaging some of the nation's leading scientists and engineers, the Atomic Energy Commission, the National Academy of Sciences, and the United States Congress. The issue involved the risks and rewards of nuclear energy. In the end, after a demonstration that radioactive wastes from power plants could be kept at low levels, the AEC tightened their regulations by a factor of 100 and required stringent vigilence and constant monitoring. (See Figure 6.) The AEC took some pains to establish that all the requirements could be met by the utility companies without significant economic hardship.

**Figure 6.**
**Sources of Radiation**

| Source | Average dose rate[a] (mrem/yr) |
|---|---|
| Environmental | |
|   Natural | 102 |
|   Global Fallout | 4 |
|   Nuclear Power | 0.003 |
|     Subtotal | 106 |
| Medical | |
|   Diagnostic | 72[b] |
|   Radiopharmaceuticals | 1 |
|     Subtotal | 73 |
|   Occupational | 0.8 |
|   Miscellaneous | 2 |
|     Subtotal | 3 |
|       Total | 182 |

Source: National Academy of Sciences.

Note: Summary of estimates of annual whole-body dose rates in the United States (1970).

[a] The numbers shown are average values only. For given segments of the population, dose rates considerably greater than these may be experienced.
[b] Based on the abdominal dose.

The subject of nuclear reactor accidents has received a lot of attention recently. There have been hearings in Washington before the AEC on what's been called the "emergency core cooling system," which is supposed to prevent a large release of radioactive waste if the reactor loses its coolant. The results of those hearings are not yet available, but many experts think the reactors will be "derated"—that is, that the reactors will be required to operate at power levels significantly lower than those at which they were designed to run. A major accident at a reactor is really major. Back in 1957 the AEC's Brookhaven National Laboratory prepared a study that attempted to assess the worst possible damage from a maximum accident in a large nuclear installation. It calculated that a reactor blowup could kill more than 3,000 people, injure 40,000, and cause property damage of $7 billion, as well as require an agricultural quarantine over an area of some 150,000 square miles. Much would depend on the exact nature and location of the accident. Is it raining at the time? In what direction is the wind blowing? How close are towns or any concentration of population such as a school or factory? Where does the community get its drinking water, its milk, its food? The year of the Brookhaven report, an overheated reactor at the Windscale Works, the first nuclear power plant in a remote part of England, spewed radioactive fission debris over the countryside, after which the authorities impounded all dairy and agricultural products in a 400-mile area. I think one can make the case that until nuclear reactor safety has been satisfactorily resolved, nuclear power operations should stop.

While we are not talking about enormous volumes of waste, as we would, say, in connection with fly ash and hydrocarbons from coal-burning power plants, we are concerned about radioactivity. The waste is biologically active and has to be completely isolated from the biosphere—essentially forever, or certainly for periods exceeding human lifetimes or lifetimes of any social or political systems that the world has known. We're talking about assuring that these wastes are never released.

There is also the issue of disposal—though storage is a more appropriate term for radioactive wastes. Because they deteriorate so slowly, the potential risks are great. We do not yet have an acceptable method for storing nuclear wastes. There are a variety of schemes, ranging from rocketing cans of the stuff into the sun to locking them in deep salt mines or under the Antarctic icecap. The problem persists, though reactors continue to be built as if there were no problem at all.

Finally, there are important and unresolved issues that have received little or no public attention. This is mainly by design, because the industry strives to limit any discussion. One involves safeguards—that is, the means designed to keep countries that do not now have nuclear weapons from acquiring nuclear material to build a nuclear arsenal. Scientists call this the $n$th country problem. Any nation that has a civilian nuclear power industry—even one reactor—has the capacity of joining the Nuclear Club. The technology is there, and the material is there. It is assumed, therefore, that India and Israel, with their nuclear reactors, now possess a small nuclear weapons stockpile or enough ingredients and know-how to assemble a few "nukes." Worse yet, a number of other nations will soon have that capacity, if they don't already. It's hard to imagine that this state of affairs contributes to world stability.

Another problem related to safeguards usually goes under the term "diversion." This worry is that so-called special nuclear materials or reactor fuels such as uranium 235 and plutonium, which are basic ingredients of atomic bombs, could be diverted to unauthorized channels—that is, to people, or groups, or nations that may act irresponsibly. It is not far-fetched to conceive of a nuclear coup d'état or nuclear blackmail. It is not possible to buy plutonium at the supermarket, but it might be possible to steal a quantity or connive with some unscrupulous technicians, businessmen, or politicians to obtain nuclear material. Botulin toxin, the poison that turned up recently in canned mushrooms and vichyssoise, happens to be one of the most lethal biological agents that we know. But it can hardly be compared with plutonium, which is dangerous to humans for 200,000 years.

It will not be enough to limit the release of plutonium into the environment. It will have to be prevented. The safeguards will have to be rigidly imposed at several stages—at fabrication plants, at reactors, at reprocessing centers, and in transit everywhere—not only because of the inherent toxicity but of the inherent danger that it will fall into the hands of mischief makers, terrorists, extremists, and crackpots. A few grams—enough to fit into an ashtray—could be exceedingly disruptive. To be disruptive, it need not be in the configuration of a weapon—that is, portable, reliable, and of known explosive yield. What I am suggesting is that nuclear energy, particularly the way the proliferation of it is now proposed and pursued, carries with it the peril of Doomsday. My own view is that the nuclear route to energy is completely unacceptable. Nuclear energy is an option that should be pursued only as the last choice, when all other sources are exhausted, when we are desperate for power.

## NUCLEAR ALTERNATIVES

Apart from nuclear power, the technology and material of energy sometimes complicate environmental problems. The greater use of petroleum has resulted in the greater production of its by-products—chemicals, plastics, and synthetics of all kinds, from rubber to textiles. Many of these by-products can have—indeed, some already have—profound effects on the environment.

In some instances, these substances raise problems of pollution and waste of their own.

Are there ways of preventing environmental deterioration? There are a number of remedies. The first one was discussed by Dave Freeman, and that is the necessity to look at growth rates as a way of limiting the use of energy. Freeman also said he thought that our energy consumption could be reduced by 30%. I'm willing to accept that figure, but I believe that it could be cut by 50%, merely by introducing more efficient technical means of using energy and with no major disruption in our life-style. Freeman was right in saying it can't be done overnight. It can be done over a short period, however, by practicing conservation.

How much time lag is there in the public's response? My own feeling is that it will take years to minimize the flow of resources and maximize the life expectancy of goods. The market will not respond quickly enough to prevent rather serious disruptions.

Moreover, we have to look at ways of using fossil fuels, particularly coal and oil shale, in environmentally and socially acceptable ways, regardless of whether or not nuclear power supplies increase. At the moment, we don't know how to best use many of our resources, and we don't know how to clean up their residues. The attention that these matters have received is incompatible with the severity of the problem.

I think, too, we should take a serious look at those energy options that would least disrupt our social institutions and our biosphere. That means two— solar power and nuclear fusion. How soon can we have these? It certainly won't be in 10 years; it certainly will be within 100 years. One reason for the slow development is that our efforts to attain both are feeble. They are low priorities if we judge from the research budget. Money for solar and geothermal research and development amounted to only $3 million last year and reached $8 million this year. Even though it is being doubled to $16 million in the administration's new budget for fiscal year 1974, this is a low sum. Compare it with the $120 million proposed for coal research and development in 1974. The nonmilitary research and development on controlled fusion, which increased from about $28 million to $37 million in the past few years, would go up to $44 million next year—an amount that is of a low order of magnitude in contrast to the $323 million the AEC is to receive in 1974 for its work on the fast breeder reactor.

The new budget also creates a $25 million "central fund" for energy research in the Department of the Interior. This sum would go to "promising technologies" and would seem to be a step in the president's announced route to transform the Department of the Interior into a new Department of Natural Resources with central authority over national energy policy, both nuclear and nonnuclear. That transformation is apparently to take shape soon.

40

# Discussion

Are these figures for government research only?

> *For solar research there probably isn't much else but government support, with some money being channeled through the National Aeronautics and Space Administration and the National Science Foundation into a few private operations—Honeywell, Grumman, Textron, Raytheon, Arthur D. Little. For fusion it is very largely federal money. Here again there are a couple of private concerns— Gulf Research, Keith Brueckner's KMS Industries, that's about all. The efforts are very difficult and very expensive.*

Dr. Melvin Gottlieb, who heads the fusion project at Princeton University, was telling me about three years ago that the Russians would probably be at the threshold of a fusion breakthrough about 1981. This leads me to ask why there isn't a cooperative effort to pool the resources and know-how of both countries.

> *Apparently the Soviets have put substantially more into fusion than we have. Their work to control the fusion reaction with a "tokamak" design is a variation of one of our methods using a toroidal magnetic bottle, the Adiabatic Toroidal Compressor. To a large extent there is an exchange of people and reports between Soviet labs and our own. But that exchange breaks down on laser-triggered fusion. The idea is to heat small pellets of hydrogen fuel (deuterium and tritium) with a laser pulse so rapidly that the reaction is reached and contained. This research is highly classified because it has military implications. But there are peaceful implications as well because it holds a promise of spin-off into clean energy.*

Could you compare fusion with fission, particularly since you have called fission energy unacceptable?

> *Well, let me take the major problems: The heat releases are really about the same for fission and fusion, but the radioactive wastes produced by the fusion reaction are of an order of magnitude far less troublesome than with fission. In the first place, fusion wastes are not biologically active. They are produced in much smaller quantities, are much easier to manage, and don't concentrate in food chains.*

*Fusion is not pollution free, as some people insist quite wrongly, but its radioactive wastes are less long-lasting and, so, more manageable. Also, the major accident problem does not exist with fusion reactors, because there is no plutonium whatsoever and, therefore, no toxicity. Finally, the chilling prospect of diversion and proliferation is removed, and the need for safeguards against such risks would not be pervasive.*

Why is there no safeguard problem?

*Because there are no special nuclear materials that are needed for atomic bombs—no uranium, no plutonium. Instead, there is deuterium, tritium, or lithium—the stuff of hydrogen bombs. In order to set off a hydrogen bomb, you would first have to have an ordinary fission bomb, and those materials are not involved in fusion power reactors.*

To go to a much more prosaic matter, what about coal gasification? One hears that we have huge reserves of coal waiting to be used. Could coal gas replace natural gas for, say, home heating or industrial power?

*If our consumption of energy grows at present rates, and we become totally dependent on coal, we have proven resources to last 70 to 100 years. The nation's coal reserves are known to exceed 500 billion tons, enough to last, at the current rate of production, for 800 years. So, from a resource standpoint, we could be self-sufficient using coal.*

You mean burning coal as coal, right?

*That's right. I don't know what the efficiencies are in converting coal to natural gas, but I suspect that they're quite high. Certainly the losses are not as high as in producing electricity from coal, where only one-third of the coal is converted into usable energy. The transportation problems are obvious, of course. All you need is a pipeline, in one instance, or a transmission line, in another. It depends on whether we are shipping gas or electricity. But back at the coal mine or the gasification plant, there is still a problem: How do we keep the sulfur and other particulates out of the atmosphere?*

Are we on our way toward achieving coal gas?

*We know how to make gas, which appears to be the scarcest of the fossil fuels, out of coal, the most abundant of the fossil fuels. There*

42

are several variations of the process. The basic idea is to use steam to react chemically with the carbon in coal to make a hydrogen-rich gas. Then the gas is cleaned of its sulfur by an additional chemical reaction. This would permit otherwise environmentally unacceptable low-grade and low-cost coal, high in sulfur, to be used in the form of a synthetic gas.

There are some coal gasification systems operating — a few in Europe, others ready for pilot operations in the United States. A number of firms have announced that they are planning to go to the next stage of development — that is, demonstration plants. Still, it may be at least fifteen or twenty years before coal gas contributes significantly to our energy supply. There are still problems to overcome. We don't know how to remove the pollutants from emissions of the gasification plant, and the heat content of the synthetic gas is not as high as in natural gas.

What about coal liquefaction? What promises and what problems are involved in this process?

Synthetic liquid fuels can be made from a number of things. The Bureau of Mines has converted cow manure and carbon monoxide into oil. Most kinds of solid wastes can be changed into oil. Coal can be converted into either oil or gas. But the economy of doing this is substantially higher than natural oil or natural gas. In most instances, the technology has been demonstrated in the laboratory. Deposits of oil shale, which contains a waxy substance called kerogen that can be refined to a burnable oil, are extensive in Colorado, Utah, and Wyoming. Research indicates that it would be possible to extract 25 gallons of oil from each ton of high-grade shale that is mined and processed. But processing shale oil results in a high proportion of shale waste.

Can you see any way in which we can meet our energy requirements in the next few years without building nuclear power plants?

You used an interesting term — "energy requirements." I think we can meet our energy requirements very easily, but I also think that our energy requirements are substantially less than our present consumption. So, if you will allow me to affect demand while increasing supply, I'll say yes, without any qualifications.

But suppose we don't allow you?

> *If we suppose that our present growth and consumption rates are maintained, then we can clearly meet our energy demands in the next few decades from fossil fuel with present technology at high environmental costs. We have to live with strip mining. We have to learn how to reclaim strip-mined land. We have to do something about miner health and safety. We have to do something about pollution and noxious emissions. I agree with Dave Freeman that these certainly should be manageable problems.*
>
> *During these few decades, we should take a very serious look at alternative energy sources—solar, geothermal, fusion, and other types.*

Many people believe that solar energy offers the only inexhaustible supply. What are the present possibilities of massive utilization of solar energy?

> *First, it's not inexhaustible. But very large quantities are available. Fusion is also inexhaustible in the same sense. Its source is essentially water, and there is plenty of that around.*
>
> *The potentials for solar power fall into two distinct classes: very large power complexes of, say, 1,000 megawatts, and small local devices that would heat water or run air conditioners. There are other forms of solar power, such as hydro, wind, and burning of solid wastes. I think that smaller uses have large potential and could be implemented fairly quickly. The little work that's being done indicates that it's much more economically attractive than was previously thought. Solar water heaters are already in use in Australia, Israel, and Japan. Sunshine has powered many of our spacecraft by way of photovoltaic cells that convert sunshine into electricity.*
>
> *Major power plant use is another issue entirely. First, there are very serious questions of land use. It would involve vast spaces. At the University of Arizona plans for a solar farm call for some twenty-five square miles of desert plus $1 billion. Apparently, the technology is available, but the cost is unclear. Then there is the problem of energy storage. You can't store electricity. If we become dependent on solar energy in any major way, we would have to have a system of storing and smoothing the supply. So we're faced with pumped storage or the production of hydrogen or something of that kind.*

*I don't see that any technical breakthrough is needed, but some pretty hard-nosed engineering is needed. We have to rethink the distribution systems for the energy. I expect demonstration solar plants will be built in the fairly near future.*

**Would you give us the pluses and minuses of geothermal energy?**

*One important plus, of course, is that there are no fuel costs. The mechanism involved is quite straight-forward. Underground heat in the form of hot water and steam, like the geysers at Yellowstone National Park, would be harnessed to generate electricity. The only geothermal field now being tapped is near San Francisco. In the Imperial Valley of California, the San Diego Gas and Electric Company is constructing a $3 million pilot plant to convert geothermal hot water into electric power.*

*Among the pluses is the fact that geothermal energy is probably a renewable resource—that is, the heat flow up from the hot core of the earth probably persists over time. The disadvantages include earthquakes and things of that sort, for many of the hyperthermal zones exist near geological faults or areas of volcanic activity.*

*Questions abound. If you seriously alter the hydrology—that is, the underground water movement patterns and underground pressures—you might, perhaps, trigger earthquakes or something equivalent. In California's Imperial Valley, there is highly saline water underground; in fact, it's being used now as a mineral recovery mechanism—that is, when the water is pumped to the surface it contains certain minerals. But we have to learn how to handle the brine and contaminants in the water. There are also noise problems and land use problems. The Department of the Interior has proposed leasing out some 59 million acres of geothermal resources in fourteen western states.*

**Is there any concerted effort on the part of the nuclear power industry or AEC to discourage solar and fusion power research?**

*Well, they clearly aren't enthusiastic about using AEC money to support these programs. Whether or not they actively discourage the research, I just have no evidence at all.*

**Should the United States concentrate on fusion research?**

*I think that fusion should be pursued as vigorously as possible. It is*

*one energy source that is, from a resource standpoint, inexhaustible.
It has a minimum of environmental problems. Of course, no energy
source is wholly without heat releases into the ecosphere. Fusion
research should be our number one energy priority in the long-term.
I think the number one research priority for short-term is to find ways
to use fossil fuels that are acceptable from an environmental and a
social standpoint. There are other areas of research—transmission
systems, energy storage, and other matters.*

**Will you comment, Dr. Abrahamson, on the safeguard systems
of nuclear power plants?**

*First, we should look at the geographical structure of the nuclear fuel
cycle as it is now. Fabrication plants are in one part of the country,
reactors someplace else, fuel reprocessing plants in New York, and
radioactive waste depositories in the South and Midwest. We are
maximizing the possibilities of accidents and diversion. The remedy
suggested by Alvin Weinberg and a number of others is to create
nuclear parks where fabrication plants, reactors, and reprocessing
plants would be at the same site. This would make it easier to establish normal security.*

*Second, the risks can be minimized by turning to an essen-
tially military operation—that is, to have armed guards at every
point in the system, to have extensive screening of all personnel,
and so on.*

**Would you also deny nuclear materials to certain countries?**

*I don't know. Would you feel comfortable with every small country
of, for instance, South America and Africa having nuclear weapons?
On the other hand, can you deny them a power source that is not
dependent on the fossil fuels? I have no qualms about exporting
fusion reactors. I have no qualms about exporting solar or geothermal
technology. But exporting the capacity to join the Nuclear Club by
possessing atomic bomb material gives me a lot of trouble.*

**Could you sketch the scenario of how nuclear material would
eventually get into the hands of a terrorist group or a
hostile country?**

*There are two ways about which people worry most. One is that some
employee, for example, in a fuel fabrication plant or a chemical
processing plant will just routinely steal small quantities.*

## What would he steal?

*He would steal plutonium in one of its chemical forms — that is, either the metal, the nitrate, or the dioxide as it exists in the fuel.*

*The other worry is about a hijacking in transit. The AEC announced last February 1, 1973, when the rule was published, that it was greatly strengthening the security measures for transit of nuclear material. Until that time it had been shipped in commercial aircraft, in trucks, handled just like a package of Post Toasties. Now the AEC is requiring armed guards on shipments and more stringent accounting methods. You don't worry about these things happening at the reactor. But such things can happen at the processing plant or the fuel fabrication plant.*

## What would a terrorist do with the stuff?

*The most disruptive thing that I can think of to do with plutonium is to crunch it up into small particles and throw it into an air conditioning system someplace, for instance, the Pentagon or a World's Fair. The danger is in inhaling the small particles. Plutonium's physical properties are such that it is deposited in the deep tissues of the lung and stays there a long time. It cannot be readily cleared. It's a radiological hazard, not a chemical toxicity.*

## How do you die?

*In two ways: It can induce cancers, leukemias, and the like — and that takes a fairly long time; in larger quantities, it destroys lung tissues, like fibrosis, and destroys epithelial tissue.*

## Is a terrorist likely to be able to design a weapon or something that he could use to blackmail a country?

*The blackmail could be done in any number of ways. He could threaten to release it in an inconvenient place as particles of plutonium dust, or he could make a weapon — though there is some uncertainty as to how long it would take and how many people would be involved. There are certainly tens of thousands of people in the world who have the technical knowledge to make this weapon. It's not like making something out of Tinker Toys. On the other hand, it's certainly within the capacity of a fairly modestly supported group if they had one or two nuclear chemists with some technical knowledge. It would not even be necessary for them to have worked on a*

*weapon before in a government laboratory. There's enough informa-
tion in the open literature to tell you all that you need to know.*

Dr. Abrahamson, we started out asking you "When is Doomsday?" and we went full circle. It seems as if we may be closer to
it than we think.

# Chapter 3

**Charles A. Zraket**

# The Global Energy-Environment Problem

Let me make my position clear: I believe that we have an energy crisis, but that there are infinite physical resources on the planet earth to meet the crisis. I believe that we do not have an environment crisis, but that there are some serious, potentially long-term and barely perceived problems which require research, time, and money. I believe further that the issue of growth, as originally conceived by Malthus and reinforced by the Club of Rome and similar groups, can be approached as omnidirectional—or, in the words of Herman Kahn, "there is an expanding pie for everybody to share in." Therefore, we are not confronted by the question of what kind of growth we *can have,* but rather what kind of growth we *want to have.*

Outside of certain sections of the United States, and possibly Europe, the world is becoming what I call a "super-industrial society." The limits of growth are restricted primarily to the people of Northern Europe and to about 10% or 15% of the population in the United States. The rest of the world is entering the super-industrial stage.

During the next fifteen years, the big action will take place in the Pacific Basin—nations or areas washed by the Pacific Ocean, meaning, most notably, Australia, Japan, Southeast Asia, Indonesia, Canada, the Soviet Union, and the United States. I would offer a few exceptions: China is the premier limited-growth country today, and Brazil, though not bounded on the Pacific, ought to be included among the super-industrials. The Pacific Basin is growing economically at the rate of 10% a year. For this region, the era of the automobile has yet to come. There are now about 200 million cars in the world, half of these in the United States. By the year 2000, it is projected that there will be 1 billion cars, most of these outside the United States.

The determinate issue for energy over the next thirty years is the capability of oil, originating mainly in the Middle East and Soviet Union, to support the growth of the West. By West I mean to include Europe, Japan, the

**Figure 7.**
**World Primary Energy Consumption**

Million Tons Oil Equivalent

| Country/Area | 1972 | | | | | | 1971 | | | | | |
|---|---|---|---|---|---|---|---|---|---|---|---|---|
| | Oil | Natural Gas | Solid Fuels | Water Power | Nuclear | Total | Oil | Natural Gas | Solid Fuels | Water Power | Nuclear | Total |
| U.S.A. | 776.2 | 555.0 | 325.0 | 22.7 | 5.6 | 1,684.5 | 719.3 | 545.6 | 301.8 | 22.1 | 3.0 | 1,591.8 |
| Canada | 79.9 | 41.3 | 18.5 | 13.7 | 0.8 | 154.2 | 75.8 | 38.5 | 17.6 | 13.1 | 0.3 | 145.3 |
| Other Western Hemisphere | 160.2 | 32.2 | 13.1 | 11.0 | — | 216.5 | 149.4 | 30.5 | 12.5 | 9.9 | — | 202.3 |
| Total Western Hemisphere | 1,016.3 | 628.5 | 356.6 | 47.4 | 6.4 | 2,055.2 | 944.5 | 614.6 | 331.9 | 45.1 | 3.3 | 1,939.4 |
| Belgium, Luxembourg | 30.7 | 5.8 | 12.9 | 0.3 | — | 49.7 | 28.4 | 5.1 | 12.6 | 0.2 | — | 46.3 |
| Netherlands | 40.1 | 25.7 | 2.9 | — | — | 68.7 | 36.0 | 21.1 | 3.6 | — | — | 60.7 |
| France | 114.2 | 12.3 | 30.5 | 4.4 | 0.7 | 162.1 | 102.8 | 10.7 | 33.5 | 3.9 | 0.6 | 151.5 |
| W. Germany | 140.5 | 21.2 | 77.0 | 1.8 | 1.1 | 241.6 | 133.5 | 16.8 | 80.3 | 1.6 | 0.5 | 232.7 |
| Italy | 100.8 | 11.7 | 10.8 | 3.9 | 0.3 | 127.5 | 93.8 | 10.1 | 10.6 | 3.6 | 0.3 | 118.4 |
| U.K. | 109.3 | 26.5 | 72.4 | 0.4 | 2.3 | 210.9 | 103.1 | 18.5 | 82.1 | 0.3 | 1.9 | 205.9 |
| Scandinavia | 56.6 | — | 4.4 | 9.8 | 0.1 | 70.9 | 55.1 | — | 5.0 | 9.3 | — | 69.4 |
| Spain | 31.5 | 1.0 | 12.9 | 2.6 | 0.3 | 48.3 | 27.6 | 0.6 | 12.5 | 2.5 | 0.2 | 43.4 |
| Other Western Europe | 80.3 | 4.4 | 38.7 | 7.6 | 0.2 | 131.2 | 75.0 | 3.8 | 38.5 | 6.9 | 0.1 | 124.3 |
| Total Western Europe | 704.0 | 108.6 | 262.5 | 30.8 | 5.0 | 1,110.9 | 655.3 | 86.7 | 278.7 | 28.3 | 3.6 | 1,052.6 |
| Japan | 237.2 | 3.8 | 61.3 | 7.1 | 1.0 | 310.4 | 219.7 | 3.3 | 60.4 | 7.1 | 0.7 | 291.2 |
| Australasia | 30.5 | 3.1 | 24.2 | 2.1 | — | 59.9 | 30.0 | 2.2 | 22.6 | 2.1 | — | 56.9 |
| U.S.S.R., E. Europe, China | 396.3 | 217.5 | 952.5 | 17.2 | 1.6 | 1,585.1 | 361.1 | 196.8 | 933.9 | 15.9 | 1.2 | 1,508.9 |
| Other Eastern Hemisphere | 205.7 | 22.5 | 122.3 | 5.7 | 0.3 | 356.5 | 187.6 | 19.8 | 117.7 | 5.5 | 0.2 | 330.8 |
| Total Eastern Hemisphere | 1,573.7 | 355.5 | 1,422.8 | 62.9 | 7.9 | 3,422.8 | 1,453.7 | 308.8 | 1,413.3 | 58.9 | 5.7 | 3,240.4 |
| World | 2,590.0 | 984.0 | 1,779.4 | 110.3 | 14.3 | 5,478.0 | 2,398.2 | 923.4 | 1,745.2 | 104.0 | 9.0 | 5,179.8 |

Source: British Petroleum Statistical Review of the World Oil Industry, 1972.

Soviet Union, and the United States—their economies being based on Western science and technology. Together, these advanced industrial nations presently use about 90% of the world's energy. Their economic development clearly parallels their energy development. (See Figures 7 and 8.)

**Figure 8.**
**Primary Energy Consumption, 1950–1972**

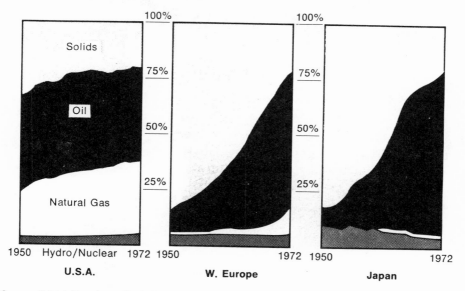

Source: British Petroleum Statistical Review of the World Oil Industry, 1972.

Even if the rest of the world grows economically by a factor of five in the next thirty years, the amount of energy that it would need would still be a relatively small proportion of the world's total energy—from 10% now to about 15%. In real terms of energy consumption, the demands for the world beyond the most advanced nations would increase from some 100,000 megawatts today to 500,000 megawatts in three decades. So, by the year 2000, that part of the world will be using the amount of energy that the United States is consuming right now. (See Figures 9 and 10.)

## THE POWER OF OIL

Oil is the name of the energy game for the next thirty years. The growth of the West will depend on the resources of the Middle East and Siberia. One important source of power is Saudi Arabia, which possesses, under its desert sands, the largest quantity of oil anywhere. It produces some 5.7

**Figure 9.**
**World Oil Consumption**

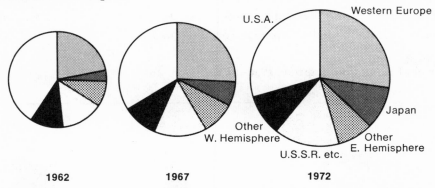

Source: British Petroleum Statistical Review of the World Oil Industry, 1972.

**Figure 10.**
**Petroleum's Share of Energy Consumption**

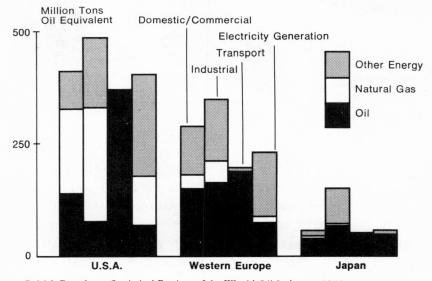

Source: British Petroleum Statistical Review of the World Oil Industry, 1972.

million barrels of oil a day, and, according to present projections, it will produce four or five times that quantity by 1980 in order to meet its percentage of the world's needs. (See Figures 11 and 12.)

Consider the critical significance of Middle East oil. In 1960 the Federation of Arab Emirates, Kuwait, Iraq, Iran, and Saudi Arabia yielded about 30% of the world's oil. In 1972 they produced 42%. By 1980 these coun-

**Figure 11.**
**World Oil Production**

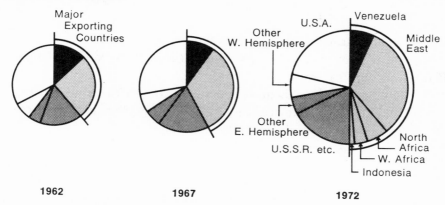

Source: British Petroleum Statistical Review of the World Oil Industry, 1972.

**Figure 12.**
**Total Discovered Oil**

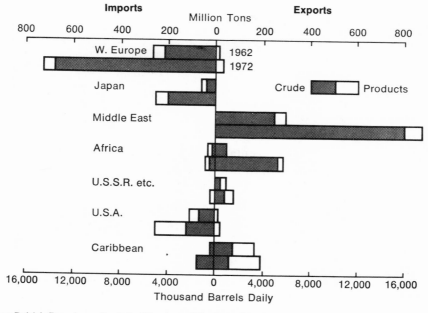

Source: British Petroleum Statistical Review of the World Oil Industry, 1972.

tries will need to supply between 50% and 70% of the world's needs. By contrast, the percentage of world oil output in the United States is diminishing from 45%, which it was a few years ago, to something like 15%, projected for 1985.

Nuclear energy does not seem to offer a ready solution to the nation's power problem. The nuclear power buildup in the United States between now and 1980 is already fixed. It is not going to make a strategic difference in the supply of energy. It will satisfy only a small percentage of our needs. Even if the pace of nuclear power plant construction is accelerated, it will make a difference only after 1985.

The big questions about nuclear energy concern the environment and health. These questions have been discussed for many years, but only recently have they become critical. Ralph Nader and some scientists who have been addressing the issue of emergency core cooling are now talking about lawsuits to prevent construction of any new nuclear reactors until this matter is resolved. It's a technical problem, and some of my friends at the AEC tell me it may result in building nuclear plants at least fifty miles away from population centers. Such nuclear-free zones, requiring up to seventy-five square miles, may make it impossible to accelerate the program so that nuclear power would not make any real difference before the year 2000.

## MINIMIZING IMPORTS

Another dimension of the energy crisis is our balance-of-payments problem. Regardless of how much we push our options over the next twenty years—and our biggest option is coal—we are still going to have to import large quantities of oil. (See Figure 13.) I am one of those who believe we should try to minimize the amount of oil we import, but not because of our balance of payments. Those who argue for limiting oil imports for economic reasons often state: "We are going to have to import as much as 7 billion or 8 billion barrels a year at $4 or $5 each, and, by multiplying those figures, it comes to a balance deficit of between $30 billion to $45 billion a year."

This argument may be answered, first, by showing that the multiplication factors are wrong. For one thing, much of the cost of domestic oil consists of internal transactions that stay within the United States economy, in terms of transportation, insurance, dividends, and so on. For another, exports to foreign oil-producing countries in terms of refineries, pipelines, materials, and reinvestments by the Organization of Petroleum Exporting Countries (OPEC) result in revenues to us that would tend to balance out the whole thing.

There are two larger factors that, I think, mitigate this matter further: First, oil imports, which now account for only 10% of our external trade, will still be a fraction—though a significant one—of our total trade in the 1980s; second, we can't look at energy as an end in itself. Energy is a commodity which

**Figure 13.**
**Oil Imports and Exports, 1962 and 1972**

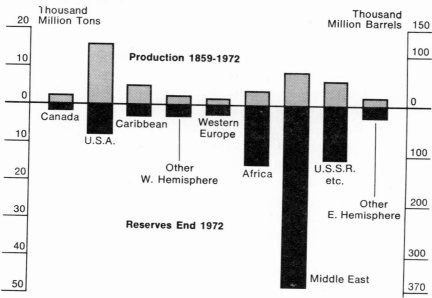

Source: British Petroleum Statistical Review of the World Oil Industry, 1972.

makes other things happen—in our agricultural system, as few properly recognize, as well as in our industrial system. We put in something like 100 Btu's of energy for every Btu of food we produce. By contrast, the Chinese, for example, put in ½ Btu besides their manual labor for every Btu of food they produce. So, we have a 200 to 1 ratio in the quantity of energy that we put into our agricultural system. This extra energy is what it takes to make chemical fertilizer, to make and run tractors, to transport crops, and so on. When the price of energy increases or energy becomes scarce, the price of food goes up, the cost of growing it goes up, etc. Energy is so critical to many sectors of our economy that it has a very positive effect on the balance of payments.

Oil is a real, not a rhetorical, issue of national security. There is a tremendous amount of world competition for this resource. It is questionable whether even the Middle East is capable of meeting the world's energy needs over the next ten or twenty years, even if the Arabs wanted to.

## OIL ALTERNATIVES

There are few options. One is nuclear energy. In the United States, as I have said, the nuclear issue concerns the natural environment and health safety; for the rest of the world, the nuclear issue concerns capital and technology. Another option, fortunately, is coal. The issue here, as far as I am concerned, is strip mining. It does not involve the money needed to develop such technical operations as coal gasification or coal liquefaction. The citizens of Colorado, Wyoming, Utah, and elsewhere are not, however, going to take very kindly to large-scale strip mining. The United States has the world's largest coal resources. The resources are rich, abundant, and fairly low in sulfur, though most are bituminous, containing up to 10% sulfur. So we are confronted by the question of whether or not we can solve the strip-mining problem by pouring enough money back into the system to reclaim the land.

There is plenty of money in the sense that we need only to increase the price of coal, including transportation, by about 10% to defray the cost of reclamation. The problem is that the inherent value of that land, once the coal is mined, is only a few hundred dollars per acre. Not very surprisingly, people don't like to spend $5,000 or so reclaiming an acre of land that is worth much less. It is an economic issue. It is also a technical issue. We don't really know how to reclaim the land—either to make it look good or to make it useful for agriculture or anything else. Once strip mining takes place, certain changes occur in the soil which make it difficult to restore. Research is now underway into land reclamation.

Europe, in contrast to the United States, has fewer options. It has the North Sea oilfields which, at best, are likely to supply about 15% of its needs. It has got to start, then, looking seriously at alternatives to oil. Yet, as far as I can tell from conversations that I have had with them, Europeans are not doing that. They seem very sanguine about their situation. The French believe they have a firm hold on the Middle East for all the oil they need. From our viewpoint, the French defected to the Arabs a few years ago. We brought this up with one of our French friends and he said, "You have got it wrong. We are leading the way."

The English are in love with the idea of limited growth, and so it appears that they are not doing very much about energy. The same applies to the Germans and Scandinavians. Japan has the worst problem of energy supply by far. The Japanese are running around the world making deals with everybody—Arabs, Canadians, Australians, Russians. They are writing long-term contracts for oil supplies.

What does all this mean with respect to the environment? We are just entering the age of the automobile and the airplane. Moving all this oil around the world is going to mean a 10% to 12% growth in marine transport—

and a lot more ocean pollution than we have today. Building all the oil infra-structure—deep ports, pipelines, ships, refineries, canals, power plants—is going to mean an exponential increase in environmental troubles. Providing more energy in agriculture—by the use of fertilizers and mechanization—is also going to increase environmental problems, as well as the automation of industry.

It seems likely, therefore, that most primary and secondary industries producing energy will be set up in the Third World, those developing countries like Korea, Taiwan, and Singapore. Very recently in Korea, to cite a case, they have been wrestling with whether or not to industrialize. They keep asking their Western friends, "Can we get clean industry here?" We tell them, "You could become the Ruhr of the Pacific." Well, they have chosen to become the Ruhr of the Pacific and to accept all the pollution that goes with it. The developing countries are concerned with getting rich first and cleaning up later.

My own feeling about the conventional pollution problems—con-tamination from power plants, autos, and so forth—is that we can solve these problems with an expenditure of time, money, and good strong government policies. But the really serious, longer-term problems—like hurling thousands of organic compounds into the biosphere without knowing the synergistic effects in the future—will require more deliberate thought and research. The fact that lots more krypton and tritium will turn up in the next thirty or forty years as by-products of fusion reactors—if we ever attain fusion power—re-quires attention. Then there is the carbon dioxide "greenhouse effect," which could well cause a significant problem in global heating. We already have local "heat islands" in many parts of the world, where some cities are ten degrees hotter than their surrounding areas because of all the energy that is being burned.

One of my friends at the National Center for Atmospheric Research made a calculation using Herman Kahn's "20-20 world." Kahn has looked at a future with 20 billion people, with $20,000 per capita, with each burning 20 kilowatts of energy per year—or twice the rate of energy consumption in the United States today. It turns out that with that growth of population and energy there is a possibility that the temperature of the earth would be raised by two degrees. If this occurs only over the northern land masses, it means an increase of up to maybe ten degrees. That may be enough to melt the polar ice caps, which, over a period of years, will change the climate and cause cities like London and New York and Boston to be inundated.

This would seem to indicate a catastrophe. But the history of the earth reveals that we have had events like this in the past, even without industrial pollution. Some 60 million years ago, the northern hemisphere was twenty degrees warmer than it is today. Then the earth encountered an Ice Age. So it's not clear, at least to most responsible scientists, that from a physical point of view the "20-20 world" of Herman Kahn would make much difference in the scheme of things. There may be social tensions and economic pressures as a consequence of our growth, but environmental transformations probably will have little to do with it.

# Discussion

Do the people in developing countries approach the energy-environment collision as an emotional thing or have they carefully calculated to industrialize no matter what the risk of pollution?

*I think it is a very sophisticated, calculated decision. If you talk to the Brazilians or Koreans or others, they will tell you they know exactly what they are doing, and they want to do it. They recognize that until they get the affluence to live in a clean environment, they are never going to make it. There is no easy way to industrialize without the attendant effect of pollution. To the guy making $200, $1,000, or $2,000 a year, a car spewing hydrocarbons or beaches smudged with crude oil mean nothing at all. He wants to share some of the action of the affluent.*

What will become of Israel in the next ten or so years if the United States comes to rely on oil for most of its energy?

*I'm not a political scientist or soothsayer. The general feeling is that the Arabs will be responsible because they have a big stake in the concept of private property. They fear any strong country that seeks to take them over—politically or economically. They have to behave responsibly to the West because they have no alternative. And so the general consensus is that our increasing dependence on Middle East oil will not result in holdups or extortions in connection with Israel.*

*There is no uniformity in the Middle East—either in oil or politics. Jordan, Lebanon, Tunisia, Morocco, and Yemen have virtually no oil; Egypt has little; Algeria and Libya, somewhat more; and the countries in the Persian Gulf, gigantic reserves. So, too, in politics there are differences. The Saudis don't view Israel as emotionally as do the Egyptians. Yet Saudi Arabia's King Faisal, who has said repeatedly that he wants to be friendly with the United States and believes that communism is a mortal danger to the Arabs, informs every visitor that our policy in the Middle East is pro-Israeli so that ultimately all Arabs will be driven toward the communist camp.*

What happens when we are mainly dependent on Middle East oil? Do we turn our backs on the Israelis and leave them naked to their enemies?

*I hope we don't. I am on the side that wants us to be as little dependent as we can. We have worked out strategies on limiting oil imports to 25% of our oil needs. One calls for using coal and providing incentives to develop oil resources offshore and in Alaska.*

*The reason that American oil companies are concerned about imports is that they have a huge investment in infrastructure— refineries, drill-rigs, pipelines, and ships. They need eight to fifteen years lead time; then they write it off over twenty years. So they are talking about something like thirty years into the future, and they say: "Where are we going to get oil? We don't even know where we are going to get it twenty years from now, so why should we make this big investment unless we can assure ourselves that we have a secure supply under our control."*

*Also, it is much more expensive to hunt and drill for oil offshore and in Alaska than it is in the Middle East. The cost of producing oil at the Saudi wellheads is now 8 cents to 10 cents a barrel. Dividends, royalties, taxes, transportation, and everything else makes up the rest. Anytime they have a mind to do it, the Arabs can drive out the oil companies or sell their oil below the world price. So the companies are not about to make a $500 billion investment over the next twenty years unless they know where they are going to get the oil to refine and ship. That's what it's all about.*

We can always turn to coal—though we would face the specific problem of the 1970 Clean Air Act. In your opinion, do those standards have to be relaxed in any way?

*We have done a lot of studies for the Environmental Protection Agency in this area. There are three kinds of standards for coal-burning power plants. There is the federal primary standard, the federal secondary standard, and state emission standards. There is no question that over the next four or five years the secondary standards will have to be relaxed because we need lead time to start opening new mines and getting low-sulfur coal or gasifying and liquefying coal. It turns out, also, that if we are very sophisticated about it on a state-by-state basis, we can make differentiations in the emission standards so that we can eliminate the worst polluters and burn the cleanest coal. So the answer to your question is yes, both the emission standards in certain states, like those in the Middle West, and the secondary standards will have to be relaxed for the next four to five years if, in fact, we want to limit the imports of oil.*

*The alternative, of course, is not to relax the standards and to import more oil until such time as we can start using coal in a clean way. It's only partly an economic question. The issue of the effect of sulfur oxide on health is a very squishy issue. I don't think that the standards we have today are really addressing the question of people's health.*

## Is the world headed for an energy recession?

*I think we are heading for energy shortages in terms of the projected demand. I think energy will get more expensive. But it's not going to get so much more expensive that the rich countries can't afford it. My own feeling is that the energy shortages and higher costs over the next ten years are going to hit the developing countries much more than the United States. There will be some rationing and some shortages here, but it's going to be the guy on the low end of the totem pole who will suffer when the electricity bill and gasoline price goes up. But it shouldn't make a difference in the life-style of the people or affect the growth rate of the economy. It will, however, hold back the advances of a lot of developing countries that won't be able to afford more expensive energy.*

## Do you think that we can buck OPEC by negotiating separate contracts with individual oil-producing countries?

*Well, so far I haven't seen the need to do that. The Arabs have been extremely responsible in selling their oil at, or below, the world price. None of the countries except Kuwait has said anything about limiting production. The Saudis have said they will continue to expand production to meet the demand. So have the Iranians. As far as I can tell, those suffering the most in all of this are the oil companies. They are the ones who are worried about their future. They face two major problems: One is that they don't have a secure supply, so they are afraid to make a massive investment in infrastructure; the other, paradoxically, is that the world is now burning about 53 million barrels of oil a day, and, if the present rate of consumption continues, it will be using more than 100 million barrels each day in the year 2000. But there are many people who believe that by that time oil*

*will no longer be the name of the energy game. That worries the oil
companies more than prices.*

**Do you foresee any problems in the accumulation of capital by
the Arab countries?**

*In the April 1973 issue of the journal* Foreign Affairs, *James Akins,
the State Department's leading oil specialist, who has been named
Ambassador to Saudi Arabia, wrote: "With the possible exception
of Croesus, the world will never have anything like the wealth
which is flowing and will continue to flow into the Persian Gulf. There
have been and still are countries which are richer than any country in
OPEC, but there is none which is so small, so inherently weak, and
which has gained so much for so little activity of its own."*

*Akins figures that the Arab countries alone, excluding
Iran, which is not Arab, will boast a cumulative income from 1973
through 1980 of more than $210 billion. Assuming that they spend
more than half that, their capital accumulation could be about $100
billion by 1980. At 8% interest, the income on this money — in a sense
unearned — would be $8 billion, which is larger than the current
expenditures of Kuwait, Saudi Arabia, and the Federation of Arab
Emirates combined.*

*It is projected that the Saudis will be earning about $25
billion a year in 1980; Iraq, Algeria, and Kuwait, between $5 billion
and $6.5 billion a year. Iran may be deriving revenue of some $13
billion in 1980.*

*What are they going to be doing with all this money? The
answer is of crucial importance to the world. There have been several
suggestions. At the Algiers Arab Oil Congress in mid-1972 it was
proposed that the Arabs could set up an inter-Arab development
bank for projects in the Arab world. Akins has suggested that the
oil-rich countries invest in the energy industries of the United States.
At a recent meeting in Kuwait there was a proposal to simply float
the money from country to country, moving it around depending on
how each country reacts to Arab problems. Of course, the Arabs could
decide, with so much accumulated capital, to leave the oil in the
ground. As Akins has observed: "This would cause a problem for the
developed world far greater than the floating billions."*

**If the Middle East decides to hoard its oil, how much of a dis-**

ruption would that cause in our supply?

*We are now importing about 3% of our oil from the Middle East, which means about 20% of our oil imports come from other places — notably Canada and Venezuela. So an Arab boycott would not be devastating, but we would suffer shortages. The United States maintains only a seven-day supply, while most European countries, having learned lessons from the Suez Canal crisis and the Six Day War, maintain reserves for ninety days.*

Why do we not maintain a larger stockpile?

*There has never seemed to be a reason to do so because most of our supply has been domestic. Up until the last few years, all of our oil has been from our own wells. We don't even have long-term storage facilities in the United States.*

The Europeans seem to have considered the national security aspects of importing oil better than we have. I wonder why we don't increase our oil explorations in this hemisphere and husband the resources where we discover them, while continuing to meet our needs as much as possible from abroad?

*I think we need to do both. If we don't develop our domestic options — shale oil, tar sands, coal, nuclear power — and there is an interruption of Middle East oil, we should probably have five to ten years before we confronted a real crisis.*

Do you see any way we can avoid constructing new refineries and deep-water tanker ports?

*No. The oil companies can start investing in that kind of infrastructure once they have some assurance they are going to get oil to keep their refineries and ports operating. That's what's holding up investments in additional infrastructures.*

The oil men say this is the first time in history that we aren't building refineries. Is this because of environmental restrictions?

*They are businessmen. We need five more refineries each year to keep up with the increasing demand. Why should the oil people make an investment of about $100 billion a year, which will take five to ten years to write off, when they don't know where the additional crude* *oil will be coming from to keep those refineries operating? So it's strictly a business proposition.*

But the oil companies always invoke the environmental questions and blame the environmentalists for their problems.

*I think that is a smoke screen. The oil men are reluctant to build refineries until they are assured of oil from the North Slope in Alaska, until they are assured they can sink wells off Long Island, until they can make a deal with the Canadians. They don't want to depend on the Middle East exclusively for their crude oil. All other arguments— balance of payments, environmental protection, and others—are secondary to the increasing flow of oil and the alternative sources of energy.*

Do you visualize coal playing an important role in the future? If so, how long do you think this will take, bearing in mind the need to solve certain environmental problems like strip mining and particulate scrubbing, as well as the need to develop new mines?

*Well, that's the $64,000 question, of course. I started out by saying that I think we are in an energy crisis. If we mounted what I would call a "crash" program, we could resolve our problems in five to seven years. But the administration doesn't seem to be looking at the crisis that way. So it's probably going to be more like fifteen or twenty years. If you asked me what's probably going to happen, I would say we are entering into a period of indecision and debate; we are going to slide into a situation in which we are importing more oil and living with more shortages—what has just been called the "energy recession." That's what I think is going to happen, not what I think can happen. If we went into a kind of wartime high gear in developing coal and relaxed environmental standards for five to seven years, we would be able to limit imports of oil in the 1980s to 25%. I don't see this happening because few people are taking the problem seriously. So I will not be surprised when President Nixon, in his energy message, calls for business as usual, with some adjustments.*

How do you explain that? The documentation on this is solid. Why did the administration fail to adopt a more urgent approach than many people had expected?

*I suspect that some of the big oil people said, "Look, if you just guarantee us a supply and a price, we will fix the problem. Don't worry about it." Maybe they are right. Maybe it isn't a problem, let alone a crisis. I happen to be one of those who thinks there is a problem, and it's going to erode further over the next ten to fifteen years. As a technologist I think that, with the right policies, we can get out of this bind, that there is a way out. But I don't think we'll do it.*

I wonder if I could turn your attention for the moment to nuclear production of energy. Do I understand that you are not concerned about the question of nuclear waste?

*Not really. There was a comedy of errors in the last few years with respect to the abandoned Kansas salt mine for nuclear waste. For two years the geologists and chemists kept trying to tell the AEC that the salt mine proposed for storing the waste wasn't secure from a hydrological aspect. The guy in the AEC who had picked that salt mine in Lyons, Kansas, literally selected it off a map. Nobody even looked at it, because in our society a physicist is at the top and a geologist is at the bottom of the pecking order. It's very difficult for them to talk to one another. I'm not making a facetious comment. Only in the last year or so has the story come out in the open. It was revealed at professional meetings. The fact is that the salt mine approach is good. There are salt mines where you can store nuclear wastes for hundreds of thousands of years.*

*Then there is the scheme James Schlesinger talked about when he was at the AEC—to shoot the stuff at the sun. It so happened that when they tried the experiment they fired rockets three times and they failed every time. People lost confidence in the idea. But the idea is basically right, if we can build rockets that are more reliable. So I think most technical people don't feel that the waste problem is really a serious issue.*

*On the other hand, transportation of nuclear wastes is a problem because we are talking about shipping around megacuries of nuclear material. No system of transport—railroad, airline, trucking system—is without risk from accident, loss, or theft. So, stringent precautions are going to have to be taken in transporting fuels all over the place.*

Isn't there a threat of someone hijacking some of this stuff and holding us all up?

*People who want to do something clandestine with fuels can get it today. Certainly it will be more plentiful in the future, and some people with whom I work feel that sabotage in nuclear power plants is a very critical issue. Safeguards would have to be imposed.*

We have had a couple of speakers tell us that there are enormous savings that could be made in energy, that the heart of the matter is trying to influence demand rather than trying to provide supplies. Would you comment on that approach?

*Conservation of energy in the broad sense is a very useful strategy. But let me modify that by saying that conserving energy at the demand end of the spectrum is of secondary importance. If you look today at the overall efficiency of the energy system in Btu terms of the fuel that's in the ground compared with what you end up using at the other end, it's about 10%. You need energy to explore for the stuff; you need energy to extract it; you need energy to process it; you need energy to transport it. The power plants that burn it are only 40% efficient, and then it must be distributed and used in other inefficient ways.*

*We could conserve energy supplies by increasing the efficiency of extraction, which in many cases is only 30% to 40% today. There is tremendous leverage in increasing the efficiency of processing and burning fuels — going from power plants that are 40% efficient to 60% efficient by magnetohydrodynamic generators and fuel cells. There are tremendous efficiencies to be realized by more efficient engines and automobiles, by insulating buildings and so forth. So, in fact, we could get increases in efficiency and conservation of energy without affecting the demand at all.*

*My own feeling about this is that those who concentrate on the demand end of energy are really addressing the life-style issue. They are not addressing the energy resource issue.*

# Chapter 4

**Harry Perry**

# How Much Energy Do We Waste?

Do we waste our precious energy resource? The answer depends on who is being asked; it is subjective, parochial, biased. In our electricity generating plants today, about 60% of the fuel being used is not turned into energy, so only 40% of the fuel in our most efficient processes turns into electricity. A plant can be built that will achieve an efficiency of 42%, but this would require a great capital investment, something economists and executives consider a waste of another resource. To an engineer the 60% loss is "reject," not waste, because that is the way the laws of nature operate, the application of the first law of thermodynamics.

Waste in the minds of consumers is something else again. When I set the thermostat in my house below seventy-five degrees in winter, my wife turns it back up again. She doesn't consider the extra heat a waste.

If, indeed, we are in the grip of an energy "crisis," do we want to tell people that they can't do certain things? In other words, how much restriction do we want to place on people?

I think it is fairly wasteful to operate pleasure boats in terms of energy and other kinds of resources, but I wouldn't want to tell people they couldn't buy a yacht. I would like to maintain as much freedom of choice as possible, consistent with other goals that we have in our society. The community has to make judgments about where there are opportunities for saving energy. Cutting the number of electric toothbrushes in half won't get you very far, but improving mass transportation will. We must put things in perspective.

## ECONOMY IN PRODUCTION

Almost everybody who talks about conservation does so in terms of consumption. There are other areas where significant savings are possible, and this is particularly true in the production of fuels. The average amount of coal that is extracted from underground mines is only about 55% of what is there, and what we now leave behind will probably be lost forever. We are only extracting 31% of the oil in a reservoir and about 80% of the natural gas. It is hard to put an extraction value on nuclear fuels because in mining nuclear minerals a given grade is cut off arbitrarily.

The best underground coal mines actually extract as much as 90%. In some of the leases on the western coal deposits, where the coal is very thick, it may get as low as 25%. So there are some real opportunities for conservation during the production of fuels.

Over the years, I have tried to determine whether the production and upgrading of the fuel consume a lot of energy. There are only two places where this is important. A refinery consumes about 12% of what goes into it, and there are opportunities to reduce that. In the electrical transmission of energy, we lose about 10% of all the energy that is moved. These are the only two large opportunities for saving. The energy used in producing coal or oil, to upgrade coal or natural gas, to transport all of these taken together consists of 2% or 5% of the energy in the fuel, and is not really important.

Inherent in any discussion of the desirability of using coal in the future is the requirement for converting it to either a liquid or a gas. The minute we do that we have a disincentive for conservation, because when we go from one to the other it is about 75% efficient, and when we go from fossil fuels to electricity it is about 40% efficient. Gas turbine efficiencies are even poorer than that. So every time a fuel resource is converted to a more useful form, some of the original energy in the fuel is lost.

## THE ENERGY USERS

One out of every five units of energy consumed in the United States goes towards moving people or goods. Transportation is the single biggest consumer of energy—whether directly in fuels to run the whole system or indirectly in making metals, rubber, plastics, and all the other materials to build the system. (See Figures 14 and 15.) Transportation takes 50% more energy than anything else. Space heating of homes, businesses, and industries is another large energy consumer and is the greatest user of energy in homes. In lighting the consumer has shown himself to be far more conservative than the utility people would like. But air conditioning, particularly central air conditioning as it becomes a standard item of human comfort, is a great user of energy and is increasing at twice the rate of other uses. (See Figure 16.)

Industry takes about 40% of the total energy used in the United States Electricity generation requires nearly 30% of all energy used in industry, up

Figure 14.
Energy Used in Transportation

| Transportation Market | % of Total Fuel Use | 1970 | 1985 | Change | |
|---|---|---|---|---|---|
| | | Thou. Bbls. Daily | | TBD | Percent |
| Automobiles | 53 | 4,282 | 7,395 | + 3,113 | + 72.7 |
| Trucks and buses | 22 | 1,741 | 2,665 | + 924 | + 53.1 |
| Aircraft | 13 | 1,019 | 2,415 | + 1,396 | + 137.0 |
| Agriculture and off-road vehicles | 5 | 387 | 525 | + 138 | + 35.7 |
| Ships and boats | 4 | 336 | 420 | + 84 | + 25.0 |
| Railroads | 3 | 248 | 295 | + 47 | + 19.0 |
| Total | 100 | 8,013 | 13,715 | + 5,702 | + 71.2 |

Source: U. S. Environmental Protection Agency.

Figure 15.
Energy and Price Data for Passenger Transport

| Mode | Energy (Btu/passenger-mile) | Price (cents/passenger-mile) |
|---|---|---|
| Intercity[a] | | |
| Bus | 1600 | 3.6 |
| Railroad | 2900 | 4.0 |
| Automobile | 3400 | 4.0 |
| Airplane | 8400 | 6.0 |
| Urban[b] | | |
| Mass transit | 3800 | 8.3 |
| Automobile | 8100 | 9.6 |

Source: U. S. Environmental Protection Agency.

[a] Load factors (percentage of transport capacity utilized) for intercity travel are about: bus, 45%; railroad, 35%; automobile, 48%; and airplane, 50%.
[b] Load factors for urban travel are about: mass transit, 20%; and automobile, 28%.

from just over 20% before World War II. The projections are for electricity to make up as much as 40% of industry's total energy consumption in the year 2000. Six industries—primary metals, chemicals and its allied products, petroleum refining, food, paper, stone and glass—consume more than two-thirds of all the energy in industry.

The aluminum industry in our country used 1% of all the energy consumed last year. In my view, 1% is surprisingly low, because aluminum has such a bad reputation as an energy intensive industry.

As everyone now knows, energy is the most pervasive of all the environmental degraders. I would guess that 70% of the environmental problems arise from some form of energy production, transportation, and utilization.

Figure 16.
Major Components of U.S. Energy Consumption

| | Percent Distribution of: | | Average Annual Percentage Rate of Change, 1960–1968 |
|---|---|---|---|
| | U. S. Energy Consumption, 1968 | Changes in U.S. Energy Consumption, 1960–1968 | |
| Transportation | 24.8 | 23.8 | 4.2 |
| Space heating | 17.9[a] | 16.6 | 4.0 |
| Process steam[b] | 16.7 | 14.2 | 3.6 |
| Direct heat[b] | 11.4 | 7.9 | 2.8 |
| Electric drive[b] | 7.9 | 9.3 | 5.3 |
| Feedstocks and raw materials[b] | 5.5 | 6.2 | 5.1 |
| Water heating | 3.9 | 3.9 | 4.3 |
| Air conditioning | 2.5 | 4.7 | 10.1 |
| Refrigeration | 2.2 | 2.6 | 5.3 |
| Cooking | 1.3 | 0.7 | 2.2 |
| Electrolytic processes[b] | 1.2 | 1.2 | 4.7 |
| All above | 95.6 | 91.4 | 4.1 |
| All other | 4.4[c] | 8.6 | 10.9 |
| Total | 100.0 | 100.0 | 4.3 |

Source: The Stanford Research Institute report to the Office of Science and Technology, *Patterns of Energy Consumption in the United States* (Washington: Government Printing Office, 1972).
[a]Comprised of: residential space heating, 11%; commercial space heating, 6.9%.
[b]These items refer almost exclusively to industrial usage.
[c]Of which residential and commercial lighting equals 1.5%.

If we are going to prevent energy from degrading our environment any further, we are going to have to make an energy investment. I will try to give you some feel for how much that amounts to.

For the automobile, the penalty that the Environmental Protection Agency has calculated is about 20% of all the energy costs included. In other words, we will be expending 20% more energy in driving our cars, in having them inspected, and in manufacturing the equipment that controls the air pollution from them. I made some calculations for power plants and determined that probably 5% of the energy will have to be used to control and remove the particulates and make sure the thermal pollution is not excessive.

There are positive gains to be made in environmental protection. For example, production of a given amount of aluminum requires 62,000 units of energy; if, however, we can learn how to recycle aluminum, the energy needed would be only one-twelfth as much.

There are pluses and minuses in this business. Let's consider for a moment three cases of glass bottles. The energy needed to reprocess a case of returnable bottles takes 20 units. A case of recycled bottles, the throw-away kind, takes 62 units of energy. But throw-away bottles that are not recycled take 58 units. So recycling bottles is actually a little bit more energy intensive than not recycling at all. An unusual and unexpected answer, to be sure.

## SAVING AND RECYCLING ENERGY

I mentioned earlier the efficiency problem involved in converting fuel to electricity. This process consumes 25% of the total fuel; about 60% gets rejected as heat. We can get a higher efficiency, but we have to pay for it. There are research potentials for ways to get this conversion efficiency up from 40% to as high as 50% or even 60% — magnetohydrodynamics (MHD) is one. I think MHD is probably a bad bet, but it is one that is being widely talked about. Another possible method uses a conventional steam plant with a high temperature potassium cycle and fuel cells. All have problems and none are economic at the moment. If we invest in research and development, it does increase our options to be able to convert fuels into electricity at much higher efficiencies with some real energy payouts.

There are other opportunities for energy savings in what I like to describe as a systems approach to energy use. The simplest kind of system to describe is that of Consolidated Edison in New York City. It produces steam and generates electricity from it. Con Ed doesn't try to squeeze the last bit of electricity out. Instead, it uses the steam to heat buildings in downtown Manhattan. The overall efficiency of this dual system is much higher than if Con Ed generated only electricity and created steam separately for heating purposes.

The gas industry has a system called GATE, in which gas engines or turbines are used in applications like shopping centers. They generate electricity on site and use the rejected heat to keep the area warm in winter and cool in summer. The total overall efficiency is much higher than 40% for electricity and 60% for heating and cooling.

There is a small program underway to study the effect of such things as using the heat rejected after cooling a home refrigerator in the wintertime to warm the kitchen. In the summer the refrigerator heat would be discharged outside, so it doesn't put a greater load on the air conditioner. The Department of Housing and Urban Development believes that a variety of such systems will add up to a savings of as much as 25% in total residential demand — a significant economy.

There have been proposals to construct nuclear power plants near industrial complexes and use the hot water or steam produced in the reactor for heating, a scheme similar to Con Ed's conventional system.

Opportunities exist also for reducing demand in the household and consumer sectors. The electric air conditioner is an example. When shopping for an electric air conditioner, it is common to find several models rated for the same cooling output; yet one may use two and one-half times the energy of another to achieve the same effect. That kind of a spread in efficiency can result in real savings. With the number of air conditioners increasing all the time, the labeling of energy consumption on each model would be useful to consumers. The reason that they are built with different energy levels is that the first cost of the high energy model is generally lower. People who can't afford the more expensive model look at first costs.

Home insulation is easily accomplished. In fact, insulation standards were changed in June 1971. This change was easy since 80% of all homes are financed by the Federal Housing Administration, and the agency simply changed the standards of acceptance for issuing mortgages. As a result, the speculative builder had to adopt the standards of FHA, or face rejection when a prospective buyer approached the FHA. The shady builder could cut down on insulation and keep his house costs some $900 lower than a responsible competitor. Studies have shown that use of the optimum amount of insulation could reduce fuel costs up to 50%, depending on the location of the house and on whether it used gas and electricity or only electricity.

I am not a great one for urging people to turn off lights as a means of saving electricity, because I don't think the hortatory approach is very effective. Charles Luce, who heads Con Edison in New York, claims that his "Save a Watt" campaign knocked 1% off the peak load.

In transportation the only way we can make any significant savings, as far as I can see, is to either make people buy smaller cars or use mass transportation. The spark-ignited internal-combustion engine has a theoretical efficiency of about 30%. With our driving patterns, it is actually around 18%. Our traditional transport is outmoded—overtaken by our urban congestion, population density, energy shortage, pollution problem, and other troubles.

There are some highly imaginative ways of overcoming our transportation tribulations. Most airplane travel—I don't know what the percentage is, but a very large percentage—is for business purposes. If the adequacy of long-distance communication could be improved; people might, perhaps, use a kind of video-telephone and not bother to make the flight. There are also energy benefits to be achieved from land use planning. Urban communities could be designed so that walking would be possible and the car would not be so necessary.

Industry, the largest energy consumer, has more opportunities to reduce demand than other consumers. It can change the process for making a product. In other words, if the price of fuel were to double, a process once rejected because it was too expensive for other reasons may be revived—if it is less energy intensive. I suspect that, as the price of energy goes up, industrialists will be looking at process changes.

So there are opportunities to conserve energy, but there are also problems—and these may well increase with time. For instance, as the grade of the metal ores that we use goes down, we are going to need more energy. It takes 13.5 units of energy to process a 1% copper ore. The kind of ore that we are currently using contains 0.3% copper, and this doubles the energy requirement. The same thing is true of things like titanium; if you use scrap, it is one-fourth as energy intensive as starting from scratch.

I want to cover one other subject in respect to conservation, and that is how we go about implementing conservation programs. As I mentioned earlier, I don't have much faith in hortatory efforts. I have a little more faith in solid educational methods—although Con Ed's "Save a Watt" experience in New York doesn't excite any enormous optimism. On the other hand, I think the price mechanism has worked in other resource areas.

The problem is that energy is so cheap one could almost double the price and it wouldn't make very much difference in demand. It is probably going to be a long time before price makes a lot of difference in energy consumption. The average value of energy added in all manufacturing is 3%. So, if the price of the energy goes up by 50%, which is a gigantic increase, the cost of manufacturing is only increased from 3% to 4.5%. That would not seem to make a lot of difference in energy use.

I think the price mechanism would work in the case of energy, but it is going to have a tough time because energy prices have been so low so long. There are things we can do: We can apply taxes; we can impose effluent taxes; we can provide refunds for recycling; we can try to invert the gas and electricity rate structures; we can recycle aluminum—but none of this will be easy. We have to design in advance for recycling. Otherwise we don't recycle very efficiently.

Then there are restrictive devices which change people's life-styles. This means such things as reducing the horsepower for cars, stopping the promotion and advertising by utilities to increase energy use, not allowing people to commute into the innercity, and taxing appliances that are energy intensive. All these mechanisms are undesirable unless we have to apply them. And we may have to.

Government energy policies up to the last three or four years had been shaped by the nation's surplus of energy at very low prices. The government sought to encourage the use of energy because there was a correlation between energy consumption and economic growth. We have the Rural Electrification Administration and the Tennessee Valley Authority promoting the use of electricity. We have the AEC promoting the use of energy. We have tax incentives aimed at using more energy. We have depreciation allowances which encourage people to get energy at lower costs. We *have* loan policies which also encourage energy use.

A staff study by the Office of Emergency Preparedness entitled *The Potential for Energy Conservation* (October 1972) carried the remarkable estimate that cuts in energy demands, brought about by conservation measures, could result in reducing the need for oil by 7.3 million barrels per day by 1980, a savings of some $10.7 billion in a year. By the most excruciating restrictions on energy, the OEP study states, we could conserve something like 14% of the total amount of oil that would otherwise be consumed in the United States.

The assumptions are wrong. The saving of 7.3 million barrels of oil each day is based on 1971 consumption patterns. In the years between 1971 and 1980 the need for oil will have grown at a rate of at least 5% a year. On that basis, the kind of conservation strategy that the OEP proposes would likely come to 2 million barrels a day—which is still considerable because it equals about two years of growth in fuel demand.

But the report also observes that no in-depth analysis of feasibility or survey of consumer acceptance had been done. Some of the measures advocated, the OEP admits, may not be feasible or acceptable to businessmen, managers, engineers, craftsmen, or even householders. What may well help to achieve an acceptance and implementation of measures for controlling consumption could also help in controlling pollution—some clear-cut incentives for such things as mass transit, industrial recycling, and use reduction. Our present problems weren't created overnight; they can't be solved overnight.

# Discussion

Obviously, if our energy demands are increasing by 5% each year, we have to find a lot more energy sources somewhere. Are we facing up to the problem realistically by reducing our wasted power?

*In the short-term — and by that I mean five to ten years — we are going to have to apply Band-Aids to solve our energy problems. Research and development isn't going to answer the needs in the short-term. The Band-Aids are more imports, more conservation, better allocation, and, perhaps, restrictions in demand through rationing or other devices. I, for one, don't see the country saving much energy through voluntary action. We may have to be forced to save. That, of course, would be done as a last resort. But this action may be the only option left if the country decides it doesn't want to rely on imported fuel to provide our energy.*

*There are large enough reserves in the Middle East to take care of us and the rest of the world into the twenty-first century. It is a policy matter. We, ourselves, have the domestic resources to take us into the twenty-first century. If we learn how to extract the energy in environmentally acceptable ways, but at higher prices, we can reduce our dependence on imports. We would then, as David Freeman puts it, "drain America first." Sometime in the early years of the twenty-first century, we will have to rely on the commercial use of one of the new and unlimited sources of energy, such as thermonuclear fusion or solar radiation. This being so, I think we ought to be doing something about directing significant amounts of research money toward developing this energy so that it is in place by the year 2000 or, most certainly, by 2020.*

Is our research money adequate at this time?

*Not at all adequate. The 1974 federal budget for energy research and development calls for a total of $772 million. In the White House and the Office of Management and Budget, this sum seems to be considered as the right trade-off among energy, Defense, HEW, NASA, and so forth. But I would like to examine a different matter: If there are energy problems for which research and development can provide solutions, is the 1974 budget adequate to reach those solutions in time? I think the answer to that is no.*

What about the split between federal funds and private research?

> *I worked out of the White House in 1962 when we prepared a report called "Energy R & D and National Progress," and, as far as I know, it was the last time any attempt was made to determine the split between the private sector and the government. At that time, research and development was one-third government and two-thirds private. But the individual fuel forms were completely out of line. Almost all the atomic energy research was being done by government; almost all the petroleum research by industry; as for coal, there was so little research that it hardly mattered. So there are historical differences between who pays for the research, depending on the industry.*

Is that desirable?

> *No. My feeling is that energy research and development is not going to get done by the industry alone. It is too important for the country not to increase the federal effort greatly.*

Is that because federal money will go into the more esoteric areas?

> *Yes.*

What do you see as adequate research and development?

> *I think I would triple the 1974 program, which calls for $772 million.*

Going back to energy consumption—someone once told me that one of the most outrageous things we do is to take twenty-minute showers. If you had to make a short list of the most wasteful things around the home, what would be on it?

> *I think that water heating is 3.9% of the total energy bill for the whole country. If I took a ten-minute shower, I wouldn't save over half of that, you know. You have to decide yourself whether that is wasteful. I like a ten-minute shower.*

Do you see an energy crusade—a movement to control waste and limit consumption in the time gap before power production catches up?

> *Maybe I didn't make my position on this clear. I think that, in the short run, there is little you can do, without taking restrictive action.*

*If there isn't any gasoline in that pump, I can't use it; but if there is, I am not going to slow down to save 10% or 15% of the gas. So, short of telling me I can't have it, I don't think much is going to happen. In the long run, it is extremely important that we try to do things that will result in limiting wastefulness through research and development and other routes. But the lead times are very long, and it is not going to happen by 1980 unless use is somehow limited or restricted. By 1990, if we start today doing the right things—constructing new homes and other buildings, improving building design offers, and so forth—we may be reducing energy loads.*

While we are insulating our houses, redesigning them, and so on, what about the rest of the world? Isn't our effort to conserve energy rather futile?

*You don't have to cite the rest of the world. If I were living in an innercity ghetto, I would tell you to shove your whole environmental movement. Much of the world—and that includes many people in Manhattan and Appalachia—doesn't feel strongly about energy. With money, it's there for the taking. In the United States, with 6% of the world's population, we consume nearly 35% of the world's energy. If the rest of the world gets up to where the United States is in living standards, the kinds of problems we face will be imposed on the rest of the world. And don't think they don't want to reach that point; they do.*

If the housewives of America make a concerted effort and are able to maintain a low energy profile, do you feel some of our shortages would be over?

*What brought on the meat boycott? The price of meat doubled. Meat probably takes 20% of your budget. If energy were doing that to consumers, things would happen. Energy just isn't like that, though. It is a very small part of the family budget to start with, and even doubling a small sum will not affect many people.*

# Chapter 5
Lee C. White

# A Consumer's Slant
# on the Energy Crisis

A number of consumer groups have believed that the current debate on energy policies noticeably lacked the voice of the ultimate user, the consumer himself. This is unfortunate. Although our organizations are, for the most part, well known, and some of them are even well heeled, there is something about them that industrial leaders and government bureaucrats would like to ignore. But our cause is just, and we are determined to do whatever we can to make the views we think are worthy of consideration—not only our own but those of others—heard in Congress, and the courts, if need be.

Some of the consumer groups are energy oriented. These include the American Public Power Association, American Public Gas Association, National Association of Rural Electric Co-ops. More broadly based are The League of Cities, Conference of Mayors, National Farmers Organization, National Farm Bureau, the Industrial Union Department of the AFL-CIO, and Consumers Union. We don't delude ourselves into believing there is a single, undivided, disciplined, consistent consumer position or that we are the self-appointed spokesmen for all the people all the time in this country. That is a little presumptuous even for our group.

We do think, however, that there are some factors we can stress. If we do have positions we believe are significant and ought to be advanced in Congress, we should bring them to the attention of our member organizations and enlist their assistance in letting our representatives in Congress know there is an obvious consumer interest.

Put in the simplest terms, we have been concerned that there is a feeling in the administration, and certainly in the energy industries, that the basic solution to what might be called the energy problem or the energy crisis is simply to raise prices. We are not wedded to the view that there should *never* be a price increase. The rates we are using now were not handed down to Moses on Mount Sinai.

It is evident that we are in an inflationary period, and it is obviously more costly to produce energy today than it was five years ago. Similarly, I think we are now, as the economists like to say, internalizing the costs for our concern over the environment. This is expensive. It is a legitimate case, and I think the consumers of energy ought to pay these costs. But I don't believe that we ought to use prices as a mechanism for reducing demand. I think demand is the part of the equation that requires a great deal of attention, and I think we will see increasingly sincere and strenuous efforts to work on the demand side of the equation while we are still striving to increase supply. I believe that the largest battles in Congress in this session will take place over what the news-papers lead us to believe will be the president's recommendation that Congress decontrol the rates on new natural gas.

## REGULATION AND CONTROL

We have issued a statement that contains fifteen different policy positions. It is extremely brief and skims the surface. Two of the most impor-tant items work together. I refer, first, to eliminating the distinction between intrastate and interstate gas. They ought to be treated in the same manner— either both of them are uncontrolled or both of them are controlled—by the same mechanism. More significantly, and second, I also refer to supporting a proposal to create a government-owned corporation to explore not only for petroleum deposits but for other fuel deposits on publicly owned lands.

The way the system works today there is no complete regulatory circle. In classic utility regulation, for example, the local electric utility is awarded a franchise. A particular company is selected to occupy the position of a government-granted monopoly. The privately owned company undertakes to meet all of the responsibilities for providing the utility service in a certain geographic area.

So the Potomac Electric Power Company, for instance, cannot say it is too expensive to build plants and that it is not going to meet its obligations. Pepco must make an effort. There was a utility in New Jersey about seven or eight months ago which said to the New Jersey Public Utilities Commission: "Fellows, if you don't raise the rates, to hell with you. We are not about to build another plant." The New Jersey Public Utilities Commission replied: "That is fine. We will give your franchise to somebody else who will." Where-upon the utility said: "Well, don't get huffy about it. We can work this out." The point is that the company had the obligation all along.

Now, in natural gas, the utility does not have that obligation. There is nobody today who has the authority to say to the gas producer, "We need natural gas in this country so, damn it, go out and drill." You can beg them, you can approach them with incentives or disincentives, you can do anything else you want, but the company isn't required to drill.

Industry people argue that gas is a hydrocarbon just like oil and coal. One does the same thing with both—burn them. They ask why somebody should tell them what they can charge for gas but not for oil or coal—except, of course, under the current price stabilization order. I think the answer rests upon the reason for which Congress passed the 1938 Natural Gas Act. That is the matter of mobility. Oil can be sold by a guy in a tanker truck. He can drive around to you, and, if you like his brand of oil, you can buy it, perhaps because the advertising is cute or sexy. If there is a local guy operating a home oil heating company, you can buy oil from him even though there is a little problem about where he gets it. But, insofar as the householder is concerned, there is a choice. There is likewise some choice for coal, although coal presents another problem about which we are concerned—the increasing concentration of ownership in fuels across the board.

This cannot be done with natural gas. Natural gas has to be treated in a pipeline system where it involves expenditures of hundreds of millions of dollars. The natural gas industry, at least the modern industry, is only thirty years old. Yet it is the fifth or sixth largest industry in terms of capital investment—about $35 billion.

We don't have the capability to tell a gas company that it has got to get the gas out of the ground and run it through the pipeline for distribution to customers. It is different with a major petroleum company. The company president says, "We need oil. Where shall we put our exploration and development dollars this year?" The head of his foreign investment division says, "Let's drop it in the North Sea where there is a lot of untapped oil and gas." Another says, "Indonesia or how about the coast of Ecuador?" Then there is a guy who wants to drill in the Gulf of Mexico on a lease from the Department of the Interior or in western Texas or Oklahoma. The management is concerned with getting the most for its bucks. The management doesn't quite say it has a soft spot for the beleaguered American consumer. Stockholders are very interested in how good a job management has done, not in supplying energy to a whole bunch of people, but in making money. That is the atmosphere in which the managers grow up and operate, and there is nothing wrong with it, except when a critical situation arises.

## A GOVERNMENT ENERGY CORPORATION

I would like to see a corporation that is concerned with service to the consumer as well as with dividends to the stockholders. I would like to see a corporation board concerned about the imbalance between supply and demand of natural gas, for instance. I think that can be accomplished by a government corporation.

Fortunately, the American public owns very valuable fuel deposits. We know how valuable these are because we have already heard and read about how much was bid for the rights to explore the continental shelf or the North Slope. I would like to see the public take some of this reserve of oil and gas and develop it.

I have one more proposal: I would like the newspeople in this symposium to demand from the energy industry the necessary data, statistics, information, and studies that are so vital, not only to enable government regulators to reach an informed judgment, but to enable the press to provide informed judgments to the public. I don't know how people can operate so much in the dark. For the past fifteen years, the Federal Power Commission, whether under Republicans or Democrats, has been uniform in its desire to get more data. Its members have all supported legislation which would give to the FPC the same authority to get information about gas that it presently possesses on electricity, all to no avail.

If the United States were running an energy enterprise or were a partner with somebody, the information would be available. The United Kingdom went into a partnership with Royal Dutch Shell, and together they found gas in the North Sea. When that gas is brought into the United Kingdom, it will be sold to the National Gas Council for distribution to the public. The National Gas Council, a British government operation, sets the rates. It is very convenient for them to have all of the cost data available in establishing the rates. They got the data because they were a partner, 50-50. Nobody could say, "Sorry, old chap, business confidentiality won't allow me to tell you what it cost to produce gas because my competitors might find out." A second major benefit from a government corporation in the energy field would be the ability, at long last, to be able to get some accurate data.

Finally, in support of the corporation concept, I believe we are going to require drilling in areas where it is not now being done—particularly along the Atlantic and Pacific coasts. There are many environmental groups that will not believe a United States energy corporation is the answer to their prayers. Many of them are terribly disillusioned with my old agency, the Tennessee

Valley Authority. In many ways TVA today is indistinguishable from the private power companies that surround it. It bugs me that TVA is one of the nation's biggest strip-mining operations.

I would hope that my proposed government energy corporation would have, at least in the early years, the same vigor, dynamism, imagination, and public concern that TVA once had. Maybe these enterprises need a self-destruct mechanism—in fifteen years they would collapse. I think people will have more confidence in a United States corporation drilling in the Atlantic than in Mobil or Exxon or Texaco. I would envision the legislation establishing the new energy corporation as requiring it to be extraordinarily careful in activities that have an impact on the environment. I even foresee a considerable profit in this business. I would like to see a provision for plowing back those profits into research and development in an environmental field. There are some other subordinate reasons for the corporation concept, but those are the principal ones.

Initially, this concept was offered as a prod to private industry. But I first realized that it was a fairly serious proposal when the American Petroleum Institute's statement of energy policy, in its first point, stated that the federal government should not engage in energy production or sales. I felt then that we had come to the point where a government energy corporation was worth discussing openly. Senator George McGovern even mentioned it casually during a speech in April 1972. Now there is the remarkable development that Senator Henry Jackson has expressed a positive attitude about this project. Such acceptance of the idea is encouraging.

# Discussion

**Has a bill proposing a government energy corporation been introduced in Congress?**

*No, no bill has been introduced. Senator Warren Magnuson was quoted in* The Wall Street Journal *several months ago as being sympathetic to the idea. I don't think there is anything stronger than that. But Senator Jackson, in a speech at the National Press Club in Washington, expressly listed it as one of the things he thought ought to be considered.*

**As I understand it, you don't argue with the idea that the price of natural gas should be allowed to rise?**

*Absolutely correct.*

**You want to relax regulations, not eliminate them.**

*No, I don't want to relax them. I want the rates set where they belong by a mechanism. The 1938 Natural Gas Act says the FPC shall set "just and reasonable" rates. "Just and reasonable" has been interpreted judicially. It has a fixed meaning in the law. It's that rate sufficient to provide a satisfactory return to the industry for incentive and investment. Yet it is to be the lowest possible rate to achieve that objective. I can tell you, having sat there, how difficult it is to come to that nice fine print when you know that the rates you have set meet the requirement.*

**Why are you so firm in saying that the price structure should not be used as the device to reduce or, if not reduce, at least alter demand? Why not let the price of natural gas rise and thereby shift industrial use into other fuels which are cheaper?**

*Well, I guess I should reveal some of my prejudices now: I'm against higher natural gas prices partly because I think the industry has all the characteristics of a monopoly, and I don't want to see windfall profits go to somebody operating a monopoly. I don't believe the reason we have a gas shortage is because the rates were set "artificially" low, even though that is a popular view. Believe it or not,* The Washington Post *said so editorially. I canceled my subscription when I read that editorial. I believe the argument is phony. If the reason the country has a natural gas shortage is because the rates are low, why don't we have more oil, which has no set rates?*

**What is causing the shortage then—if there is a shortage?**

*There is a shortage. But there has been a lot of discussion as to whether it is a genuine shortage or an artificial shortage. Is it a contrived one, because guys are sitting on their gas? Or is it something that is the result of a set of economic and physical factors that have brought us to where we are. As far as I am concerned, there is an imbalance. There is not enough gas to meet demand. But, in large measure, it is because the demand has gone ape.*

*This is an industry which grew at the rate of 4% to 5% annually through the 1950s and 1960s until 1968. In 1968 it jumped to around 9%. Of course it was raising a bigger base all the time. In large measure this was because of the completion of the pipeline network across the country, but also because of the new concern with the environment. As air pollution began to be a problem, cities like Los Angeles, St. Louis, and New York warned the electric utilities and other large fuel users: "Gentlemen, you can't use those old dirty fuels any more. You have got to use clean fuel." The most attractive clean fuel, of course, was natural gas. It's a very premium, flexible, and desirable fuel. So the demand went up.*

*The industry didn't foresee this. The FPC didn't either. Congress didn't provide the money for a natural gas survey that the FPC asked to run. I don't know if we would have found anything that would have prevented the current shortage, but at least it would have prevented me from blaming Congress for being a tightwad.*

**Another reason demand went up was because gas is so cheap, right?**

*Correct, in part. Don't forget, cheapness is a relative thing. We are not talking about a uniform price. We have had what we call valley gas, the bargain stuff sold at greatly reduced rates to industries on the basis that service may be interrupted. If there were not enough, the industry said, it would cut off. Well, nobody ever got cut off, because during those periods a lot of gas was being discovered.*

*It was beneficial at that point in time because, with that kind of a customer, smaller communities were able to be served by gas, and residents who lived there were able to get the benefits of it when they otherwise might not have had a sufficient load to warrant the extension of the pipeline into their region. But conditions are very different now. Facts that used to be accepted in the electric utility industry, for example, are no longer valid. Everyone now claims that more is better. The more it was used, the more it could sell. The more sold, the newer, the better, the more modern the technology and the lower the per unit cost. And lower unit cost meant the nation's standard of living would rise because the public would be using more electricity.*

*Suddenly, it doesn't work that way any more. When you add a plant today, gas costs more than the average price, whereas ten years ago it used to cost less. Now we have to use sophisticated rate-making and price-fixing mechanisms because there is a big dispute going on between incremental and rolled-in prices. Yes, I think the fact that natural gas was attractive financially and environmentally did increase the demand.*

Then why don't you want to use pricing as a way of reducing demand?

*I am willing to use pricing, as long as it is on a cost-based formula. I don't think, in other words, that we ought to say it costs 20 cents to produce 1,000 cubic feet of gas, which includes a 15% to 18% rate of return on the investment. At 20 cents, too many people are going to want gas. So let's put it up to 30 cents, and they won't use it so much, then give the additional 10 cents as more profit to the guy who produced it. That offends me. I don't think it ought to be done.*

Others are speaking to the whole energy picture when they say natural gas is artificially low. They are saying it is low in comparison to the costs of oil and coal. But you are saying that gas prices are based on the cost of producing the gas, not in relation to other fuels. Is that right?

*That is correct.*

So it is like comparing apples and oranges. There are two different bases for setting the rate?

*The gas industry wants it set on the basis of value—on what the market will carry. At this stage of the game, when we are encountering shortages, I would rather see the allocation take place not through pricing, but through end-use control by the regulatory mechanism in the government.*

What do you mean?

*Well, right now the FPC has adopted rules which I think are reason-*

*able. It says when you have to curtail, there are some priorities—the use of gas is not just one category. I would prefer to see, as the FPC apparently does, too, the residential consumer, who uses gas to cook his food and heat his house and water, have a priority position as distinguished from the fellow who uses gas to fire a boiler for whatever purpose, whether to generate electricity or to distill gin out of grain and juniper berries. The commercial user can burn oil, corncobs, coal, or wood.*

If you are representing consumers, why contribute to higher prices for electricity by requiring the power companies to use some fuel other than gas?

*We are not suggesting there is any magic here. We expect to pay more for energy, including gas. But I don't want to pay more than what it costs. I don't want to let some company experience a windfall in a regulated business. The reason I think it ought to be regulated is because people ought to have that particular fuel available to them.*

How, constitutionally, are you going to deregulate gas interstate and regulate it intrastate?

*Just pass a statute.*

What about interstate commerce?

*I don't know what the Supreme Court would do, but I can't believe even the "Nine Old Men" would not find that this affects the national interest.*

Would you like to regulate the price of gasoline and other energy sources?

*Electricity, yes; gasoline, no. It is because of mobility. I can tell you when natural gas is not going to be regulated: first, when there is enough of it again, as there was up until 1969, and, second, when liquefied natural gas and synthetic natural gas are available. Then there will be mobility in gas. Then the local distributing company is not at the end of a pipeline. It will work out port arrangements and terminal arrangements, then move the stuff around. Competition at that time will do what regulation does today.*

How can you conserve energy without using price as a mechanism for reducing demand?

*One of the ways is through design requirements. We are rapidly approaching the time when we will see controls on the design of automobiles, either directly or through tax policies. Frankly, we are really at that point where we are willing to let somebody tell us about emission controls and that we can't have a big car.*

*Further, I expect us to make some considerable strides in mass transportation. When the highway trust is broken—it's not broken yet, but Congress shows a disposition to do so—the movement will grow toward public transit.*

One of the reasons you seem to be against paying more is because of the profits going to industry. What about raising the price through taxes—let's say taxes earmarked toward fusion research?

*I don't have any problem with that. We vigorously support greatly expanded research and development programs.*

What can the consumer do? How can he protect himself against the energy crisis?

*One way, I believe, is to mount a campaign to make sure gas is not decontrolled—because I assure you that would result in a drain on the consumer. When price increases are proposed as a way of limiting use, it is the consumer who has to pay for the dearer product, and sometimes the consumer who is already using the minimum finds he cannot afford to use even that amount. So continue regulation.*

*Then there is rate design. Rate design is very important. We are seeing some fairly sophisticated presentations by consumer groups —for instance, the Urban League, which has started studying how rates are structured. You ought to read, if you haven't already, a very perceptive speech that Judge Skelly Wright of the U. S. Court of Appeals for the District of Columbia Circuit made about three years ago. He expressed a sneaking suspicion that the cleancut white families in suburbia were riding on the backs of the harrassed black people in central Washington and all the other major metropolitan areas in the country. That got the Urban League thinking and looking. So one of the answers to your question is rate design.*

*Rates should be imposed to achieve the results you think are in the public interest. One of the ways to do that is through adversary process. Get your lawyers in there arguing with their lawyers, and let the regulators reach their judgments.*

Basically, it means charging big users more at different stages of consumption.

*At the very minimum, I would say that.*

**What else?**

*Certainly building and auto designs need to be regulated. I think we will see very soon — and I am willing to see it considered now — some device for pressing Detroit to emphasize construction of small vehicles rather than huge gas-guzzling monsters. That is where a great deal of our national energy goes. Transportation takes 25% of it. We have a love affair with the automobile, but I would say we are now at the stage where, along with women's fashions, we are going to have to do with less elaborate and more skimpy modes.*

**You have been describing group political action. How about individuals?**

*President Lyndon Johnson set the tone for that by turning off lights that weren't in use in the White House. Would you believe we have in suburbia today more ornamental gas fixtures on front lawns than we had to light the whole United States in 1890.*

**One speaker told us of a campaign in New York called "Save a Watt," which cut only 1% off the peak load of electricity after thousands of dollars were spent on advertising.**

*Consolidated Edison's rates of both growth and consumption were around 1½% this last year. So 1% isn't bad when you are talking about that incremental part of it which is where it's expensive.*

**You spoke earlier of windfall profits by the energy industry if rates and prices were unregulated. Wouldn't the excess-profits tax guarantee against such windfalls?**

*That's an idea which has been kicked around a little. After the Supreme Court said in 1954 that the FPC had to regulate well-head prices, we tried it on a company by company basis and gave up. We then tried it on an area basis and it took too long. Afterward, the industry itself asked that it be done on a nationwide basis through rules so that the FPC didn't have any problems other than picking a price.*

*We thought maybe we ought to do what was done in World War II when the country needed an economic engine to wage war.*

*There were critical shortages of essential supplies and major industries were slow to begin producing war materials. Manufacturers, miners, power magnates and Pentagon officers came before the Senate Special Committee Investigating the National Defense Program, which was headed by Senator Harry Truman of Missouri. The Truman Committee, as it was called, found that some contracts had been negotiated unfairly — meaning, with business profits rather than public interests at heart. So a process known as "renegotiation" was created. Under it, contracts were changed, priorities were set, and the government funded research and development through various programs to get the war effort moving. Once the guns, ships, and planes were made, the companies had to bring in their accounts. If a firm made too much war profit, the government took some of it. If a firm didn't get a good enough return for its outlay, the government gave it some more.*

*It occurred to me that this system might not be bad for the energy industry. We would say, "Look, fellows, you run some risks and put in big investments and so you ought to make a reasonable return. Bring in your accounts to our renegotiation board, where we will have a full and fair review of the ledgers. If you haven't made enough while operating in the public interest, we'll figure out some way to help you; if you made too much, we'll take that money and prime the pump of research and development."*

*This is an interesting idea. But so far there is no backing for it in Congress.*

# PART TWO

# THE SECURITY FACTOR

# The Authors

**Frank N. Ikard**
*The Oil Industry and the Energy-Environment Problem*
Mr. Ikard has been president of the American Petroleum Institute since 1963.
A law graduate from the University of Texas, he has served as a judge in his native
Texas, as a five-term member of Congress from Texas's Thirteenth District, and
as a United States delegate to the 1972 U.N. Conference on the Human
Environment at Stockholm.

**Morris A. Adelman**
*Cartels and the Threat of Monopoly*
An economics professor at M.I.T., Mr. Adelman is one of the nation's leading
authorities on antitrust law and international trade. He serves on advisory committees
to the American Petroleum Institute, the Federal Power Commission, and the
National Research Council's Maritime Transport Research Board on nuclear
merchant ships. An editor for *The Journal of Industrial Economics,* Professor Adelman
has written articles for the *Harvard Law Review, The American Economic Review,*
and other scholarly journals. His latest book is *The World Petroleum Market.*

**Lawrence Rocks**
*Energy and Foreign Policy: How Dependent Must We Be?*
A research chemist trained at Purdue and in Vienna, Mr. Rocks is at C. W. Post
College, Long Island University. He is co-author (with Richard Runyon) of the
1972 book, *The Energy Crisis.*

**Richard P. Runyon**
*Energy and Foreign Policy: How Dependent Must We Be?*
Educated at Yale as a psychologist, Mr. Runyon is dean of the Division of Science
at C. W. Post College, Long Island University. He is co-author (with Lawrence
Rocks) of a controversial book, *The Energy Crisis.*

# Chapter 6

Frank N. Ikard

# The Oil Industry and the Energy-Environment Problem

A decade ago, in 1963, the United States consumed 10.5 million barrels of oil a day. Of this, we produced 8.6 million barrels a day—82% of our daily needs. We imported 2.1 million barrels each day, which was more than we actually needed, and we even exported on average about 210,000 barrels of oil a day. I think it is an instructive comparison to note that this past year, 1972, we used nearly 16 million barrels of oil a day, producing 11.2 million barrels—70% of our needs—and importing all the rest. Obviously, we did not export any oil last year.

## THE U. S. OIL MARKET

Looking ahead, by 1985 the oil requirements of the United States will be on the order of 25 million barrels each day, and, if present conditions and trends persist, we will be producing less than 12 million barrels ourselves. Oil will be at the top of our shopping list of imports from abroad. We will be dependent on importing about 13 million barrels a day—more than one-half of our daily oil requirements.

By our increased imports, the United States in 1985 will be creating a demand for nearly half the combined daily output of Saudi Arabia and Iran, two of the largest oil producing countries in the world. Our oil purchases from others lands, to make another comparison, will be equal to the entire anticipated daily capacity in 1985 of the Soviet Union. *We will be the world's most insatiable importer of oil.*

Some people are inclined to shrug off the seriousness of this implication, confident in the belief that other energy sources will be available by then. There is no question that huge deposits of oil shale and tar sands, along with gasified and liquefied coal, will contribute substantially to the nation's future energy needs. But these synthetic fuels will provide, at most, no more than 1%

of our demands by 1985. So, as almost everyone knows by now, we must have massive research and development programs initiated just as soon as possible.

At the very earliest, according to all the reports that I have seen, the more exotic energy sources (breeder reactors, thermonuclear fusion, solar power, geothermal steam and any others) are still twelve to fifteen years away, under the best of circumstances, from making a substantial contribution to our needs.

The problem, then, breaks into three segments: (1) for the short-run, certainly until 1985, there is no substitute for the conventional hydrocarbons—oil, coal, and natural gas; (2) until the year 2000, the usual sources will have to be reinforced by the products of research; (3) for the long-run, the results of research and development will predominate the energy industry.

Right now, crude oil and natural gas provide 78% of the energy we use in the United States. Year by year this percentage increases because of the restrictions placed on other energy sources. Coal, once the chief source of fuel to generate electricity, is being replaced in larger quantities each year because of environmental considerations. Atomic power, the great clean hope of the 1950s and 1960s, has not met our expectations because of environmental and technical reasons. What's more, until the fast-breeder reactor is fully operational, we have, as I gather from the data, only some thirty to forty years' supply of atomic fuel resources.

## SELECTIVE USE OF OIL

As we face up to our growing appetite for energy and our worrisome shortage of gasoline, fuel oil, and natural gas, Congress and the industry debate about who is responsible for what. In an effort to assist in that debate, let me provide some telling statistics: In 1967 we used 8,000 barrels of oil distillates a day to generate electricity; in 1972 the need was for 186,000 barrels a day.

If the additional oil that went to the electric power industry last year had gone to heating and transportation, there would have been no cold schoolhouses or closed gas stations across the country. It is inefficient, uneconomic, and downright wasteful to use oil distillates to generate electricity. But that is what we are doing.

All this is happening while the nation's refineries are operating at an unprecedented rate of production. As a matter of fact, in every month beginning with August 1972, a new record of distillate production was established.

Yet stocks of distillates on hand for that period were lower than they were in 1971.

So our production is going up but our stocks are going down. We think the problem could have been relieved if administrative actions were taken so that, without sacrificing the quality of our air—in the industry's judgment at least—coal would be used for generating electricity during certain periods. Simply stated, the country cannot afford any longer to increase the use of distillates or residual oils in power plants at the expense of home heating and transportation.

Something which would, I believe, have an effect on the short-term energy supply is a law, administrative procedure, or independent authority (either local, state or federal) to determine or decide where oil refineries and power plants and tanker ports can be located. The decision by one agency or authority is desperately needed.

A companion step would be the start of a vigorous educational program—and I am not talking about a government educational program, but one jointly organized and operated by the energy industry, transportation field, agriculture business, and the government—to try to get across to the public a basic truth: The United States is now a "Have-Not Nation" in energy, and we will have to conduct our personal, private, and business affairs accordingly.

This will mean, for all of us, smaller automobiles, better designed buildings, some un-American conservation practices like five-minute showers in the morning and chillier homes in the winter. While I think the energy industry has a large part to play, a public realization of the problem is essential. There isn't anything we can do to make everyone across the country decide that he is going to change life-long habits about using energy until he understands the implications of the energy shortage.

# Discussion

Could you repeat again who would have the burden of education?

> *We all would. It is not the burden of industry alone. Government, the media, the schools, all have a responsibility to articulate the fact that we are, as I said, a "Have-Not Nation."*
>
> *In our industry we are also going to have to start educating ourselves. We have initiated some programs in our organization, and so have a large number of companies. You have no doubt seen some of our efforts in newspapers and magazines and heard them on radio and television.*
>
> *We feel that there is a desperate need to use the greatest treasure trove of energy locked into the North American continent, the petroleum in Alaska's North Slope. The field at Prudhoe Bay appears likely to contain about 10 billion barrels, making it twice as big as the East Texas field which was the largest previously found in the United States. M. King Hubbert, one of the nation's foremost energy experts, estimates rather roughly that there may be from 30 billion to 50 billion barrels of oil in Alaska. At the present rate of consumption in this country, 30 billion barrels is less than a six-year supply.*
>
> *When the Alaska pipeline is operating, it is estimated that about 2 million barrels a day will be flowing to the other states. This would make a significant contribution to our critical energy situation. The pipeline already has been delayed for more than five years. At the very earliest, and under the best circumstances, it is going to take another three or four years—assuming the decisions are made as soon as possible, before any "black gold" arrives in the "Lower 48," those contiguous states on the North American continent.*

Even with the Alaskan oil, a large gap between supply and demand has been predicted unless the industry builds additional refineries to process oil from abroad. Is that right?

> *We estimate that we will need about five refineries, with capacities of 250,000 barrels a day, built each year until 1985. Currently, for the first time in our oil history, there is no refinery under construction in the United States. Local zoning restrictions, environmental con-*

*straints and other factors have limited construction. Only three large refineries have been built since 1969, one of which went up in the Middle West in the past year.*

*The lack of refining capacity is the result of four factors: the site problem, the supply of crude oil, the lack of deep water ports, and the absence of any definitive knowledge about the products that will meet new standards, such as low-lead gasoline and low-sulphur heating oil.*

Senator Henry Jackson has suggested that one reason we had a shortage of heating oil this winter and will have a gasoline shortage this summer is that the oil refineries failed to produce to capacity because they didn't want a surplus which would tend to suppress the prices of oil and gas.

*I have great respect for Senator Jackson, of course. There has been a great deal of confusion about the level of refinery operations. We have just conducted a survey of refineries, and we find that the average refinery in this country is operating at about 93.5% of capacity. If you have been around any kind of machinery, you know that 93.5% of operating capacity on a steady basis is about as effective as you can get. What's more, where there has been an ample supply of crude, the refineries have been operating at 106% capacity. Then, of course, there were also a few inland refineries—for instance, Allen in Oklahoma—which shut down for lack of crude supply. What I am saying is that the refineries that have been able to get crude have been operating at capacity.*

You disagree, then, with Senator Jackson's belief that there was a holding back of refining capacity in order not to produce a surplus?

*Yes, I disagree with that. I think there is some problem of definition.*

Senator Jackson has argued that the refineries misjudged the need for No. 2 oil and made too much gasoline. Now, you have shifted into making a lot of No. 2 oil, resulting in a gasoline shortage. That doesn't appear to be clever planning.

*It is much easier to look at something with twenty-twenty hindsight. All our predictions last winter were wrong. We had theorized. We hadn't figured on a cold, wet fall, particularly in the Midwest, where they had some real problems. But we did not hold down supplies or create shortages.*

*The other morning I heard a news broadcast that, first, reported the sales of new automobiles were up 25% last month, then, immediately afterward, announced that some 1,200 gas stations had closed for want of supplies. So we have a greater demand as a result of more cars, trucks, motorcycles, and campers on the road than ever before, with many of these carrying the additional weight of safety equipment and larger low-compression engines and pollution control devices. At the same time, we have a reduced stockpile of oil and gasoline even though our refineries are running in a virtually all-out effort.*

*Other factors compound the shortage. The delay of a tanker getting to port can shut down a refinery. The turnaround period required to change the mix of distillates and gasoline can vary widely with the age of a refinery. These things happen and do affect output. When there are no surpluses or stockpiles on hand, shortages are sure to occur.*

The Office of Emergency Preparedness has accused the refineries of being on a gasoline binge. Isn't it a case of everyone's expecting George to do it, and so nobody does it? What's to prevent it from happening again?

*Nobody is tampering with supply. We simply do not have the capacity to meet demand. The industry tries to predict the market demand. Every company does it differently. There is no way under the antitrust laws of the United States that an industry can get together and agree on production, price, or anything else. Everyone in oil would be in jail before morning if we met and reached an agreement. So every company and every supplier is on his own.*

Do we have the tanker capacity to meet our increasing need for crude from overseas?

*In a word, no.*

It would seem to me that the high cost of building tankers combined with the high cost of crude from the Middle East would make us think hard about delaying the construction much longer for a trans-Canada pipeline to move our Alaskan oil.

*Both superports and supertankers will have to be built, conceivably, say the experts, at an investment of $15 billion to $18 billion. That alone should impel us to reach a decision on the pipeline. I think there is one inescapable point, though, and that is that the Canadian government has a great deal to say about it, and they have indicated, according to information I have, that they don't want the pipeline. So I think we are being somewhat presumptuous when we talk about building a pipeline across Canada when Canada has said, "We are not going to export any more oil to you; we are concerned about our own supply. If you do build a pipeline, we are going to take a certain part of the product."*

**Is the American Petroleum Institute in favor of legislation to tax horsepower on cars or to require Detroit to produce a more efficient automobile?**

*We are not on record as having a position. I don't know how you could require Detroit to build a more efficient automobile. We have publicly stated that we hope they will build one, and we have publicly stated we are for smaller engines and smaller automobiles. As long as people want to buy the big automobiles, Detroit is going to produce them. But, of course, you could tax horsepower, as some of the European countries have done.*

**Why are we troubled about being a "Have-Not Nation," as you put it? We import minerals like bauxite for aluminum. We import rubber. Importing oil, if anything, would benefit the oil companies since they control much of the oil in the Middle East. We are actually trading with ourselves.**

*In the first place, I don't think there is any great hangup about importing oil. I think the question is to what degree—25%, 50%, or even more? I think we develop a dependence on that source of supply which, to some degree, causes us to lose economic freedom. Then, secondly, there is a great misunderstanding that the American oil companies control the Middle East. That is certainly not true.*

**Why are we worried about dependency? Japan and Europe are dependent on foreign oil. They don't seem to have any problems.**

*I sit in a number of meetings with the Japanese, the English, and others, and I have never seen people as nervous as the Japanese are about their energy supplies. England is very fortunate because it has been about 25% self-sufficient; within a period of five or six years, it will be about 75% self-sufficient because of coal and nuclear power, as well as the North Sea oil and gas fields. So England is relaxed about energy.*

**How long do you think the oil sources available to the United States, including Alaska and the Continental Shelf, are going to last?**

*The hydrocarbon age, which we are in, will reach termination some thirty or forty years from now. By then we will have shifted to some other basic energy source. Through technological break-throughs, we will probably have solar, thermonuclear, or some other kinds of energy sources.*

*I don't think that you can say we have a certain amount of oil and gas reserves today and, from those figures, determine that we have a supply that will last X number of years. There are too many imponderables. There is no way to project what the demand will be. Projections that were made by the government, by the energy industry, by the independent agencies, by the professional academics in no way approached the great surge of energy demand. Our experience indicates that when you explore, you find new resources.*

*Within the last twenty years, for instance, Australia has become a source; so has Alaska. We know that discoveries have been made recently off Nova Scotia. There is no accurate way to assess energy reserves.*

**What preparations are the oil companies making for either going out of business or shifting to another fuel source?**

*I think if you look at it objectively, the oil industry is probably more research-oriented than any other large industry. Some would challenge that statement, but it is true. For instance, in our opera-tion most of our funds go into research. There is, in addition, a great deal of controversy, as I am sure you are well aware, about the oil companies in other kinds of energy—coal, nuclear research, reactor facilities, and so on. Some companies are doing a great deal of work in oil shale and tar sands in Canada. Geothermal energy sources are largely being developed by oil companies. Even one of the large solar projects has oil company support. More and more, the oil companies are beginning to think of themselves as energy companies and are trying to work toward the end that they become energy companies.*

**Do you have any estimates on the capital investments required on research and development and exploration?**

*Just in exploration alone, we project over the next twenty years that we will need something like $200 billion. In addition, each new refinery costs, roughly, about $250 million, and there will probably have to be about thirty of them. So the sum of $7.5 billion looms ahead for refineries.*

**How does the cost of offshore exploration compare with inland or continental exploration?**

*I grew up in the oil business in north Texas. I remember when I first started practicing law in the oil and gas field, we would talk about being able to put a well on connections to pipeline for $50,000. That was a big expenditure. Today a cheap well offshore will cost $1 million; more complicated ones will cost $5 million or $6 million. The offshore drilling platforms may well cost $10 million or $15 million.*

**Do you get as many dusters offshore?**

*Sure you do.*

**What percentage—one in six?**

*About one in nine. That means you get a good productive field about one out of the nine times you drill. Offshore you will probably get something like one in three or four.*

**Do you know where the oil companies at this point in time would like to locate some of these suggested one-stop refineries or expand some existing refineries?**

*The Northeast simply has to have some if the consumers are to have the kind of price treatment they want. You can't ship oil from the Middle East to Beaumont or Port Arthur, Texas, make products out of it, then transship it to Massachusetts or Vermont with the hope of any reasonable retail price.*

*So the Northeast is one place. But the oil companies can't construct refineries in Delaware, and, as I understand, New Jersey has similar legislation under consideration. One of the odd things about this is that a modern refinery can meet practically all the environmental standards.*

Who wants to go swimming in the shadow of a refinery. This is the big argument in New Jersey.

*I would be the last to try to defend the flats of New Jersey, which I think are horrible in appearance. I can understand that. But what the industry is trying to say is that there should be some determination by proper authorities—federal, state, or local—regarding the appropriate zoning and location of refineries.*

Are there any refineries in the Middle East?

*No significant ones. There are some in Iran.*

Wouldn't it be logical to build refineries in the Middle East and bring the products here?

*Historically, the industry has built refineries near the demand, not near the product supply. The problem with building refineries in a country like Kuwait (which has 30% of the world oil reserves) is that there is a population of about 750,000, few of whom have the expertise to run a refinery or an industrial complex.*

You made the point earlier, Mr. Ikard, that it is inefficient and wasteful to use distillate and, I presume, natural gas, as well, to generate electricity. What are we to do about this?

*We should free both fuels for heating and transportation and turn to coal for electricity. Coal can be burned in ways that are not harmful to air quality. You see, the current regulations deal with fuel quality, not air quality. I suggest that standards of air quality be established and monitored, then whatever fuel is available should be used as long as the air standards are not violated. In this way, if the air in a metropolitan area meets the standards, the fossil fuel power plant should be able to use whatever fuel it wants. This plan would be in effect until a synthetic fuel is developed or until atomic reactors replace the old generating plants. In some areas coal would not disturb the quality of air; in others, where the density of industries of all sorts already affects the air quality, coal might very well be forbidden. We prefer this system to a blanket requirement that prohibits the burning of high-sulfur coal.*

Wouldn't that plan conflict with a coherent national energy policy and a comprehensive national environmental standard?

*I am simply suggesting that, until our technology can provide alternatives, there should be some flexibility.*

Is the oil industry as dismayed by the fragmentation of authority in the federal government as are some other groups involved in the energy-environment conflict?

*I don't know about others, but we are dismayed. In the executive branch alone, there are scores of places to which we have to go for answers. In the Congress it is equally confusing.*

Nearly all the statistics we have received at this symposium come from industry sources. Wouldn't it be helpful to have a single government agency acting as a clearinghouse for what Senator Jackson calls "honest figures" in energy?

*I have no quarrel with that. But I think it is important to understand that these figures are developed by the industry and monitored by the government. There also are academics—engineers, geologists, economists, and other professionals who have nothing to do with management—preparing these estimates. The government could take on the job, but the irony is that the same people are going to be making the estimates because, well, they are the only ones who can make them.*

What about the Government Accounting Office?

*I was at a White House meeting the other day when this whole subject came up. Someone questioned the reliability of the gas research figures, even though these were checked out by the Colorado School of Mines. When a Federal Power Commission study was discussed, somebody else questioned the FPC figures. Well, the Department of the Interior had statistics. Again the reliability was in doubt.*

In all cases the figures come primarily from industry?

*There's no disputing that. What's more, most of the figures are projections, so they are necessarily inexact.*

# Chapter 7

Morris A. Adelman

# Cartels and the Threat of Monopoly

The world "energy crisis" or "energy shortage" is a fiction. But belief in that fiction is a fact. It leads the public to accept higher oil and gas prices as if they were imposed by nature when, actually, they are fixed by collusion.

There is at present a world oil monopoly consisting of the big oil-rich states, the eleven-nation Organization of Petroleum Exporting Countries (OPEC). This much was said by an important executive of Royal Dutch Shell when he was elected president of the Institute of Petroleum in London. "A basic situation of surplus crude oil availability has prevailed from the 1950s on and remains with us today," he stated. "Today we have a paradoxical position in which the underlying situation of supply and demand remains one of potential surplus. Yet the producing countries manage to reap the rewards of a seller's market by monopoly." So the supply is abundant and more is available, but a cartel exists to thwart any surplus and maintain prices at ten to twenty times the cost of bringing forth additional oil. In this, the multinational oil companies are only the tax-collecting agents of the oil-exporting cartel.

## UNITY AND CONTROL

Monopoly means insecurity, for monopoly is the power to control supply, to withhold, or, in another sense, to overcharge. The cartel was organized in January 1971 at Tehran after the United States State Department, acting in the interest of "stable and predictable" prices, supported the OPEC demands for higher oil taxes. After the intervention by the State Department—and not before—the OPEC repeatedly threatened to impose oil embargoes and boycotts. The genie was out of the bottle. The OPEC states have wielded their weapon of embargoes and boycotts with great success. From time to time, some sheik or minister warns the West that the OPEC knows the power of its weapon but possesses a "moral responsibility" to use it for constructive, not destructive, purposes—a message nobody can mistake.

The OPEC monopoly has provided strength and solidarity where there was neither. The producing countries are not united on any political issue or ideology. They are united only as a monopoly cartel. Resistance to the OPEC demands in 1971 would have shattered the nascent cartel. In the same month the OPEC was organized, the Shah of Iran told the press: "If the oil-producing countries suffer even the slightest defeat, it would be the death knell for OPEC, and from then on the countries would no longer have the courage to get together." Ignoring the Shah's view, the United States, in its desire to appease the producing countries, buying popularity with someone else's money and trying to reduce Arab-Israeli tension, bargained directly with the OPEC instead of accepting the price levels negotiated by the oil companies. The irony is that the Arab-Israeli conflict is irrelevant to the supply, availability, and price of oil. Non-Arab Iran, the acknowledged leader of Persian Gulf nations in 1971, has cooperated with Israel on an important project—the trans-Israel pipeline, which was opposed by the State Department back in 1957 and again in 1968. What happened during the 1967 Six-Day War is instructive. When Arab nations cut off supplies to Britain, Germany, and the United States, non-Arab oil states, producing 45% of OPEC oil, refused to go along, not to romance the West or to humiliate the Arabs, but to profit by the transaction. The boycott failed then and it will in the future.

## THREAT AND RESTRAINT

The cartel is very harmful to United States interests. Over the nine years from 1972 to 1980, the consuming nations will be paying the producing nations around $360 billion. The richer the OPEC nations, the greater their power to impose boycotts, raise prices and, thereby, make us more insecure. It is a self-aggravating ill. Worse yet, the world monetary system will be endangered by the huge hoards of money accumulated by the OPEC members and available for speculation, for investment, and for just sloshing about. Additionally, the expected deficit in the United States balance of payments caused by oil imports will almost certainly result in our restriction of imports. Such a move will surely provoke our trading partners to retaliate. Then, too, the political consequences of the immensely rich OPEC may be terrifying. Consider Libya's Colonel Muammar Qaddafi who has unleashed what he calls a "People's Revolution," which bears the message that Islam will defeat its foes even as the scattered Arab tribes once defeated the Roman and Persian empires; meanwhile, Qaddafi publicly claims he will settle the racial problems of the United States, drive the British from Northern Ireland, destroy Israel, meddle in Middle East and African affairs. The more money we pay out to such irresponsible paranoids, the more trouble we buy politically and economically.

The OPEC cartel is strong because the oil-hungry West has made it so. It is an artful and elegant maneuver to destroy the cartel by removing the essential part—the multinational company as crude oil marketeers fixing prices on a firm excise-tax base. Now it would be a misfortune if the companies were forced out of crude oil production. But they need not sell the bulk of OPEC oil and collect the taxes. The two functions are quite separate. The United States cannot do this on its own—though at this point, our blundering has so frightened and embittered the Europeans and Asians that they will not follow our lead in joint action. They are, however, pitifully eager to gain access to the OPEC oil on fair terms. Still, I suggest that we can conduct an auction of import tickets by sealed competitive bids. This scheme, in effect, would put the oil countries on notice that they have to give up something for the opportunity of trading and profiting. It would also strain the unity of the cartel by offering an opportunity to compete, which means an opportunity to use competitive business tactics, including intrigue, double cross and other devices.

The main thing to recognize is that the oil cartel is dangerous, unnecessary, and untenable—therefore, the sooner removed, the better.

# Discussion

You oppose the OPEC cartel, yet we have had a native American oil trust, which the government broke up. The courts can hardly be expected to do anything about a foreign operation, like the OPEC group.

> *If you think OPEC is favorable to your interests, then you want to support it. I offered a few reasons why it is extremely harmful to American interests.*

But the American cartel, the major oil companies, have been harmful. They live off the other cartels. The two cartels get along very well at the public's expense.

> *I don't think the international oil companies have a cartel. They haven't had one since the outbreak of World War II.*

I am talking about the Big Seven controlling how much oil comes into America.

> *The companies never controlled how much oil came in. They were in the business and did very nicely, but they have never controlled how much oil is imported — not since 1939. Anyway, we were an oil-exporting nation up to that time.*

You claim that we can solve one part of the energy problem by getting the multinational oil companies out of crude oil marketing. You are talking about a multimillion dollar business. How do we do this?

> *You can change the tax system. You can treat the taxes they pay as excise taxes — which, in fact, they are.*

Would that put them out of business?

> *I don't think it would put them out of business. It would give a number of them a hard time.*

Would they consider that discriminatory, though?

> *I don't think so. An excise tax is treated differently in law from an income tax. An income tax is credited against taxes due to the United States government, because the principle is that nobody pays taxes twice on the same income.*

Does giving the oil companies a rough time force them, in effect, to do what you want them to do—that is, get out of the oil marketing business?

> *I think it would get them out of the business. I see no useful purpose served by putting American companies out of the business so that French, Italian, or Japanese companies can get in and do exactly the same thing the Americans are doing now. I am dead set against it if for no other reason than that it wastes time and gives the cartel more years in which to consolidate its hold. Time is on their side in the immediate future, not on ours. That is why you are not going to do it except by joint action. But I don't see joint action about to happen.*

We have had academic experts, government officials, Mr. Ikard from the American Petroleum Institute, all more or less agreeing that the hydrocarbon era would be phased out within twenty-five to fifty years, depending on which particular view you accept.

> *They may all be right.*

I take it you don't agree.

> *The English sentence that is hardest to pronounce is "I don't know."*

I don't know either, but the size of the reserves has been reduced rather precipitously while the size of the demand increases, isn't that right?

> *Some thirty-five years ago the oil reserves of the Persian Gulf were being depleted at the rate of 2.5% a year. Last year the oil deposits were being depleted at the rate of 1.8% a year. There seems to be a lot more oil in the world than anybody had reason to think. Nobody knows how much oil there is until somebody has the incentive to go out and spend money to find it. (See Figure 17.) This is the kind of knowledge that scientists and engineers don't gather for the sake of knowledge, only for the sake of profit. That is why the reserves appear to grow together with the production. The more production grows, the more reason there is to establish the reserves.*
>
> > *Reserves are the available shelf inventory of the oil industry. Reserves are not the underground deposits. The standard docu-*

**Figure 17.**
**World "Published Proved" Oil Reserves at End of 1972**

| Country/Area | Thousand Million Tons | Share of Total | Thousand Million Barrels |
|---|---|---|---|
| U.S.A. | 5.6 | 6.2% | 43.1 |
| Canada | 1.3 | 1.4% | 9.7 |
| Caribbean | 2.5 | 2.7% | 17.2 |
| Other Western Hemisphere | 2.0 | 2.3% | 15.5 |
| Total Western Hemisphere | 11.4 | 12.6% | 85.5 |
| Western Europe | 1.7 | 1.9% | 12.6 |
| Africa | 13.9 | 15.3% | 106.4 |
| Middle East | 48.5 | 53.3% | 355.3 |
| U.S.S.R., E. Europe, China | 13.4 | 14.7% | 98.0 |
| Other Eastern Hemisphere | 2.0 | 2.2% | 14.9 |
| Total Eastern Hemisphere | 79.5 | 87.4% | 587.2 |
| World (excl. U.S.S.R., E. Europe, China) | 77.5 | 85.3% | 574.7 |
| World | 90.9 | 100.0% | 672.7 |

Source: British Petroleum Statistical Review of the World Oil Industry, 1972.

*mentation indicates that reserves are that fraction of the known oil which will be extracted and delivered from the facilities in place. It is not the unexploited oil in place, nor is it the oil that remains to be discovered.*

In the past few years we have looked for oil in places where a generation ago it was not economical to look. There is a point of diminishing returns, isn't there? There is a lot of oil out there to be found, but are we going to be drilling in the Marianas Trench, where it costs $1 million or so for the effort.

*What you have said is a perfectly true statement. From now on it will be harder and harder and dearer and dearer to squeeze out more oil from nature. But we are talking about cost per unit. How much do we get for that $1 million oil well? The fact is that in 1960 there were about forty-five rigs drilling in the Persian Gulf. In 1970 there were still about forty-five drilling rigs there, but these were developing three times as much capacity as in the earlier years. That is not a picture of a gradual dwindling of oil resources. It's just the other way around. But if you look at raw material prices generally over a long period of time, you find that they mostly go* *down, not up. This means that knowledge of new parts of the earth's crust and knowledge of how to get more out of it has over-come quite decisively the stinginess of nature. But that hasn't happened in oil.*

American dollars are, in effect, subsidizing guerilla activities and anti-American operations in various nations.

*That is true enough. It's one part of the picture. But I would do you a disservice if I made you think it was the major thing.*

So the only way for us to stop the flow of funds that support these activities through the Arab power structure is to pull out our oil interests in the Middle East and North Africa. I was under the impression that, at this point in time, we needed the Middle East and North Africa more than they needed us. Apparently it is the reverse.

*I think it is the reverse because there is a surplus of oil. I think, though, that if you cut down drastically on the payments to the OPEC nations, the Arab-Israeli conflict or the revolutionary struggles in the Middle East and Africa would not be affected an awful lot. Payments to these guerilla groups are in the millions of dollars. We are talking about billions.*

What are they doing with the rest of the money?

*Qaddafi shows us the way with Libya's oil wealth. He has attempted to topple the monarchy in Morocco—though the Algerians didn't like the idea. He is apparently paying people to blow things up on Cyprus and to stir things up in Uganda.*

Could you explain your suggestion for requesting sealed bids to supply oil?

*I think there would be chaos if we initiated sealed bidding right now because the Middle East would not be able to reckon on the end result. Before initiating any such scheme, you would probably want to build up a stockpile of oil.*

Do you think, Professor Adelman, the OPEC states would refuse to participate in the bidding?

*I imagine some of them would. I don't think all of them would, particularly if you offered some rebates. I believe a number of them would not want to get into a scrap with the United States because of some of the hot-heads in the area. Many of the OPEC leaders are cool-headed and clear minded. These, I assume, would ponder the rebates and realize their countries would gain, say, a three-year commitment to do business at a whopping profit.*

**Could they make more money by bidding than they do now?**

*Yes, they could, particularly countries like Indonesia and Nigeria. By a happy coincidence, Indonesia and Nigeria possess low-sulfur oil, and this is at a premium. Give them a chance to sign some big three-year contracts with American buyers, at current prices, and I think they would at least think of it very seriously indeed.*

**Would you expect Europe and Japan to follow suit if the United States took this approach?**

*I think the people sitting in precarious darkness in Europe and Asia would begin to see a great light. They are scared witless of an oil shortage.*

**Would you like to see a state trading company here that would handle oil?**

*No, it would just be too awkward and inefficient.*

**How does your proposal for import bidding differ from the present system?**

*The present system is one of imposed quotas. When a shortage or overabundance occurs, the quotas are changed.*

**Who decides how much Saudi oil is going to be in the United States next summer?**

*At this point, that is decided by the companies who use the oil in their operations.*

**Domestic companies?**

*American companies. There also is some oil that is sold at arm's length from the producer abroad to the refiner here. There would be an increasing amount of it as the amount of imports increases. There is nothing to stop them from doing this under a system of open competitive bids. Any number could play. And a government can bid on its own or in collusion with an oil company, of course.*

Do you mean that, as it is now, American companies decide they are going to import X million barrels of oil this year and then go shopping around with their contacts in the Middle East or elsewhere to buy it?

> *No, that wouldn't be correct. The American companies refine and market in this country. They produce abroad. They plan, over a specific period of time, to produce so much in a certain location and ship it to their affiliates in various places, including certain shipments to the United States.*

And what you are proposing is that the decision on where the imported oil will come from be taken away from the American companies and, instead, be made by a government agency which would open sealed envelopes submitted by foreigners?

> *The government doesn't really make the decision.*

The government would decide who wins the bid.

> *The basic rule is that the government doesn't decide; it is the highest bidder who decides. The government would do exactly as the Bureau of Land Management of the Department of the Interior does when it manages the auctions for offshore leases. The bureau says that, by a certain date, everyone should submit bids. In the same way, we would open the bids in a certain place at a certain time and see who gets the oil.*

If the oil companies enter their bids, aren't they still bound by the agreements that they have negotiated with the OPEC countries? If the OPEC countries don't get into the competition to bid against each other, what have we changed?

> *If the OPEC countries are able to agree to stay out of the bidding, you haven't changed anything. That is just the point. They have got to agree and they have got to keep on agreeing. But any one of them that wants more outlets in the United States or thinks it deserves a higher share would probably submit a bid.*
>
> *More than that, any of them that are displaced from the U.S. market because of an unwillingness to bid, would certainly have a reason to try a little bit harder next time. That is what I meant when I said there ought to be a chance to double-cross for fear of being double-crossed by others. What it means is that there*

*are no long-term commitments any more for shipment into the United States. You have either got to get in at every bidding period and pay up or you are not going to have any sales here.*

## Are there other practical ideas you might have for breaking this cartel?

*We could get together with the other nations and see to it that the contracts they have signed are invalidated. They are, I think, almost surely a violation of the domestic antitrust laws. Furthermore, Article 85 of the Treaty of Rome forbids restrictive agreements. The arrangements that the companies have with the OPEC governments are not agreements at all, because an agreement assumes there are two parties with mutual obligations. But this is not the situation in the OPEC countries today. The companies have to pay a certain amount of tax. The governments invalidate those agreements whenever they jolly well want to. The Venezuelans have spared us the trouble of this sophistry. They just legislate. But in the other OPEC countries, there are agreements for excise taxes. Iran is going to give this a new twist. They are going to sell at a certain price, which comes to approximately the same thing. The purpose of all of these so-called agreements in the Persian Gulf and North Africa is simply to set a price floor.*

*These agreements between the OPEC and the companies amount to collective price-fixing, which is illegal under the laws of two continents. This is one of the tools that you can use. And like the tool of taxation, it doesn't make much sense for any one country to do it alone because the most likely result is that your own companies get kicked out. As a nation we would lose the profits and the oil.*

## You mentioned Venezuela, in case we might get shut off. Did you mean to mention Venezuela?

*Oh, yes. If there is an Arab quarrel, Venezuela would be a source of supply, and it would enjoy every minute and coin. The mischief that has been done is the incessant repetition of Arabs, oil, OPEC, as though these were all one and the same thing. This isn't so. Some 45% of the oil is produced by the non-Arab OPEC. They are either disinterested or disdainful—or, in the case of Iran, feel themselves to be rivals and opponents.*

Are there any other nations besides Venezuela?

> *Nigeria, Iran, and Indonesia.*

If we take unilateral action, won't other nations rush in to reach agreements with the OPEC? Every big country needs oil.

> *There is a worldwide fear that the United States will stop at noth-ing to obtain all the oil it needs through the multinational oil com-panies. The fear is strongest in Japan but also exists in Europe. Sometimes the companies reinforce this fear, as when an Exxon executive testified last year before the House Ways and Means Committee that it is because of the multinationals that the United States can get access to oil on fair terms. This seems to be another way of saying that, without multinational companies of their own, the Japanese, the Germans, the French, the Italians or any other nation cannot have access.*
>
> *To pay for access through higher prices or otherwise makes no sense, no matter how one views the future. Oil supply is threat-ened by one, and only one, danger: a concerted shutdown by the OPEC. The price of crude oil is set by a world monopoly and is so profitable it is worthwhile to expand output. Therefore, even if the price declines, but especially if it increases, there will be more crude oil available than can be sold—as there is now and always has been.*

Since you claim that there is no oil shortage in the world, wouldn't it be a mistake to embark on a crash program to dis-cover new sources of energy?

> *I want to point out that I am prejudiced because I am a professor at an engineering school. It makes good sense, in my opinion, to engage in research. I would think a few million dollars could pro-vide the capability to supply energy from new sources. But I don't think it makes good sense to spend vast amounts of money to develop the new sources because, first, there is no real necessity, and, second, the British experience ought to be ample warning that this compels the use of high-cost sources and inhibits the cutting of losses, particularly when the government is involved.*

If there is no real oil shortage, there would not seem to be any pressing need for tightening our energy belts, tough conservation measures, taxes on auto horsepower, that sort of thing.

*That depends on what we are trying to do. If the price of gasoline is high enough, there will be smaller cars with lower horsepower. That may or may not reduce air pollution. I am not worried about running out of oil. I am worried about the quality of air.*

*Exhortations, preachments, apocalyptic tales, horror stories —they are all a waste of energy, except for those who enjoy telling them or the advertising agencies that appear to be making profits from the energy industry these days by churning out copy and commercials about the "crisis." The feeling of crisis is reinforced by it all. It relieves the tedium of life. It provides a new tension. It appeals to the fighting instinct in us to find a way to beat the crisis.*

*But fears of an oil crisis are unfounded. What happens to oil in the 1970s depends altogether on the consuming countries. If they are slow to learn, as they have been, then the projection of a $55 billion annual tribute paid the OPEC states by 1980 may even be surpassed. The transfer of these immense sums from the West to the East is not only dangerous, but may be unnecessary. As the Saudi Arabs, the Iranians, the Venezuelans, the Indonesians and others know so well, crude oil continues in oversupply, not scarcity.*

# Chapter 8

Lawrence Rocks and Richard P. Runyon

# Energy and Foreign Policy: How Dependent Must We Be?

Foreign policy and energy policy in the United States are becoming increasingly intertwined to a degree that is not fully understood or appreciated across the country. The dimension of our energy needs from foreign sources is underestimated. Contrary to the widely accepted view that the Middle East, North Africa, and perhaps the Soviet Union and Indonesia can provide all the crude oil and natural gas that we will require, we believe such reliance is economically unreasonable and unacceptable.

If reliance on foreign sources is futile, reliance on domestic sources is submerged in problems. *The United States has already used up half of its oil reserves and nearly the same proportion of natural gas.* The first 50% of a resource is relatively easy to find, ship, process, and deploy. The remaining 50% is something different again. To exploit the rest requires drilling deeper in increasingly inaccessible places—offshore on the Continental Shelf, in the Arctic Circle—at higher costs and lower yields.

To illustrate my point: In the 1930s we got about 270 barrels of oil per foot of exploratory drilling. Today we obtain 35 barrels per foot. So, it is now eight times more difficult to gain oil in the United States than it was some forty years ago.

## DOMESTIC RESOURCES

An analysis of the probable lifespan of energy resources in the country is depressing. Natural gas will last forty years at the 1970 consumption rate and less than thirty years at the present growth rate. Crude oil will be exhausted in twenty years at the 1970 consumption rate and in fewer than fifteen years at the present growth rate. Coal will hold out for another 200 to 300 years if it is used to synthesize oil and gas at their present growth rates. Uranium for fission power plants should be useful for 100 to 1,000 years after the fast-breeder nuclear reactor is on stream (that is, from the year 2000 to 2020 on). Deuterium and lithium would last virtually indefinitely if a controlled thermonuclear fusion reactor could be developed.

The fact that we are topping out our reserves of oil and gas would not, in itself, imperil our economic stability were it not for our failure in the past few decades to research and develop alternate modes of energy.

The truth is that the much-heralded abundance of energy provided by nuclear sources is almost as remote today as it was twenty years ago. The fuel for fission reactors, uranium 235, is in short supply. But even if it were plentiful, its energy is released as electricity, which accounts for less than 20% of our present power needs. The energy to run the nation's road and air transportation, to heat homes, offices, and factories, and to maintain farm production derives primarily from petroleum and natural gas. It is inconceivable that we could switch to electrically driven machines, engines, and other devices within the next decade or two. Moreover, the fast-breeder reactor, which is capable of replenishing the scarce nuclear fuel as an energy bank, still seems to be years, if not decades, away from producing significant amounts of electrical power to the nation, certainly not 1 trillion watts before the year 2020.

Our dilemma is deepened by our ever-increasing rate of energy consumption, now 2.2 trillion watts—an amount that rules out several modes of energy now under consideration. The potential of tidal power would amount to only 1% or 2% of the nation's energy needs. Geothermal power, which apparently has evoked romantic ideas for some people, would also provide about 2%; hydroelectric power, about 5% to 7%. Solar power could well account for 10% or much more, but it is largely inaccessible by our present technology—though perhaps some scientific or technological breakthrough may bring it within reach as the most long-lived and pollution-free energy source.

So the alternatives are not numerous. What can we do? Whether we like it or not, we appear securely bound for many years to come to the fossil fuels—oil, natural gas, and coal.

## PROBLEMS IN IMPORTING

Unfortunately, Americans tend to oversimplify problems and to seek quick and easy solutions. What is more simple and direct than importing energy from abroad? I think this is preposterous. The hope that expanding imports of oil and gas will not affect our balance-of-payments deficit, that the world is moving toward a new era of political detente, that science and technology will provide nonpolluting energy sources, are all widely shared illusions.

For our part, we think it is more than coincidental that the Soviet Union has taken such a sudden interest in the energy crisis of the West. The Soviets have already contracted to deliver about 400 billion cubic feet of gas per year to France, Italy, and West Germany by the late 1970s. The Soviets proposed to former Commerce Secretary Peter G. Peterson that they sell us 1.5 trillion cubic feet of gas per year for $2 billion. As part of this deal, the gas fields of Siberia, which already yield 7 trillion cubic feet a year, would be further explored and developed by a joint team of Soviet and American engineers and geologists at joint expense. Then the gas would be shipped to the United States in LNG tankers (liquid natural gas tankers, shaped like Thermos bottles). To do this, we would need some forty-five tankers costing at least $4.5 billion in United States funds. Finally, we would have to build deep-water ports here with regasification facilities to handle the gas.

In addition to the Soviet supplies, the United States is counting on oil from the Middle East and North Africa, which is supposedly plentiful. There are three major flaws in this approach: First, the Organization of Petroleum Exporting Countries, according to its own statements, will not be able to produce the large amount of oil that the United States, the European Economic Community, and Japan combined will need past the early 1980s; second, the dollar drain involved would be, at least, a staggering $130 billion by 1985; and, third, the capital equipment costs of importing the fuels would reach about $100 billion.

The United States has sought elsewhere for energy. Canada has been considered a likely source. It is our belief that we cannot rely on Canada for gas or oil in any major amount. Canada's proved reserves are only about 10 billion barrels—two years of supply at our present consumption level. The presumed Canadian reserves may be as much as 50 billion to 80 billion barrels, much of this unexplored in the Arctic. It would take perhaps $50 billion over five decades to explore and recover Canada's Arctic oil.

However, many Canadian leaders are opposed to both the large influx of American capital and the large outflow of Canadian energy. They are warning against a massive program to supply the United States.

The North Sea oil and gas discoveries amount to about 1 billion to 5 billion barrels—a drop in the bucket, not even one year's supply at our current consumption level. Furthermore, North Sea fuel, for economic and political reasons, will undoubtedly go to Europe.

## SELF-RELIANCE

Our thesis is that foreign gas and oil can not, in any imaginable way, close the gap between our present needs and the "nuclear future." It is physically impossible. It is financially impossible. More than that, it could well turn out to be politically dangerous. Once we commit significant amounts of our men, methods, and money to the foreign options, we will be exposed to three perils: We will have lost time so critical for developing our own alternate energy strategy; we will impose a balance of trade deficit that may well stagger our economy; we will be vulnerable to changes and conflicts in political alliances as we bid for the same energy sources or suffer the whims of the energy producers.

We believe in self-reliance. We feel that coal can supply the United States with synthetic fuels for the next 100 to 200 years, as a massive supplement to oil and gas that is available, until the phase-in time of nuclear power. If we adopt this alternate strategy, we will free ourselves of the dangers of cutoffs from abroad; we will be spared the enormous capital costs involved in developing the resources of other nations and the tanker fleet and ports required to handle the resources; we will avoid the inevitable and unconscionable dollar drain; we will probably find that the cost of energy will be less in the long run.

Even the synthetic fuel strategy has drawbacks. But this strategy must be implemented now if we are to avert more than an energy crisis.

### Richard P. Runyon

I would like to offer just a preliminary remark with respect to our capabilities of becoming self-sufficient. If Japan, for example, were to be given the question in the title of our presentation, "How Dependent Must We Be?", the answer would be quite different from ours. Japan, which imports virtually all its energy, could not conceivably develop a self-sufficient energy policy. By contrast, the United States, with its massive coal reserves, could possibly become self-sufficient in energy.

I would like to make a few observations with respect to OPEC before going on to a more thorough examination of our domestic options.

## A TRADING STRATEGY

If I were to be suddenly given the role of a consultant to the future of OPEC, what would be the nature of my recommendations? I assume that similar thinking is going on right now in OPEC. First, I would recommend that they develop a soil bank policy with respect to oil. The OPEC nations have, after all, no financial and economic viability apart from their oil reserves. If they cooperated fully with the West and provided all of the oil that the West wants, and if it were possible for them to extract oil that fast—which, we think, it is not—they would be out of business in perhaps thirty years. On the other hand, if they developed a soil bank policy—and I think that is happening right now—we would agree to extract only a certain amount of oil per year; they could, of course, artificially inflate the cost of oil in a market in which the demand is excessive and the supply is limited. We are all familiar with the economic fact that when there is a buyer's market, the sellers usually scramble and compete with one another to sell goods or services at any price they can get. But in a seller's market, there is usually widespread cooperation among the sellers to keep prices artificially high. So I think we can anticipate that this will happen.

One might argue that, by adopting such a policy, the OPEC will force the West into a synthetic fuel policy, perhaps in a crash program. That would be ultimately harmful to their own self-interests.

The truth of the matter is that, if we introduce a synthetic fuel strategy, phase-in time will be in the neighborhood of about ten years. So, in the next ten-year period, OPEC has a marvelous opportunity to bring in billions and billions of dollars. Now, if there were some intelligence behind this, OPEC would recognize that the only real way to extend the life of their petroleum resources would be to develop an indigenous petrochemical industry that would extend their economic viability for thousands of years. It would provide their indigenous population with skills and standards for a middle class, which is presently lacking.

So I think that recommendations to OPEC would be along the lines that I have just followed. And I think that we will see that something analogous to this will actually be occurring over the next several years.

Where does that leave us? There is a widening gap between our anticipated energy needs and our power sources. (See Figure 18.) What we see is that the gap can be filled to a great extent by the use of synthetic fuels. The decision on synthetic fuels must be made in the next ten years. This is why we favor a strategy of synthetic fuel, combined with a massive conservation program begun immediately, until we can reach either the atomic or the solar future.

**Figure 18.**
**If Domestic Sources Were Fully Developed**
**(exclusive of solar power and fusion)**

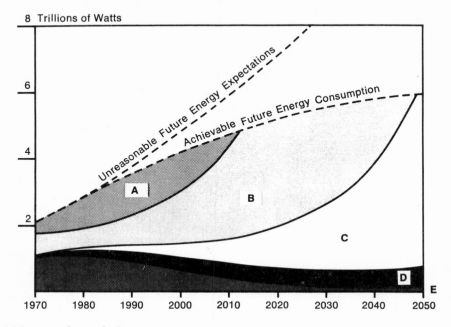

(A)  Imports of gas and oil
(B)  Coal and synthetic fuels from coal
(C)  Potential of the breeder reactor
(D)  Hydropower and geothermal energy
(E)  Domestic oil and gas

## A CONSERVATION APPROACH

Now conservation is something that can be phased in relatively rapidly, and it can have an almost immediate impact. I don't mean conservation that will give rise to all sorts of economic dislocations. One could clearly conserve gasoline by simply banning the automobile. But economic dislocations would occur if we chose to do that.

Right now, as a result of the 1970 Clean Air Act and the Auto Emissions Standards, we seem to be moving toward automobile designs that are energy profligate. The best estimates indicate that when the catalytic device is adopted by Detroit, American cars will consume somewhere between 20% and 30% more gasoline. If Detroit adopts the Wankel engine, we calculate that American cars will consume about 30% to 35% more energy.

This means that the 1970 Clean Air Act is pushing the demand curve up even higher. We have estimated that by 1985 there would be a 6-billion-barrel gap between what we can domestically produce and what we will presumably be demanding. Since the automobile already consumes about 30% of all the petroleum products in this country, and since we are making the automobile even 30% more petroleum thirsty, we are really talking about a gap of around 7 billion barrels per year by 1985.

But what if we were to take a different approach? What if, instead of the 1970 Clean Air Act, which says that we have to remove 95% of certain types of noxious materials, we substituted an automobile efficiency act requiring that automobiles must at least double the mileage they get per gallon of fuel? This can be done by moving to smaller cars in which such options as power steering and power brakes would not be necessary. These are energy profligate. We could redesign the air conditioner to make use of waste heat given off by the car's motor, rather than taking it directly off the drive train as is presently done.

Let's say we are able to reduce the consumption of gasoline for automotive use by 50%. We are talking about a reduction in our yearly needs by 1.5 billion barrels. This would be an enormous savings and, if started right now, could be realized by 1985, by which time most of the nation's automobiles will presumably be smaller and more efficient.

Other things can be done. The Maine Central Power Company asked the architects to design a computer center that would take into consideration all the energy sources that exist within the building. So this was done.

When the architects and engineers analyzed the waste heat being given off by the intense lighting (150 candlepower at desk level), and given off by the people inside (humans are 100-watt thermal power plants), as well as the waste heat given off by the machines, they suddenly realized they didn't need any other source of heat for the building. So this building in Augusta, Maine, has no heating system besides the waste heat of lights, people, and machines. Now this is rather significant because, during December, January, February, and March, the mean temperature in Maine averages about six degrees below freezing.

We feel very strongly that there must be governmental incentives to do these things. A whole new industry would be born to conserve energy if the government incentives were there. Consider, for example, the vast areas in this country where solar power could be used for heating. It has been used for heating in the past but is not used frequently now. In the Southwest and the South, many buildings could be heated completely through solar power. By making a structural change, a homeowner would include some form of solar panel device. But then the home is reassessed because of the improvement; as a result, the property tax goes up. Any savings that is gained in fuel economy is lost in increased tax. So it is going to be necessary for municipalities to recognize that improvements made for the purpose of energy conservation should not count as taxable improvements. It will be necessary for the Internal Revenue Service to allow such conservation devices as tax deductible items.

Businesses would be given a quick write-off or allowed to count such improvements as operational expenses. An analysis has been done for Grand Union supermarkets. It has been estimated that, if the amount of waste heat given off by refrigerator units, instead of being vented to the outside, were to be recirculated, the whole store could be heated without any additional source. The modifications needed to do this by Grand Union would be expensive but relatively minor. With a tax incentive or a quick write-off, Grand Union, and I am sure many other corporations throughout the country, would start introducing energy-saving procedures.

One more comment: If an energy conservation industry develops as a result, we might be able to export it abroad and help to overcome some of our balance-of-trade dilemma.

# Discussion

If consumers conserve energy, it would cause demand to fall, and utilities would then have to increase their rates. So any savings at one end would be paid at the other.

> *This would be true except for the apparent fact that the gap is open-ing between our projected needs and our projected production. We are going to find out that utilities will not be able to produce all the electricity we need in the next decade.*

There is no utility in the country that will go along with a "no growth" policy.

> *You are right. The energy companies will not accept "no growth." We are saying that the projected growth rate of 4% or 5% must match physical reality. We are not recommending a static economy or a regressive economy.*

No one at this symposium has mentioned the possibility that social changes would bring about a better use of energy. Why, for instance, does everybody have to work from nine to five, just when utilities are always building to a peak?

> *We feel one aspect of the total problem is in changing public attitudes toward big cars to head off what we think is a developing catastrophe. Further, if the utilities would somehow avoid peak periods of electricity output and even things out, they could run at a better profit level and better efficiency level. So your suggestion, I think, should be vigorously pursued.*
>
> *There is also another aspect to that. Transportation accounts for about 25% of the total energy budget. We might save about half of that if all ground transportation were by railroad. Of course, we can't rebuild the railroads overnight. But natural forces are at work to constrain the transport of freight by rail rather than by truck because it is much more efficient. The government is now moving toward resurrection of mass transit systems within cities and inter- and intracity travel. So we look for a rebirth of the railroad system, for development of a fuel-efficient car and fuel-saving devices in heat-ing. All this will make an enormous difference in our total energy budget.*

What are the environmental implications of mining a huge amount of coal to convert into synthetic gas. Isn't it going to require 4 billion to 5 billion tons of coal each year?

*It will have to be strip-mined. Very little could be deep-mined. About 80% of this coal is located west of the Mississippi, so we are talking about strip-mining coal in such marvelously pristine places as Colorado, Utah, and the Dakotas. The obvious environmental implications are enormous. Strip mining does desecrate the land. It seems to me that it would require either legislation or enforcement of existing legislation to make sure that the land is restored. An interesting point is that when mountainous slopes of twenty degrees or greater are strip-mined, there is little hope of ever restoring the environment. We have seen the ravages of strip mining in West Virginia. It is an environmental and aesthetic tragedy. In Southern Illinois right now, the city of Chicago is pumping solid wastes into a strip-mining area. The solid waste produced by a city the size of Chicago can provide enormous amounts of nutrient-rich land-fill. The wastes consist of sewage sludge. A slurry is made and sent by pipeline to Southern Illinois.*

*Sometimes you run into problems. The City of Los Angeles had planned to send its waste materials to Nevada for land-fill. But the people of Nevada didn't want California's waste. So that plan was never realized.*

What about burning garbage, the fastest growing resource in America today, as a fuel source?

*It amounts to very little. All the combustible garbage in the country amounts to about 160 million tons a year. If it were all burned in a power plant complex, it would supply only 3% of our electrical needs. Pyrolisis (wet air oxidation) is a good way to get rid of garbage, but the process could never lick the energy crisis.*

# PART THREE

# THE CONSERVATION
# POTENTIAL

# The Authors

## George R. Hill
*Can Fossil Fuels Be Cleaned Up?*

A longtime chemistry professor at Cornell and the University of Utah, where he was dean of the College of Mines and Mineral Industries from 1966 to 1972, Mr. Hill is now director of the Office of Coal Research in the Department of the Interior. He has also been project director of Air Force Combustion Research and in 1971 received the Henry H. Storch Award of the American Chemical Society for his contributions to fundamental research on the chemistry and utilization of coal.

## William F. Pedersen, Jr.
*Are Antipollution Laws Working?*

Mr. Pedersen is assistant to the deputy general counsel of the Environmental Protection Agency, where he has been handling litigation on the suspension of the rigid emission standards for 1975 automobiles. A graduate of the Harvard Law School, he joined EPA in 1972 and has worked primarily in the area of air pollution.

## Bruce C. Netschert
*Are Antipollution Laws Widening the Energy Gap?*

Since 1961, Mr. Netschert has been vice president and director of the Washington office of National Economic Research Associates, Inc., specializing in the economics of energy and mineral resources. He has taught geology and economics at Cornell and at the University of Minnesota. He has served on the staff of the Materials Policy Commission (the Paley Commission), the Central Intelligence Agency, and the Energy and Minerals Resources Program of Resources for the Future.

## Stephen A. Wakefield
*Can Resources From Public Lands Be Developed in Environmentally Acceptable Ways?*

Mr. Wakefield was recently appointed to the post of assistant secretary for energy and minerals in the Department of the Interior. As such, he is responsible for administering the department's electric power, fossil fuel, and mineral resources operations and for planning and developing energy policies, conservation programs and research projects. He has been special assistant to the general counsel of the Federal Power Commission and deputy assistant secretary for mineral resources at the Department of the Interior.

# Chapter 9

**George R. Hill**

# Can Fossil Fuels Be Cleaned Up?

In a word, the answer to the question in my assigned topic is "yes." But it will take generous amounts of both time and money. The power of the purse—like the power of the press—still prevails, despite its ups and downs. We must pay the price for maintaining our phenomenal standard of living and for developing an equally high standard of environment. Coal, our most abundant fossil fuel and the one with which I am most familiar, is much more than a solid black substance made up of hydrogen and carbon atoms. With modern technology, coal can be a clean and usable substitute for natural gas or a low sulphur oil; it can be a clean fuel for efficient electrical power and a clean burning solid. *In short, coal covers the whole spectrum of energy supply and demand, from its use in the production of nuclear energy to its lesser form as a source of chemicals.*

American consumers depend on natural gas and refined oil to provide 78% of all our energy needs. Yet, natural gas constitutes only 9% of our total domestic fossil fuel resources; oil is only 8% of our fuel resource; uranium, 4%. The rest of our fossil fuel deposit—some 79% of it—is made up of some 3 trillion tons of coal. We are relying, in short, on those fuels in shortest supply for our energy requirements, while our single greatest source of energy goes begging.

At the present rate of coal consumption, the nation's known reserves could meet our energy needs for somewhere between 200 and 300 years. Even so, production has remained relatively level over the past few years, despite our rapidly increasing energy requirements. The United States, even with a stagnant production rate for coal, produced more of it than any country except the Soviet Union. We are, in fact, shutting down on coal production at the same time that we are starting up costly research and development programs to find new fuel resources.

What's the reason for this apparent paradox? Why aren't we using more coal? The answer lies, for the most part, in a combination of health and safety standards of mining, environmental restrictions on sulfur content and strip mining, and, until recently, price controls.

## RECOVERY AND CONVERSION

In the past we have had no concern at all with the despoilation of the surroundings. Coal has been strip-mined with no thought to the need for restoring the natural landscape. Underground mining has been remarkably efficient, but with a terrible toll in miners' lives when disasters have occurred — though we have come to take for granted a more ghastly rate of deaths and injuries from automobile accidents.

Both human safety and environmental safeguards need improvement. One approach is to eliminate strip mining entirely. That is not a viable option in my opinion because we are now producing oil and gas at probably the maximum rate, and we must ultimately turn to coal. We need, therefore, to build into our mining practices the requirement that the hills and valleys be restored to equivalent or better condition than before they yielded up their coal deposits.

Moreover, underground mining techniques will need to be changed. A great deal of research is required, in my opinion, to make mining safer, to reduce the number of men working in mine shafts, and to develop new detection systems for predetermining where and when underground accidents are likely to occur. Work is going on along that line in the Bureau of Mines and in several universities.

Another deterrent to using coal is that the sulfur content of much of the coal, particularly in the East and Midwest, is so high that the sulfur dioxide released on burning is above a level we now consider to be acceptable. The Office of Coal Research is engaged, therefore, in several programs for converting coal into environmentally suitable low-sulfur form. We are working to eliminate coal's dirty image.

The Office of Coal Research is developing processes for producing a low-sulfur fuel oil from coal. We are developing programs for producing low-Btu gas for power generation — gas that is clean enough that the sulfur dioxide problem is nonexistent. We are developing ways of burning coal directly in a fluidized boiler to which has been added calcium carbonate or dolomite (a form of limestone) which will trap the sulfur components in a solid form before they are released from the combustion chamber so that their disposal is no real problem.

As some ads for cars put it: "We do not have a service-free car yet, but we are halfway there." The same may be said for the cleaner uses of coal. We are at the halfway mark. But we have yet to reach the point in technological efficiency at which the economics of performance are attractive enough for commercial use.

One approach calls for low-Btu fuel gas to be used in generating electricity. The clean fuel gas would be the power of magnetohydrodynamics, or MHD, a promising method of generating electricity without a rotating turbine or any moving parts. If we can devise equipment and materials that will hold to very high temperatures, we would be able to achieve 60% overall conversion efficiency in a combined MHD-steam cycle power plant.

The most efficient overall utilization of coal uses "fluidized bed combustion." In this system, the coal is heated by electrical current in a fluidized bed of conductive char particles, where the deleterious material is trapped; the hot gases then pass through a gas turbine, then a steam turbine. We are looking at such a system here, and a supplemental project in England is operating toward developing equipment for the next generation of coal-burning plants.

## COAL GASIFICATION

The main thrust in the Office of Coal Research was to produce high-Btu gas. Together with the American Gas Association, which puts up one-third of the $120 million for research and development, three pilot projects are underway. One, the Hygas pilot plant, built by the Institute of Gas Technology in Chicago, is designed to produce coal methane, which makes up 95% of natural gas, at a price we estimate will be 20% below the price of either liquefied natural gas shipped to the East Coast or of natural gas produced by the Lurgi technique.

The Lurgi technique, developed during the 1920s and 1930s in Germany, is a well-developed off-the-shelf item. (During World War II, German planes were frequently fueled with synthetic gas.) Plants using the Lurgi fixed-bed gasifier have been proposed and will shortly be under construction. One such plant is at Rapid City, South Dakota. It utilizes the carbon dioxide acceptor process as a new way of making high-Btu gas out of lignite, mixed with dolomite. Another plant is now under construction in Homer City, Pennsylvania. All three are designed to utilize new chemical engineering

132

processes—fluidized bed, entrained slagging bed, and others. Each pilot operation incorporates different elements in its structure and each needs to be proved.

The results of these three power plants, plus the one the Bureau of Mines is building at Bruceton, Pennsylvania, called the Synthane Plant, will enable us to select the elements that are most efficient and reliable and then come up with the best commercial processes.

Conversion of coal to gas might not have been a priority if the United States had not faced a gradual increase in the price of natural gas. Besides the pilot plants, the Office of Coal Research is investigating advanced power cycles to raise efficiencies and lower costs.

A considerable amount of our budget is going into magnetohydro-dynamic (MHD) research. In this process, coal is fired at relatively high pressure and the resulting ionized gases are forced through a duct at high velocity. The gases move through a magnetic field surrounding the duct, resulting in generation of an electric current. Electrodes on the wall of the duct convey the current.

The implication of all this work with coal almost defies the imagination. Improved mining techniques could make it environmentally feasible to recover about 2 trillion tons of our nation's 3 trillion tons of coal reserves. At a conversion rate of two barrels or more of synthetic oil per ton—which is a much better ratio than that expected from oil shale—we would have more than 4 trillion barrels of oil in the form of coal, or ten times the world's proved resources. If our recoverable coal were converted to pipeline quality gas, it would yield about 32,000 trillion cubic feet of synthetic gas. By contrast, the worldwide reserves of natural gas are about 1,550 trillion cubic feet .

In conclusion, I would like to remind you of what Ralph Waldo Emerson wrote: "A creative economy is the fuel of magnificence." It is just as true to paraphrase the poet and philosophize that: A fueled economy creates magnificence.

# Discussion

What is your estimate of how much synthetic gas would be produced in the year 1980?

*By 1980, very little. We could, if we can get enough capital, gear up by 1985 to supply 10% or 15% of our needs by building ten plants producing, say, 250 million cubic feet a day. That's where the dollars come in. One plant with that capacity to convert coal would cost between $200 million and $300 million. Our current consumption is about 22 trillion cubic feet a year. If my arithmetic is right, we would need to build 300 plants to meet our total need—that is, if we didn't have any natural gas available and had to rely on synthetic coal gas.*

It might be better than 1,000 nuclear plants.

*People blithely assume that if we increase electricity production, all our problems will be solved. But electricity accounts at the present time for less than 12% of our total energy use in this country. We need to keep that in focus. We are still going to need a lot of natural gas, gasoline, and oil. My position is that we had better build all the ecologically sound nuclear plants, coal conversion plants, and oil shale plants that we can build just as fast as we can.*

*This ecumenical approach to energy may seem odd from the Director of the Office of Coal Research, but it is sincere. I ought to be pushing coal exclusively, but I am more realistic than that. I live in this country, and my children and grandchildren want to live here, and we would like to maintain a reasonable standard of living which would require, in my opinion, development of all of these energy sources.*

Do you think it is wise to burn up a diminishing resource? Hydrocarbons like coal are necessary for other uses, such as medical products. Is the "drain America first" philosophy a wise one to follow?

*The coal reserves I have spoken of represent coal in seams thicker than three feet. There is at least an equal quantity of additional coal in seams three feet thick or less that we cannot afford to mine for power production. To evaluate the quantity of chemicals we make compared to the quantity we burn for energy, look at the petroleum industry. I think 5% or less of our petroleum goes into making all of the synthetic chemicals. So we have a ratio of twenty to one in energy versus chemical demand. If we have as much coal left in the ground after we use up this 200-year supply as we now have—and only one-twentieth of it is used per year for producing chemicals— then it is really nothing we need to be anxious about.*

If the Egyptians had said that 3,000 years ago, where would we be today?

*As an answer, I offer my father's wisdom, given to me when I started graduate school. Whatever the mind of man can conceive, through diligent effort and enough faith he can achieve. If we look back at Malthus' predictions of starvation, if you read the forecasts of 1910 that our forests would all be gone within fifteen years, the future is apocalyptic. That hasn't been true because man finds alternatives or new and improved ways of doing things that foil the predictions.*

You can raise timber, but you can't create hydrocarbons.

*The total quantity of carbon and hydrogen in our system is constant. We are not losing it at an appreciable rate. We can make hydro-carbons out of carbon dioxide and sunlight, if that is the way to go. In the long term, the answer will be nuclear fusion. So we will produce all the fuel we need plus all the electricity we need and leave the coal to replenish itself under the crust of the earth in order to make nylon hose and other synthetic materials in the future.*

*The shortage, or even lack, of coal in the future is not the critical issue. Far more critical is what will happen to the standard of living in the transition period, the thirty to forty years between today and the application of fusion power.*

*In that period, we will see social, political, and economic changes brought about by our energy program. For one thing we have to provide the kind of economic matrix for the coal industry that we provided for the petroleum companies to become competitive. We provide it now for the nuclear energy industry to be competitive with the fossil fuel energy field. It is on the way for coal, and I am sure it will be available to us within the next ten to fifteen years.*

Could you elaborate on what you mean by that?

*I have done a lot of soul searching on how this country establishes its pricing system. It turns out that there are some elements in our economy that aren't, strictly speaking, free competition. For example, in order to stimulate the continued discovery of petroleum back in the 1930s, a depletion allowance was given to oil companies. This system made it possible for them to rediscover the oil they had consumed by allowing the companies 27.5% a barrel back in the early days. As time went on, that amount of money proved insufficient. Costs went up. Producers are drilling deeper wells. Smaller pools are being found. The discovery rate is considerably lower. So the replenishment wasn't fully paid for by the depletion allowance. Well, that was an artificial subsidy, plain and simple. It did, however, provide the result we were after. This became part of the economic matrix, then, that allows us to make gasoline for 12 cents a gallon or whatever it currently costs.*

*Congress got a little nervous two or three years ago and reduced the depletion allowance. The depletion allowance either makes sense at a real value now of, say, 35%, or it ought not to be there at all. To arbitrarily back a little bit away is just playing games, in my opinion. Either it was a valid concept and worth maintaining or we ought to take the whole price out of the customer's pocketbook as the price of gasoline, in which case we would be nearer a free economy.*

*As another illustration of our economic matrix, the nuclear power program has had the advantage of writing off $13 billion of research and development work that is not now being charged to the extent that we would charge the development of conventional new processes. This could be characterized as insurance that is borne by the government. There still exists the cost of storing for fifty years or so the radioactive waste products from the production of nuclear energy. As taxpayers, we are paying for this. It was done to make nuclear power competitive with fossil fuel. Everybody finally agreed to make each energy source competitive. The economic facts of life are interesting when you look at them intensively.*

*Several years ago I worked out the data on the quantity of electricity the AEC used to enrich natural, unrefined uranium into reactor grade uranium. I calculated from AEC figures that the amount of electricity used exceeded the amount we would get back if we used all that uranium 235 in power reactors. I tried to figure the economic value of using a fuel that required more electricity in its production than you would get back as a power source to generate electricity. The joker in my calculation, of course, was that most of the electricity went to enriching uranium for bomb purposes.*

Isn't an important solution to the nation's energy shortage a function of reducing our consumption of electrical energy?

*There are two factors to bear in mind as we think about turning back our consumption patterns. One is that the percentage of the total population in the twenty to thirty-five age groups, which is establishing homes, is now two and one-half times greater than fifteen years ago. Who is going to tell these young couples that they cannot buy a washing machine and television set and other power-hungry gadgets. The surge of postwar babies is a fact of national life.*

When a new household is formed, it creates a new demand for energy. It also offers the possibility for equipping the new homes with solar heating. Great new opportunities for conservation are at hand.

*There's no question about that. In my opinion, we need to move more rapidly than we now are toward houses designed to maximize the sunlight in the wintertime by having overhanging eaves, to eliminate the fireplace chimney so that heated or cooled air does not escape, to incorporate better insulation so that the energy input required to maintain a tolerable temperature level is not excessive. We can and must do these things as quickly as we can.*

What are the implications for water supplies when coal is converted to synthetic gas?

*As a rule of thumb, the water requirements are equivalent to the amount that an oil refinery needs for the same relative production. Our study shows that for 75,000 tons of coal, some 15 million gallons of water would be required.*

*In 1971 the American Gas Association made a secret study that pinpointed 176 different sites for synthetic gas works selected by the Institute of Gas Technology. Located mostly in the Rocky Mountain states, each site has sufficient access to coal and water for a plant turning out 250 million cubic feet of synthetic gas a day. Gasification plants need large amounts of water, which is consumed in the process.*

*It may well turn out that these plants would have to pipe in sea water from some distance or run in water from Canada or even Alaska.*

*In some arid regions, the value of water for chemical processing or power generating exceeds the value of water for farming. When the farmer is offered 10 to 100 times the value of water used for irrigation, he is glad to peddle it to a power plant or chemical firm. It has happened already that farmers take the money and run to the city.*

I think you said, Mr. Hill, that coal represents something like 200 years of our hydrocarbon needs in relationship to our present oil, gas, and coal demand. Isn't that demand going up every year? So 200 years now may turn into 150 years in another decade?

*Correct. Now I have heard people say we have coal for 1,000 years. I am more conservative. I think we need to understand what is meant by a reserve. We have got a proved reserve of coal, which means we've core-drilled the ground and have a pretty good notion of what's there. But we have to include some assumptions: One is that we cannot afford to mine coal that is thinner than three feet thick. We have an almost infinite supply of seams that are three, two, and one foot thick. The quantity of coal in seams less than three feet thick is at least equal to the thicker seams and probably much greater. In the West there are a tremendous number of outcrops — coal seams of six inches or less that people don't even think about. But our proved reserve of coal is that coal producible under current techniques at present mining costs. That reserve should last about 200 years, conservatively.*

Getting back to the water—is there an international legal problem in taking water out of the sea for power plants or chemical works or some other industrial use?

*No. It is a closed system. The water goes up as steam. Three weeks after it's been used, it's back in the sea. We don't destroy the water; we recycle it.*

Does a synthetic gas plant operate like an oil refinery? Could you adjust your process so that, instead of making 250 million cubic feet of gas, you make 75 million cubic feet of gas and 20,000 barrels of oil?

*That's one of the beauties of this as a feed material. What we are doing right now is building some plants for natural gas exclusively and other plants for oil exclusively. But there is a pilot operation in Princeton, New Jersey, developed by FMC Corporation and funded by the Office of Coal Research, that produces oil and gas simultaneously. If you produce oil and gas simultaneously, then, in that part of the year in which you want more gas, you crank the temperature up and produce a higher yield of gas; in the summertime, when you want more gasoline, you lower the temperature and increase the yield of oil. So you have a practical built-in flexibility.*

**What are the energy conversion figures for coal gasification?**

*You suffer a loss in energy when you convert any hydrocarbons to any other form. To make low-Btu gas out of coal costs about 10% of the original energy. The processing, in other words, costs one-tenth of what you began with. To go the next step, to make methane out of it, costs another 8%. So 18% is the loss in terms of the energy begun with. However, the cost of producing electricity is 60% of what you began with.*

**So you are still keeping a fair number of Btus in fact.**

*That's correct.*

**If you have a 10% loss in converting to low-Btu gas and a 60% loss in the operation of the plant, you have got more loss than if you put the coal there in the first place.**

*This is a very astute observation. It's the one that makes me think we really ought to look at the fluidized bed approach, where we burn coal directly. The other study in which we are engaged is the development of more efficient combined cycles so we can feed this low-Btu gas into a gas-turbine steam-turbine combination and boost the efficiency at that end of the operation by 5% to maybe 15%. Theoretically, we can go up to 50% or better, and we would gain back more than we would lose. Obviously, if you use coal in the generation, you would still be ahead. But you are very right. Every time you convert it costs you energy. As it happens, everything we do in terms of improving our environment is costing us energy.*

*I bought an Opel two years ago. A friend of mine had one which was getting twenty-eight miles per gallon. I got seventeen. So*

*I went storming into my car dealer screaming, "Fix things up." He lifted the hood and said, "Look at that anti-pollution recycling apparatus." Lowering of the compression ratio in order to meet the required purity of air out of the exhaust is costing something like 20% of the gasoline yield.*

*Every single thing we add—a stack gas scrubber, for instance—is going to cost more. It is estimated that half the cost of a power plant will be the cost of a scrubber. The operating costs are going to increase the price of electricity. A great deal of our raw material energy is consumed in cleaning up. One of these days the general public is going to become aware of this, and we are going to be criticized and nailed to the wall in a very real sense. We have not been intelligent in our analysis of the problem. We are not making the trade-offs we need in terms of conserving our limited fossil fuel resources.*

**Can you tell me what a stack gas scrubber is?**

*A stack gas scrubber is a device down which you trickle a water solution of, say, sodium carbonate over redwood slats so you get a lot of wet surface. By pumping the exhaust gas from the power plant up through a circuitous route, all the gas is in contact with that water which absorbs the sulfur dioxide and traps it as sodium sulfite, which is somehow disposed.*

**Why is this so terribly expensive?**

*Because of the size of the installation required in order to reduce the sulfur dioxide. It is an inefficient process and runs about 50% of the cost of the original plant. It could be half the size of the power plant itself.*

**Would it be necessary to relax environmental standards to make synthetic gas and oil?**

*The necessity to relax standards is to enable us to meet our needs within the next ten-year framework. If we fall into the trap of increasing our imports of oil and gas from the Middle East, we will quickly become so dependent upon that part of the world that we will be at their mercy. It has been calculated that oil tankers would be distributed every ten miles across the Atlantic Ocean in order to keep the supply coming. The relaxation of standards, in my opinion, is an immediate solution to allow us to burn coal for power generation and thus provide enough gas and oil for our current needs. Meanwhile, we would be developing environmentally suitable products from coal. The interim period would be time to prove out the processes and build up commercial projects.*

**Are you talking about state standards that go beyond federal standards?**

*No. We have almost eliminated the burning of coal. Some 90% of the coal in the East and Midwest of the United States does not meet the current standards as they stand. Power companies had to change to burning gas and oil.*

**How soon will gasification become commercial?**

*It is commercial right now. El Paso Natural Gas is investing hundreds of millions of dollars in a plant. It is being designed right now to make synthetic natural gas from coal. If all goes well—and the Indians, the Bureau of Land Management, and everybody else is satisfied—it will be on stream in three years. The plant would be located in the northwest corner of New Mexico, near Farmington. There are also proposals for three similar plants, using the older technique. When the techniques we are now developing under contract with various universities and companies come on stream, the Lurgi gasifiers (thirty of which are required to produce the same volume of gas that one modern gasifier will produce) will be scrapped in favor of putting in the new ones.*

**If an economic way of disposing of the effluent produced in the scrubbing process could be achieved, we could build more coal-fired power plants and reduce the number of breeder reactors.**

*I hope the dialogue will soon begin to happen. We must start making sensible trade-offs so that instead of one group talking to themselves and getting enthused and another group talking to themselves and never resolving the problem, we begin to debate the merits of coal versus oil versus nuclear energy and the trade-offs of different levels and grades of pollution on land, sea, and air. The choices and alternatives need to be debated and not just talked about among ourselves.*

# Chapter 10

William F. Pedersen Jr.

# Are Antipollution Laws Working?

One of the key amendments to the Clean Air Act of 1970 requires that by 1975 two of the three most offensive automobile pollutants, hydrocarbons and carbon monoxides, should be cut by 90% from the level at the time the legislation was passed. In 1970 this was considered definitely possible because new cars had already been subject to pollution controls for two to three years. The statute called for only one relief: At any time after 1972 the automobile manufacturers could apply to the administrator of the Environmental Protection Agency to extend the nonpollution standards from 1975 to 1976.

The administrator was authorized by Congress to grant Detroit's request if he found that each of four tests had been met: First, the car companies had established that the technology was not yet available to meet the new standards; second, independent studies, including one made by the National Academy of Sciences, had also established that the technology was not available; third, the applicants had made efforts all in good faith to meet the standards; and fourth, an extension was essential to the national interest or to the public health and welfare.

## EXTENDING THE STANDARDS

To nobody's great surprise, in the late winter of 1972, Detroit asked for the extension. The law requires that a decision on these applications be made within sixty days, and in early May 1972 the applications were turned down.

The opinion basically addressed only the first of the tests—that is, whether the applicants themselves had borne the affirmative burden of proving the technology was not developed. The conclusion was that there was still a way to go before certification tests began for the 1975 models which would take place in October or November of 1973, and that the technology seemed to be advancing quite rapidly.

I think the principal reason for denying the request was a method of statistical adjustments to the actual test results purporting certain corrections for the lack of all the most advanced elements on the cars that had actually been run. The auto companies took the decision to the courts, and, in February of this year, the Court of Appeals in the District of Columbia handed down a sixty-page opinion which, I think, amounts to about 80% of an order to grant the suspension. Looking at the record, the court said it appeared that the economic cost of the decision to deny the suspension could be so great that some companies wouldn't be able to pass their cars through the certification tests. More than that, the manufacturers might not be able to achieve the standards even if the cars had passed. In addition, the environmental costs of a one-year extension would be relatively small. The court characterized the one-year extension as a safety valve, which was an integral part of the scheme to really put it to the auto industry no later than 1976, and cautioned the administrator against closing the safety valve too tightly.

If William D. Ruckelshaus, EPA's administrator, had been convinced the evidence showed, despite what the court had said, that a denial was still necessary, he would have ordered it. Still, the court decision played a major part in shaping public attitudes toward the problem.

As to the specific findings, the court concluded that the technology is available and listed three standards the makers would have to meet: first, certification testing, which means EPA approval of emission levels based on prototypes that are run 50,000 miles; second, the ability to mass produce the cars which are still in the prototype or preproduction stage when they are certified; third, the ability of the emission control system to perform adequately enough to really reduce pollution.

We investigated each of these three points. On the first point, everyone here knows that Honda, Mazda, and Mercedes-Benz are able to pass the standards with, respectively, the stratified charge engine, the Wankel turbine, and a light-duty diesel. What I don't think has been as well publicized is that General Motors, for one, is almost as far along using a catalytic converter. GM has run six of its test cars through the required 50,000 miles. Of those, three passed the standards, and two others failed by a couple of hundredths of a gram of hydrocarbons. That is five out of six.

Although the Court of Appeals hit us pretty hard on adjustments to the data that had been done the last time, we have gone back and readjusted the data. We have made some assumptions to correct for the fact that the best systems were not on the cars that were tested. We have taken individual systems, and said, "Look, this car did better with that on it," and we have corrected the data for that. On the other hand, since it takes about five or six months to do a certification test—somewhat longer than that if it is part of a development program, when you are continually interrupting it and looking at the car—we have been working with data that is a year old, and we have not made any corrections. The court forbids us to make a correction for the general progress of knowledge and know-how during that year and during the additional six months until certification testing has to begin. In addition, all the results have been adjusted to a 95% confidence level, which is the standard statistical confidence level for saying you are really sure of something. This means a car which just barely passes the standards will be counted a failure because the random variation in the test results is such that you cannot be 95% sure it would still be there if you tested it again. By this calculation, which we view as conservative, we predict that model lines amounting to 93% of GM's production would certify in 1975, 55% of Ford's production would certify, but none of Chrysler's production would certify. So, we say that 66% of the market is not enough for 1975, but we think it is a most excellent indication for 1976 and proves that achieving the standards is technologically feasible.

On the second component—the ability to mass produce these cars—all the industry people told EPA that they would phase in across a portion of the model line, moving slowly to shake down the assembly lines, but that they weren't able to do this to meet 1975 standards. In their defense, Detroit says that it can put the catalysts on if it has to, in the sense that all the necessary contracts and construction commitments have been made, but that it is sure to go wrong because the bugs haven't been worked out in the normal leisurely way; and other experts from outside the car industry say the same thing.

Now some people in EPA are somewhat suspicious of this argument, because it rests, to a large degree, on industry evidence. But the record, as it now stands, is strong on that point, particularly in light of what the court said about balancing the environmental harm relatively lightly against the economic risk.

## THE CATALYTIC CONVERTER

The third component of the technological test—certainly the one that causes the most public uneasiness and about which the auto companies yell loudest—is catalyst failure in use. I know there has been a lot of talk about this untried technology and what it will mean. The record is absolutely clear: The court opinion says that all a failure in use means is that the catalyst will not control the pollutants. A catalyst is a metal cannister containing either a ceramic honeycomb with all the little passages in it each about one-half millimeter thick or a bunch of pebbles of aluminum ore. This material (no matter which one) is coated with a thin mixture of platinum and palladium, which is the catalytic material. The exhaust gases pass through this chamber on the way out, and the catalytic material causes them to react with each other so that the reaction product is harmless gases—water, carbon dioxide. It needs no moving parts.

We think the evidence shows that there are certain ways in which the catalyst can be damaged so it will not react with the exhaust gases. But there is no way the catalyst can fail and either endanger the driver or damage the vehicle. So, we reduce the problem of the catalyst failure to a cost-effectiveness problem—that is, if X number of catalysts fail, then a given degree of air quality becomes that much more expensive. As to what that failure rate will be under all the conditions of actual use, we just can't be 100% sure because it has never happened before.

We think the claims of catalyst failure that are made are probably exaggerated. Chrysler claims it has a 40% rate of catalyst failures. Chrysler runs its cars on an engine testing cycle that typically causes component failure rates about ten times above the experience in the field. In other cases, an analysis was made of one of the failures of one of the tables where Ford claimed failure rates. We analyzed the catalysts that were said to have failed because they had melted to some degree—as the catalyst will do when it gets overheated—or had cracked from vibration or thermal stress. These so-called failures, we found, had essentially no effect on the performance of the catalysts in reducing emissions.

The technology is still advancing. There may be devices which all the companies are working on to reduce the activity of the catalyst when a sensor says it is overheated. All things considered, we do not think the possibility of catalyst failure in use is worrisome enough for us to say that it is faulty technology or unavailable technology.

As for the cost, the estimate put forward by the National Academy of Sciences is that the entire emissions control system for a 1975 car will cost $160 more than the emissions control system on present cars. However, $100 is accounted for by various modifications to the engine, which also reduce pollution and which all the auto companies, without exception, propose to put on their 1975 models. So the actual cost of the catalyst itself, as opposed to these other engine modifications, is an extra $60.

It isn't so much the cost that I want to stress, although we think that is a good price. Part of the notion that you have to distinguish between the cost of the catalyst in 1975 cars and the cost of other engine modifications lies in the distinction that has to be made between the cost of the catalytic system for the 1975 car and the cost of the entire system to control the nitrogen oxides to the level required in 1976. We have found the preponderant evidence indicates that there will be little or no fuel penalty associated with the use of a catalyst, which automatically reduces the cost of the system greatly. It appears there will be a significant fuel penalty associated with the use of a catalyst in 1976, however, and it also appears that the level of nitrogen oxides in the atmosphere has been overstated. The reason EPA has called for reexamination of this is really that the original standard was met using instruments that read 4 when they should have read 1.5 or something like that. It is just a simple problem in the instrument. So we don't think it is legitimate to assume the 1976 standards will require a catalyst and then to attribute that to the 1975 system.

So, making those two distinctions, let me suggest the public interest. I have already talked about fuel economy; the next point is performance and drivability. We have compared the drivability of 1973 Ford production cars with the drivability of its prototype fleets, which in many cases are calibrated to be not very drivable because they are seeking maximum emissions control. We have found virtually no difference. We also have a letter from General Motors which says, in effect, that they expect drivability will improve, if anything, by 1975.

## NEW ENGINE ALTERNATIVES

Another component that we address is alternate technologies, which is another part of the court decision that has caused a great deal of public concern. We concluded that we cannot say the Wankel engine is a superior technology because of its fuel penalty. Mazda has about a 15% fuel penalty over an equivalent-sized conventional engine. The diesel has much better fuel economy, but there are some other problems associated with it. People just don't seem to like to buy it. It is noisy. It creates particulates. It has a bad smell. We can't clearly conclude that these things are preferable technology either.

So we come to the Honda engine. Everything that we have seen about the Honda engine is good. But we haven't seen all that much. So we praise it, but we don't go overboard.

In last year's decision, I remember we said that the monolithic catalyst, the honeycomb type, was clearly best. This year it appears that the pebble catalyst is clearly best. GM is the only company using the pebble catalyst, which is better than anything else.

The technology is constantly changing. We have not nailed our colors to the mast on the Honda engine. The big point about all these technologies is that everyone who testified claimed it would take a minimum of four years to get a significant changeover to these new engines—the Wankel and the diesel and, possibly, the Honda—and it will take a total of ten years before all cars on American highways are equipped with these new engines.

If we are to have emissions controls anything like the amount that the Clean Air Act mandates for this decade, it looks as if the catalysts will be necessary. We don't think that is so bad. It is General Motors' opinion, as well as the opinion of all the catalyst companies, that the catalyst is pretty good.

The way we sign off on the alternate technologies is to say that the only way to make sure they are adopted is to let the marketplace do it. It is hard enough getting the auto industry to accept any degree of emissions control—though the car makers now concede it is a legitimate public purpose and something the government should bother them about. I think if we were to try to tell them how to make the engines that they have been making for fifty years—whether or not you think it is a good idea—it would be a most difficult regulatory task.

The only other problem is the issue of Chrysler's good faith, which is addressed in detail in the court opinion. Chrysler has spent one-sixth to one-tenth as much on emissions control in absolute terms as the other two of the Big Three—about one-third as much per dollar of sales or per car sold. From a detailed analysis of the documents that we subpoenaed from Chrysler, it appears that on two or three occasions, probably three occasions, they put off the commitments that would have moved their program to another stage or they chose a technology that did not appear to be the best one in order to save money. On that basis, the EPA administrator expressed his serious doubts as to whether they really had tried as hard as they should have. But since the consequence of a finding of bad faith would be to shut them down, he did not make that finding.

The Clean Air Act requires, in effect, that we reduce emissions by a factor of about 85% from the levels of today's cars. The levels which are set forth for national use, which it is anticipated will not require the general use of a catalyst, reduce the emissions by about 50%. The levels for California, which will probably require the use of a catalyst, will still be high enough so that the manufacturers will not have to worry too much about passing the certification test, reducing emissions by a factor of about 75%. These are far more significant reductions than any which have taken effect since the amendments were passed—although they do not go all the way to the 1975 standards. They are designed to prepare the ground for going all the way in 1976.

# Discussion

What is your reaction to the auto industry's testimony that they may not be able to meet even the interim standards you have set?

> *Well, all I can say is that this is not the judgment of our technical people. I think that, more than any other issue, is one which is likely to end up in litigation.*

You mean you expect them to come back and sue again on the interim?

> *They may well not sue on the California interim.*

Speaking to the Chrysler case, although the company didn't spend as much money in researching this matter, it did spend more money in lobbying against it. Have you any comment on that?

> *I want to steer clear of that. It is their right of free speech to say that the Clean Air Act is a lousy law. I think we should avoid even the semblance of punishing them just because they are vociferous in that opinion.*

Has the production of low-lead gasoline reached the stage where there is a possibility that low-lead or no-lead may not have to be used?

> *Last January, regulations requiring low-lead gas were promulgated. Service stations will have to carry one pump of low-lead gasoline by the beginning of the 1975 model year. The court opinion cites four or five letters from oil companies in which they say that they plan to do that. Since catalyst cars will not be as numerous in 1975 as was previously anticipated, maybe there will be some rewriting of that regulation. But, in general, low-lead gas will be available nationwide.*

What is the purpose of this law on low-lead gas? Does lead foul up the catalyst?

> *Yes, the lead physically settles on the catalytic surface, so there is lead over the platinum. Once that happens, the platinum can no longer react with the exhaust gases.*

Apparently the decision had been made to operate on the side of the marketplace as opposed to public interest. What would tip the balance in the larger context?

> *Well, it appears that the Honda engine may be somewhat less expensive and may have marginally better fuel economy than the catalyst on the open-to-mistake view. It also appears it is likely to be far more durable.*
>
> *Let me just sketch to you my understanding of how the Honda engine works. Ordinarily the air fuel mixture is injected into the piston top where it is ignited by the spark plug and pushes the piston down. Now you need a relatively rich air fuel mixture — more fuel to air — for that mixture to ignite, which means a couple of things. It means it burns hot, and hot combustion produces nitrogen oxide. Also, the mixture burns incompletely because there is so much fuel, and this incomplete combustion produces hydrocarbons and carbon monoxide. But there must be a rich mixture or the spark plug won't work. Now, what Honda has done, in effect, is to put a little cylinder on top of the big one, with two intake valves. The one in the little cylinder lets in a very rich mixture; the one in the big chamber puts in a very lean mixture. The spark fires and ignites the rich mixture. When burning, the rich mixture is enough to ignite the lean mixture. But the overall mixture is quite lean, so you get much cleaner combustion. And because it is right there in the piston, it should be more durable in use. In ordinary circumstances, the consumer wouldn't care about that. But in many cities and counties where there will be yearly car inspections and catalyst replacements, this will be an incentive to buy the Honda engine. Let me say another thing about the Honda: One of the somewhat surprising things at the hearing was that Nissan and Toyota were really as bad as the domestic companies — probably worse — and wanted the standards suspended. Honda is a small company just moving into the automobile industry. It is run by one man who is a mechanical genius. It is a company that was made to order to invent something like this, regardless of its being in Japan or not.*

The National Academy of Sciences recommended a year's delay with the expectation that the time would be used to create some new technology, not to follow the same old route.

> *The evidence indicates that the year's delay will not have any significant effect in allowing them to install any new technology. Further,*

*although everything we know about the Honda engine looks good, the jury is still out. The whole field is too undeveloped. It is conceivable and even asserted, not only by the catalyst makers, but also by General Motors, that the catalytic converter may, in fact, be the best technology. Then, too, I just don't see how the government could order or persuade the auto companies to manufacture one particular engine rather than any other. I think that if the sales of Honda cars and a couple of American cars that have converted to the Honda system really start to go, this will be more effective than anything the government could do.*

Sometime last fall, **Mr. Ruckelshaus** said that if cars were reduced to an average weight of 2,500 pounds, we would be saving $2.5 billion a year in our balance of payments through oil purchases by 1985. Can you see the government regulating the weights of cars?

*Some of the weight increase is caused by safety regulations. Nevertheless, EPA did make a study, in which no one has really put a dent, that shows the emissions control devices contribute a 7% to 10% fuel penalty. An air conditioner or an automatic transmission adds to the fuel penalty. The fuel penalty is almost linear with the weight. In other words, a car that weighs twice as much will consume twice as much gasoline.*

Do you think, **Mr. Pedersen**, that other states will follow California's example and not allow cars without any catalytic burners by 1975?

*The Clean Air Act says: "No state shall set an automobile emission standard more stringent than the national standard except California." The California Standard is sort of a legal hybrid, and there are legal doubts about it. I think there is a good case in favor of requiring that special status be given to California. For nitrogen oxides and for hydrocarbons, we have just granted California's request to be allowed to present more stringent standards. For carbon monoxide, we have not granted their waiver; we have set a more stringent federal standard. There is hope that California will go along with it and accept it as their standard, in which case all the legal doubts disappear. If not, then the defense is that the court read the statute very broadly for us to act in the public interest.*

*There are many reasons why the limited phase-in in California is an especially good option. Auto pollution is awful in California. The big cities are on the coast, far away from other states, so it's geographically a separate area for automobile use. The state has a lot of experience in this. Its air pollution control people are experienced in taking new inventions and seeing how they work.*

*Mayor John Lindsay once testified that he thought any dual standard for New York City, which is one of the three or four other worst pollution areas, would be absolutely unworkable because of the great flow of traffic through the area.*

If, in fact, you do wind up in court on the interim standards, how long might one suspect that that case would last, and what would that do to the whole timetable?

*I would think we would get a quick decision, because certification, the description of how the 1975 cars must behave before they are approved, will be coming up before EPA in the fall. So the auto companies will want to know with finality, sometime in advance of that date, what the standards are.*

What caused Mr. Ruckelshaus to change his decision about the cutoff date for car pollution?

*I think it was a choice between phasing-in the catalysts in California and setting some other standard which would be stricter than the present national standard but not as strict as California's.*

But Mr. Ruckelshaus ruled once that the auto maker should not have the extension. Obviously he reconsidered the order and came to another conclusion. What are some of the factors that led to his decision—influence, sellout, what?

*I don't believe that he sold out. I am not at a high enough level in the agency to know with whom he talks. But I know it was a staff opinion, once they had digested the Circuit Court's ruling and once the companies had come in with the figures on their test results, that we would not be able to make a denial stick this time.*

As I understood it, EPA's first position on emission control standards would mean shutting down Chrysler, something the government didn't want to tackle. At what point does an industry become subservient to the public interest?

*I am not sure shutting down Chrysler would tend to make it subservient to the public interest. In his press conference, Mr. Ruckelshaus stated that, if he had some intermediate sanction like a fine (such as the one imposed on Ford), then he might well have decided otherwise. I wouldn't be surprised if some environmental group appealed that part of the decision.*

There is a body of opinion which holds the view that there is no way to clean up the internal combustion engine. Maybe we ought to set about getting rid of this great noxious beast.

*If the 1975 standards are achieved, air quality will improve dramatically in the next decade. But in the late 1980s it will begin to deteriorate again. Even the National Academy of Sciences, which I think was relatively soft on regulating the auto industry, said that there is no cure for our major cities except to diminish the number of automobiles. It certainly is clear in a case like Los Angeles that you just cannot do anything without a lot of public transportation. In Boston they have stopped all new road construction inside Route 128 and they are expanding the subway system. I think we will see a lot more of that.*

What was that about air quality beginning to deteriorate again in the 1980s?

*The projected increase is such that, after all the old cars that aren't 1975-level cars have been retired, the inevitable increase in the number of automobiles will begin to raise the pollution levels again.*

What responsibility, if any, does EPA have to investigate the potential pollution and other environmental problems arising from water diversion, nuclear power, and the production of shale oil and coal gasification? Does EPA conduct any research in these areas?

*Well, I don't think we have much formal or line authority to deal with those things. They are basically problems for other agencies. EPA has programs to develop expertise in energy use. The big legal handle we have is that environmental impact statements have to be reviewed by EPA. There is an EPA office that comments on them and says whether they are considered good or bad. And there seems to be some impetus to give EPA veto authority, even over matters that are the province of other agencies. The administration's strip-mining bill would give a veto or consultative role to EPA. I think we already have it in the area of aircraft noise. But our basic business is air pollution control.*

Do you think EPA will build up enough confidence so it won't be at the mercy of the automobile industry by 1975?

*In a sense the automobile area is the one in which we are most comfortable because we don't have to be competent or anything. We just have to say: "There is the law; as long as the law is the law, you manufacturers must come here and have your cars certified to meet it."*

*In other areas where we, as an administrative agency, set the standards, those standards have to be based on evidence and are subject to challenge as being arbitrary.*

You are making your decisions with regard to the automobile industry on test data supplied by the industry, isn't that correct?

*That's right. One impression I got from attending the hearings is that that's the problem. On the other hand, if you had a lot of EPA inspectors crawling around the industry so they got a handle and knew what was going on, the big bureaucracy, with intensive regulatory powers, would have undesirable aspects too. We are dependent on the auto industry and it is dependent on us. It's just a great process that churns along.*

What agency in the United States Government has responsibility for determining the basic changes to be made in society fifteen or twenty years from now so that we can live in a tolerable environment?

*The answer is the Council on Environmental Quality which is part of the White House staff. Each year it issues a report on environmental quality. It is supposed to take an overview of the government and society and think about such things. EPA, although it's formally only involved in pollution control, is, in fact, concerned with the whole environment, so it speaks to other points, too.*

Are you satisfied with the efforts and people that are needed in this area?

*I don't know. I think that concern for the environment has to percolate and a consensus has to develop.*

# Chapter 11
Bruce C. Netschert

# Are Antipollution Laws Widening the Energy Gap?

To begin with, I would like to illustrate Barry Commoner's observation that, "Everything is connected to everything else."

First, the case of natural gas. The Clean Air Act of 1970, affecting coal production and utilization because of federal and state standards on emissions of sulfur oxides, at the same time advanced the production and utilization of natural gas, which could meet the standards of air quality. So, when the Environmental Protection Agency set ambient air standards to limit sulfur oxides and other pollutants, it was creating a large potential demand for natural gas. The consequence, as might be expected, was that the demand exceeded the industry's ability to supply natural gas. For one thing, the demand increased so quickly that the industry couldn't possibly respond.

The unfilled demand for gas spilled over into the other acceptable low-sulfur fuels, notably oil and especially No. 2 oil. Not surprisingly, the demand for this, too, increased at a rapid rate because the sulfur limitations were reduced. I am talking here about oil with only 0.5% sulfur or, in the cases of many large cities like New York, Boston, and Philadelphia, 0.3% sulfur.

The demand for oil, in turn, outstripped the ability of the oil industry to produce residual oil with that low-sulfur content. So, one of the ways in which the demand was met was by diluting high-sulfur or medium-sulfur residual with No. 2 oil. Moreover, No. 2 oil was used to replace other fuels, particularly natural gas, which most consumers would have preferred for heating homes and other buildings.

Second, the case of nuclear energy. At the same time that sulfur restrictions were imposed, a storm of public opposition to our new nuclear capacity suddenly swept across the land. Just how much the delays in getting nuclear power are actually due to environmental battles is a subject of much armchair argument. According to *Electrical World,* there are ten nuclear plants that will not be operative this summer, as scheduled, because of delays in licensing due directly to environmentalists.

Now, with the electrical utilities faced with a shortage of nuclear capacity, the power companies turned as a stopgap measure to gas turbines. Gas turbines are a misnomer for jet engines. The companies had bought them as jet engines from Pratt & Whitney, but they are now designed specifically as turbine generators. These turbines were installed by the utilities to provide extra capacity during periods of extreme peak loads in the summer months. They were not intended for use except at peak times. But, when nuclear stations were delayed, the companies turned to the gas turbines for more than just peak periods. The fuel for these gas jets happens to be No. 2 oil.

In short, what started as pressure on natural gas was compounded by pressure on nuclear power, which further put pressure on oil. This is the picture of our energy crisis. This is the basic cause of the gasoline shortage. The emphasis on producing No. 2 oil for both home heat and power resulted in a lowered supply of gasoline.

## RESTRICTIONS AND INHIBITIONS

To continue my illustration of how "Everything is connected to everything else," I will remind you that the National Environmental Policy Act called for state standards of air quality. This happens to be the year in which the states submit their "implementation plans," as these standards were called, for approval by the EPA. In many instances the states have gone beyond EPA's own standards.

The EPA standards, promulgated in 1971, apply to power plants. While the regulation was stated in terms of the sulfur content of emissions related to the number of Btu's, it meant, in effect, that utilities could not burn fuel with a sulfur content higher than 0.7%. In the states of Ohio and Kentucky, the standards applied not only to new power plants but to existing ones as well.

In Ohio there are utilities located virtually on top of coal. Many of the power plants were built practically at the mine mouths of some of the largest coal reserves in the Eastern United States. Unfortunately there is no coal in Ohio with less than 1% sulfur. As it is now, Ohio utilities have certified that they will comply with the standard by 1975.

Since the utilities will not be able to burn Ohio coal, what about using other coal? The plain fact is that there is not enough low-sulfur coal in the East for their use. For electricity, billions of tons of coal are required. The supply of low-sulfur coal in the East is relatively modest, and most of it is already committed to the steel industry as the basis of coke, which is vital to steel production. So, what about coal from the West where, as Mr. Hill has stated, there are vast reserves? To transport it to Ohio would require the construction of many more steel hopper cars for the railroads. This would take time, increase the cost of shipping the coal, and put an increased burden on steel production. What's more, it is not at all clear that a power plant designed to burn coal of 1% sulfur content can operate on coal of 0.5% sulfur, because when the sulfur content changes so does the ash content. The ash may melt and form slag in boilers designed for a different kind of coal. In instances where the Tennessee Valley Authority and Mississippi utilities have turned to coal from the West, enormous problems have resulted and the practice had to be abandoned. For Ohio electricity plants, then, the options may be as clearcut as either violating standards or shutting down.

Still another illustration comes from the automobile industry. One of the unfortunate consequences of the emission control devices on cars is the reduction in gasoline mileage. EPA claims it has been reduced no more than 7%; the oil companies say 10% to 20%; my own experience leads me to put it at as much as 25%.

Last year we came close to having gasoline supply problems. The 1973 cars have greater pollution controls than the 1972 models, and their mileage, as a consequence, is even lower. The percentage of 1972 and 1973 models on the roads is now higher, and the effect on gasoline consumption this summer will be even greater.

So, in addition to gasoline supply difficulties unrelated to demand, there is the increase in demand brought about by the emission controls. An additional complication is that no additional refining capacity is scheduled to be built in this country, nor has there been any significant refining capacity added over the past several years.

## COSTS VS. BENEFITS

It may sound as if I am trying to argue that we shouldn't have a pollution abatement program, and I want to emphasize that this is not my point. My point is that *antipollution laws tend to widen the energy gap.*

At the same time, I do believe that environmental measures cannot deal in terms of absolutes—in other words, one cannot say that because pollution abatement is a socially desirable thing, anything that furthers pollution abatement is justified. Every environmental measure, it seems to me, should be subjected to a comparison of trade-offs between costs and benefits.

One of the problems created by our lack of attention to comparisons is illustrated by the 0.3% sulfur limitation imposed on fuels in some of the big cities. I don't know whether a 0.3% sulfur limitation is justified; nobody else does either. In New Jersey, to make matters worse, the sulfur limit is now 0.2%.

The fact is, if these sulfur limitations had been done in an economically rational manner, some marginal calculations would have been made. It's clear, for example, that when cities reduced the sulfur in fuels from 3% to 1% an enormous improvement in ambient air standards resulted. The air in New York City is remarkably cleaner than it was in terms of sulfur content. But it does not follow that because 1% is so much better than 3%, than 0.3% is also justified.

We know that costs rise in the process. To give you a very dramatic example, it costs more to remove particulates from stack gases by putting in precipitators. It costs more to go from 99.5% to 99.7% than it did from zero to 99.5%. It seems to me that changing the standards a few tenths of a percentage point should certainly involve some recognition of sharply increasing costs. There ought to be some measurement or comparison of the incremental benefits derived from incurring those incremental costs. With that lesson, I will open myself to questions.

# Discussion

For years Commonwealth Edison in Chicago said its boilers were designed for high-sulfur coal and could not be changed, but a year ago the public discovered that the company could use low-sulfur coal in those boilers. The point is the company could, at some cost, modify its boilers.

> *I would not make the engineering problems my main argument. I agree with you, though, that solving these problems is a matter of relative cost. In some instances, however, it appears to have been absolutely impossible for plants to continue normal operations. There were such massive accumulations of slags on the boiler tubes that they had to shut down every month or so to clean them off. A plant is not designed, built, or intended to run only a month at a time.*

You talk about a cost-benefit appraisal, but you are not going to use the kind of cost-benefit appraisal with which managers, accountants, and even journalists are familiar. What kind of cost-benefit analysis is involved?

> *Somebody makes a reasonably based estimate, however crude it might be, of the costs involved and some estimate, crude as it might be, as to the benefits. The fact is nobody has shown in any way what the difference is between the cost and the benefits of using 0.5% and 0.3% fuel.*

In New Jersey they have shown a difference. Since going from 0.7% to 0.5% to 0.3% to 0.2% fuel, some 70% of the sulfur dioxide has been removed from the air we breathe. This is a measureable impact.

> *But you don't know how much of that removal is due to the move from 1% to 0.5% and down to 0.2%. Would you have had a 68% reduction if you hadn't gone the last three-tenths of a percentage point?*

We have considered the benefits of not inhaling sulfur dioxide, of lessening the harm to lung tissue, and of reducing the acid rainfall on the crops we eat. Can you measure that?

> *I don't think you can yet.*

160

If you can't measure the impact, why set the sulfur content at some arbitrary percentage?

> *Because we know what the results were with 4% sulfur content. We had measurements; we had health effects.*

If that is the case, why can't you find out what the effects are with 1% sulfur?

> *You could with experience.*

Isn't it better to have a little overkill than take the chance?

> *That is exactly what the philosophy has been to date. One of the results of that philosophy has been a major contribution to our energy problem. You may argue—and this is certainly something that reasonable people can differ on—that the energy shortage is worth living with if we are a healthier people by keeping our air purer. You can argue about it but I don't know how you can prove it. I don't know how you would prove the converse, either. My point is that I don't think we were under the compulsion to move as fast as we have on environmental measures. If we had gone even at the pace originally scheduled, it would have helped a bit with our energy problem.*

Our charts show that over the past seven years we have removed 70% of the sulfur dioxide from the air. What effect does the remaining 30% have on the asthmatics and the elderly? What effect will it have on the rest of us? This is why I challenge you about the economic benefit.

> *That is the problem. And since we don't know the answer, it seems that we should be careful in adhering to the philosophy that argues it is better to do too much rather than not enough. I can provide an argument that can be used against that philosophy. If you talk about the impact of the existing sulfur level on old people with respiratory problems, you can also talk about the costs of brownouts at the peak of the summer heatwaves when air conditioners and kidney machines can't work. So the health and lives of heart cases and kidney sufferers are impaired by electricity shortages or failures.*

There is something wrong with that argument. If we reduced the size of our cars and cut down the number of airplane flights, a large quantity of oil would be free for diversion into electricity production. So maybe the building of Cadillacs should be banned while air conditioning should be encouraged.

*This is an interesting point and certainly it is relevant. But I would be consistent and say that the extent to which Cadillacs are made and used should be determined by the democratic workings of our market economy. If Cadillacs use more resources in their production and operation than smaller cars, then that is reflected, in general, in the cost of buying and operating the car. This, in effect, serves to ration Cadillacs. Most of us can't afford them.*

*Normally, I would say that is enough. On the other hand, when you can show that our environment is worsened by the production and use of Cadillacs, or any large and heavy car, then there is a legitimate question of public policy as to whether or not Cadillacs should be banned. In terms of economics, however, there is only one rational way to achieve such a social policy. You do not forbid the manufacture and use of Cadillacs, but you put a tax on the horsepower or the weight of the car to discourage its purchase. In other words, our only disagreement concerns the method, not the goals.*

I have heard about putting environmental quality on the cost-benefit scale since 1965. It's now 1973 and we are still only talking about how clean a cubic foot of air should be; meanwhile the air is getting filthier and filthier and more irritating and more irritating. At what point do we get alarmed?

*I'm glad we've returned to this issue, because you are challenging the closing point in my opening remarks—that there are no absolutes. I would continue to hold to that point. If you assume that any risk of a nuclear incident in a power plant is intolerable for society, you appear unrealistic because you are demanding absolute certainty or zero risk, which does not exist anywhere under normal circumstances. We live in a world of risk. We always have, we always will. And we have gladly tolerated an increase in risks on all kinds of fronts because of the benefits that flow from them. If we considered the risk involved in riding in automobiles, we would never get in one. The fact is, you have to make a judgment in some way about the risk you are willing to run versus the benefits you derive from accepting the risk. The least defensible position, it seems to me, is the position that we must get everything down to zero.*

Nature creates some of the worst risks—earthquakes, floods, volcanic eruptions, tidal waves.

*Yes, and there are cosmic rays from space, bombarding us all the time with radiation that can cause cancers and cataracts and, in general, debilitate us all.*

What do you recommend?

*My recommendation—which the President may well follow it in his energy message—is that there be a pullback from the rate of increase in the severity of the regulations in those instances where it can be clearly demonstrated that very serious widespread problems are created by adhering to the schedule. For example, in the case of Ohio, which I presented to you, it would make sense to move back the 1975 deadline—by how much I don't know, without more investigation.*

*I am not calling for an abandonment of all environmental standards. It seems we should tailor environmental preservation and pollution abatement to the circumstances in which we are trying to apply them. I am not arguing that the EPA administrator, whoever he is, should cave in anytime anyone raises his hand and says no. But there are clear instances, it seems to me, where we have been pushed too far too fast and have created unnecessary problems, the cost of which exceeds the incremental benefits. One such instance is Ohio; another is New York City. The people of New York City are paying millions of dollars in electricity bills because they are burning 0.3% sulfur fuel when 0.5% would be acceptable and would certainly help supply the power which is essential to the functioning of the city.*

There is a certain point in your formula where it is just too costly for the economy to operate, so we would have to risk lives for our economy. Is economic growth anti-life?

*It may be. And if it were the will of the electorate that we cut back our standard of living because we were leading ourselves to the grave, then that would have to be our course of action. But this certainly has not been expressed in any way in the policies of the officials that have been elected at any level. In other words, it is safe to say that most people today are not willing to give up the essentials of our standard of living in order to perhaps prolong life or improve health.*

Didn't we make great sacrifices during the Second World War, rationing gas, meat, clothing, sugar, all in the name of a national emergency? Don't you think the economic-environmental situation today warrants a similar sacrifice by the public?

> *Not at all. The cities are far better off today than in the nineteenth century. The air is far purer, the water safer.*

Doesn't your proposal suggest another economic quandary? For example, in the mountains and valleys of Virginia, only 60 miles away from Washington, D.C., the air is pure enough to afford a utility plant using fuel with 1.5% sulfur. So electricity rates out there are cheaper and, consequently, business can operate more competitively than around Washington.

> *That's right. So, according to the way economics works, industry moves out there and less of it stays in the city, which is what you want anyway.*

I am not sure we want to dirty up the air out there.

> *Why not?*

Take the problem you cited for Ohio. If the Dayton Power and Light Company spends $700,000 a year on advertising, why can't they use that money on sulfur oxide removal? Instead, they file suit against the standards.

> *I'm glad you brought that up. The best way to meet the requirements being imposed on the utilities is to remove the sulfur from the emissions. Then it doesn't matter how much you are burning. They could burn Ohio coal and everybody would be happy. The problem is that there is no reliable system for removing stack gas sulfur.*
>
> *Now EPA will not agree with this. EPA says the Japanese have demonstrated that it can be done. Well, one of the methods which the Japanese use is, in effect, an exchange of air pollution for water pollution. They are dumping the waste product into the water. We couldn't do that here. Furthermore, the scale of operation is much, much smaller.*
>
> *But we are working here on stack gas desulfurization. There must be at least a dozen different processes which are being tried out on a semicommercial scale with existing power plants. And when they work, they work very well. These systems have removed*

*some 90% of the sulfur. The trouble is in keeping them working. There isn't one system in this country that has worked for more than thirty days at a time.*

*Now, is this right for the consumer? The person who pays for this in the end is the consumer, not the utility. So is it right to have consumers burdened with the cost of installing these plants, which run $20 million to $100 million, when it isn't demonstrated that they are workable?*

**Do you know how much energy is used in cleaning up the environment?**

*The only hard figure I can provide is one released last month by the Edison Electric Institute. In a survey of its utility members, the Institute asked them to determine how much power used by their industrial customers was attributable to pollution abatement activities. The figure they came up with was 7%. It was calculated that the power used in cleanup activities would be 10% by 1975. That would include such efforts as the pumping of water for water treatment, the precipitators on emission stacks, and so forth.*

**I am trying to determine how your argument applies to the environmental problems of the United States. We are not grappling just with a few percentage points of sulfur dioxide, but with a whole range of problems.**

*I wouldn't agree with you. I think the sulfur problem in New York City has been pretty well licked. The reduction is dramatic—something like 70%.*

**But there is 30% less oxygen in Manhattan because of internal combustion. Shouldn't we deal with the collective impact of everything in the area?**

*No, you can't relate auto exhaust gases to gases coming out of a stack. They are totally different.*

**But if you have got the proper concentration and then add 0.1%—boom!**

*Are you saying they are synergistic?*

Do you know the synergistic effect of sulfur dioxide and nitrogen oxide?

> *The major problem in New York City is carbon monoxide. The major problem in Los Angeles is nitrogen oxide. There sulfur might very well have a much more important effect. Los Angeles has gotten around that by banning it entirely. My personal opinion is that the ban was probably justified. Los Angeles is, perhaps, closer to crisis conditions than anywhere else in the country.*

The kinds of environmental pollution we have been talking about are all man-made. If man made them, he can correct them, through the application of technology, the dispersal of population, the conservation of energy—all of which we have failed to do.

> *I guess I haven't gotten my argument across.*

How much energy would we save by copping out?

> *The whole point of my opening remarks was not that we would be cutting back on a demand, but that we would be creating an additional flexibility in supply to meet the demand. Our big problem right now is not that we don't have the energy resources; it is that we don't have the right ones that will meet the conditions we have imposed on ourselves.*

# Chapter 12

Stephen A. Wakefield

# Can Resources From Public Lands Be Developed in Environmentally Acceptable Ways?

Not content with having the longest title in this symposium, I would like to add a second question: *Can environmental protection goals be achieved in economically acceptable ways?* Since these questions are interdependent, they can't be addressed or answered separately.

I think the word "acceptable" should be defined, because every development project has an environmental cost. So the trade-offs become inevitable, and the balance point between the environmental cost and the economic cost represents the "acceptable."

One of the difficulties that we encounter initially is trying to ascertain what the long-run costs are going to be before the development even begins. For example, most people in positions of authority thought in 1964 or 1965 the costs of the Vietnam War would be acceptable, but by 1967 or 1968 many people had come to the conclusion that the costs would not be acceptable. We have to be very careful not to repeat that experience in the area of environmental protection—that is, not to bite off more than the American people can chew.

There are enormous difficulties in distributing the costs and the benefits among all Americans, because the costs and the benefits of either development or protection don't often affect the same people. This can lead to great inequities.

A good, if not classic, example of this was the proposed Louisiana offshore gas sale, which the Department of the Interior advertised in December 1971. The sale was blocked in the courts by environmental groups, mainly on technological grounds. This, I assume, would be considered a benefit to the people of Louisiana who would be offended by more offshore rigs, pipelines, and so on. But against this benefit was the price which had to be paid in the Midwest and Northeast by people who would not obtain Louisiana's offshore natural gas.

Santa Barbara, California, suggests a similar trade-off. Some of the benefit gained by Santa Barbarans, who would no longer have oil derricks off their majestic coastline or run the risk of additional oil spills, results in an additional cost to people hundreds of miles away where the oil and gasoline supplies may be running low.

Santa Barbara's environmental problem had another effect. In 1969, after the Santa Barbara blowout, the Department of the Interior revised and strengthened the standards for safety and pollution controls on the Outer Continental Shelf (OCS). As a result of the OCS operating standards, the increased inspection of drilling sites, and probably good luck, as well, there were no major oil spills last year, and minor spills were reduced by 45% from 1971.

## OFFSHORE OIL LEASES

The energy potential of the OCS is enormous. It is considered to be the best region around the Lower 48 in which to discover oil and gas. I think the United States has leased approximately 7 million acres offshore, which is about 2% to 3% of the whole OCS—and that is only to the 200-meter isobath. The offshore areas of the United States are believed to contain 186 billion barrels of crude oil and more than 844 trillion cubic feet of natural gas resources, all recoverable with existing technology. This represents about 40% of the nation's undiscovered oil and gas reserves.

Considering what I have just relayed to you, it may seem surprising that my original topic was to be the limits of our natural resources. I have to rely on what the U.S. Geological Survey tells me, and the geologists there insist that the OCS holds close to a fifty-year supply of oil and gas before the marginal reserves in very deep waters are explored and recovered by advanced, still unknown, methods.

The federal government has leased OCS areas since 1954. Some 16,000 wells have been drilled and only four major spills have posed any danger to the environment in all that time. My understanding is that none of these have caused any permanent damage to the environment. My computer tells me that OCS drilling carries a 99.99975% reliability against significant spills. That is still too much. We would like to get it down to zero—though the statistics show that the risks of blowouts, serious spills, or other mishaps from offshore drilling is negligible.

Coast Guard studies have shown that, of all the oil polluting the world's oceans, less than 2% comes from offshore drilling and production. Some 30%, by contrast, comes from tanker spills and tanker discharges. Just as the Coast Guard patrols the OCS for unusual events like these, the Geological Survey carries out inspections and surveillance of offshore drilling operations and producing platforms.

One alternative to drilling on the OCS is greater reliance on imports, particularly from the Middle East, which means more deliveries by tanker to the East and West Coasts, as well as to the Gulf Coast, and a greater strain on our balance of payments. Economists talk in terms of $20 billion and even $30 billion a year in adverse balances of trade. Energy experts predict an even greater shortage of natural gas than we now have, because, price aside, there is no way we can get anything like the needed amounts of gaseous fuels into the country short of domestic production.

## STRIP MINING AND LAND RECLAMATION

Another alternative is coal, our greatest hydrocarbon resource potential. Our discovered reserves that are readily available, not the total resource base, amount to about 390 trillion tons. We mine something like 600 million tons a year. At that rate we have literally hundreds of years of supply in proved reserves, and we could be entirely self-sufficient in energy through our coal resources alone. Approximately 40% of our coal reserves are on federal lands, especially west of the Mississippi. It is to a large extent high-sulfur coal. The record of the coal industry indicates that there is a great deal for which it can make amends, and it is doing so. Through 1972 about 4 million acres of land had been disturbed by surface mining, more than half of this unreclaimed and unrestored. In 1969 alone 73,000 acres of lands were disturbed and, of this amount, 86%, or about 63,000 acres, was reclaimed.

I think the critical factor here is that in 1972 surface mining provided more than one-half of all the coal that was used and about one-fourth of all the electrical power generated in the United States. A great deal of opposition persists in Washington and elsewhere to surface coal mining, and there are a few bills in Congress right now that would ban it altogether. The position of the administration and the Department of the Interior is that under proper safeguards strip-mining operations can extract coal in an environmentally acceptable manner, and that before mining begins a suitable reclamation plan should be presented and approved. Before strip mining gets any go-ahead, it must be demonstrated that the landscape can be properly reclaimed. Land can be surface mined and reclaimed with a greater usefulness than before it was mined—with certain exceptions, such as on very steep slopes or under very arid conditions. But we consider mining to be a legitimate claim on the use of public lands.

A ban on surface mining could well turn out the lights from Chicago to Harrisburg because there is no near-term alternative to coal for power generation. There is not enough oil available that can be readily used. We have already put the squeeze on No. 2 distillate fuel oils when power plants turned to low-sulfur oils.

The suggestion to go to deep mining as an alternative to surface mining doesn't take into account the five-year lead time that it takes to develop a deep coal mine, the number of miners to go down and do the deep mining, or the large amount of capital that would be needed in an industry that does not possess the best prospects for the future.

Another difficulty with coal, which has nothing to do with mining or with federal lands, concerns the environment. Under the 1970 Clean Air Act and its amendments, the states are required to meet primary and secondary air quality standards, which most of the nation's coal resources, being high in sulfur content, cannot approach. The upshot is that if all the state plans are implemented by 1975, as presently proposed, we may be eliminating between one-third and one-half of all the steam coal presently being mined in the United States.

## OIL SHALE DEPOSITS

Another area of consideration is oil shale, the most significant energy resource known to exist, with possibly as much as 2 trillion barrels of hydrocarbons in our own Rockies. The Green River shales rival those of the Middle East. As much hydrocarbon may exist there as has been found to date in the entire Persian Gulf area. An estimated 600 billion barrels of oil could be commercially produced from shale with present technology.

Of the 11 million acres of land bearing oil shale deposits of potentially commercial value, some 8.3 million acres, or about 72%, are owned by the federal government—primarily on public lands managed by the Department of the Interior. Someone once wrote *The Elusive Bonanza,* a book about the ultimate potential of oil shales, but we haven't had any production to date, at least not commercially.

Last Friday, I toured the oil shale country and saw a couple of the projects that are going on out there. The general method involves mining, retorting, and refining. The retort stage requires a huge plant. The enormity of the amount of rock that has to be mined, moved, and retorted is just overwhelming. One demonstration plant I saw was under consideration as a commercial venture. It was huge, and to scale that up to commercial size, they would have to go sixty-six times the size of the plant they presently have.

We went into a shale mine that was thirty feet high, about sixty feet wide, and approximately 1,000 feet long. I asked how much a mine of that size would yield on a commercial basis. I was told about two to three weeks' worth. So there are obvious problems—the environmental difficulty of disposing of the spent shale and the technical demands of moving that amount of rock around.

A good bit of these problems could be solved if we are able to develop *in situ* processes, on which several companies, along with the Bureau of Mines, are working. In this process the petroleum liquid could be recovered from the shale in place without hauling that volume of rock around.

The Department of the Interior proposes to lease six oil shale tracts—two in Colorado, two in Utah, and two in Wyoming. I think there are twenty-three companies interested in bidding on the leases, which is quite different from the department's prototype leasing program in 1968 when there were no bidders. Environmental impact statements will be filed with the Council on Environmental Quality in the not too distant future. The statement now runs to some 30,000 pages.

## GEOTHERMAL DEVELOPMENT

Another potential power source is geothermal energy, the natural steam heat in the earth. About 1.8 million acres of land—90% of it in the western states—have been identified by the Geological Survey as being within Known Geothermal Resources Areas (KGRAs). An additional 96 million acres are listed as having prospective value as geothermal sources. But estimates of how much geothermal energy is usable, and for how long, vary widely. The world's total installed geothermal electric capacity is now about one kilowatt, which equals a single large fossil fuel or nuclear power plant. About 40% of the geothermal power is harnessed in Italy, with the rest originating in New

Zealand, the Soviet Union, Iceland, and our own California. One geothermal source at the Geysers area presently supplies about one-third of the electricity needs of San Francisco, and plans are being developed for additional electricity-generating facilities. Just last week another geothermal source in northwestern New Mexico began generating electricity.

At a local level, geothermal energy could contribute significantly. But it offers no solution to our national energy problem. Located in the western states, the potential of geothermal energy is small — less than 0.1% of the nation's total energy needs may be available by the year 1985.

The Geothermal Steam Act in 1970 gives the Department of the Interior authority to lease public lands for geothermal resource development. The final environmental impact statement, which deems the environmental risks to be acceptable, will be ready soon. Environmental problems do exist, particularly in the wetter steam areas. Sometimes minerals appear in the water and their disposal can be a problem.

In conclusion I would say that the decisions to be made in all these areas, whether by the president in his energy message or the secretary of the interior, have got to reconcile economic interests, on both a national and an individual level, the environmental needs of the nation, and the national interest, which includes the national security.

# Discussion

Mr. Wakefield, the National Petroleum Council points out in its reports that federal lands hold 50% of the oil and gas, 40% of the coal, 80% of the uranium, and so forth. It asks the administration to open up this land and let the interests in. What is the likelihood of the federal government's opening public lands to the energy companies?

> *These lands will not be opened to the extent that we say, "Here it is, come and get it." They will be opened in a manner that is acceptable by environmental standards.*

You are saying this will be done?

> *Yes, we will move forward, but in a timely manner. Another consideration, of course, is the value of the land. This is a public resource and we are landlords for it, so we are not going to give it away, as I think was evidenced by the latest OCS sale, which brought $1.3 billion into the federal treasury.*

Is the government giving consideration to setting up a public corporation to exploit those resources?

> *There are certain people in Congress who have advanced the possibility of doing this. But it is not likely to occur in this administration. Personally, I am philosophically opposed to it.*
>
> *Consider TVA or any of a number of federal corporations— they were set up under circumstances where private industry either could not or would not do the job. That is not the situation here; it is quite the contrary. I think that private industry is willing and able to do the job, and that it will do the job when lands are made available to it and it is released from other restrictions. But I don't think this administration would consider a public development corporation.*

One of the problems is that private industry wouldn't develop resources offshore because it wouldn't make enough profit.

> *But private industry is doing it.*

It seems we are heading in the direction of coal to meet the nation's energy needs. Will we have to waive primary standards by 1975?

> *It is too early to say definitely yes or no. I don't think we are seeking a change in legislation or a waiver of the primary standards. We would like to try to meet the primary standards and work with some relaxation on the secondary standards.*

In your opening statement you mentioned one-third to one-half the coal being forced out of the market?

> *If all of the state plans are implemented by 1975, between 155 to 250 million tons of coal could be prohibited from use in the marketplace by 1975, and we have about 490 million tons being used as steam coal right now.*

Have the courts decided who can preempt those plans?

> *There is still an open legal question as to whether the EPA or the federal government can instruct the states to modify their implementation plans.*

Do you think we can get through the next fifteen years without a substantial increase in oil imports?

> *No, and I think that time is approaching faster than even the most pessimistic once thought.*

We have heard that there are committees involved in making energy policy. Do you think the energy committee or an energy czar is going to improve the situation?

> *I think the energy council that the President set up with Charles DiBona and his staff are to coordinate policy at the highest levels. Within the administration it is quite likely that there will be the proposed Department of Energy and Natural Resources, which would go far toward resolving conflicts between government agencies.*

# PART FOUR

# THE SURVIVAL STRATEGY

# The Authors

## Milton Shaw
*Is Atomic Power the Answer?*

Mr. Shaw was director of the AEC's Division of Reactor Development and Technology from 1964 to 1973. Prior to that, he was one of Vice Admiral Hyman Rickover's "whiz kids" in the Navy's nuclear submarine program. He has twice received the Navy's Distinguished Civilian Service Award and the AEC's Distinguished Service Award.

## Richard E. Balzhiser
*Fuels for the Future*

As assistant director in President Nixon's Office of Science and Technology, Mr. Balzhiser is responsible for energy, natural resources and environment. He is on leave to the OST from the University of Michigan where he was chairman of the Chemical Engineering Department. In 1967 he served as a White House Fellow at the Department of Defense, where he worked under Secretaries Robert McNamara and Clark Clifford.

## Stephen J. Gage
*Who Should Pay for Clean Energy Research?*

Mr. Gage is a member of the Federal Impact Evaluation Staff of the Council on Environmental Quality. As a White House Fellow in 1971, he was technical assistant to the director of the Office of Science and Technology for energy and environment. Mr. Gage taught nuclear engineering at the University of Texas from 1965 to 1969 before becoming director of the university's Nuclear Reactor Laboratory, the post he held until coming to Washington in 1971.

## Charles J. DiBona
*Reconciling Our Energy and Environmental Demands*

In February 1973, Mr. DiBona was named special consultant to President Nixon for energy policy. When President Nixon appointed Colorado Governor John A. Love to head the new Energy Policy Office in June 1973, Mr. DiBona became Mr. Love's chief assistant. Mr. DiBona has been special assistant to the under secretary of the Navy and president of the Center for Naval Analyses at the University of Rochester.

## Henry M. Jackson
*Is a National Energy-Environment Policy Possible?*

Senator Jackson has represented his native state of Washington in Congress for six terms in the House of Representatives and four in the Senate where he is chairman of the Interior Committee. He is the author of many conservation bills and is currently directing a National Fuels and Energy Study ordered by the Ninety-second Congress.

# Chapter 13

Milton Shaw

# Is Atomic Power the Answer?

The beginning of the Atomic Age is dated officially as December 2, 1942, when the world's first nuclear chain reaction was produced under the west grandstand at the University of Chicago athletic field. That sustained reaction in the Chicago nuclear pile No. 1 (known among scientists as CP-1) did not create enough energy to light even a small electric lamp. The Atomic Energy Commission, organized in 1946 to develop and operate the nation's nuclear programs, set up several experimental reactors, and in 1951 a reactor at Arco, Idaho, generated enough electricity to keep a light bulb glowing. Two years later the AEC authorized the first commercial power reactors, and by 1957 at Shippingport, Pennsylvania, the Duquesne Light & Power Co., together with the AEC and Westinghouse, demonstrated that the atom could yield electricity in commercial quantities.

By the early 1960s the nuclear power industry was in its infancy. Today thirty-one nuclear power plants are "on line," sixty are in various stages of construction, and eighty are on order across the nation. Yet nuclear power is providing only 1% of the energy consumed in the United States. The current nuclear capacity of about 16.3 million kilowatts is expected to increase to 1.2 billion kilowatts by the year 2000.

## ONGOING RESEARCH

Since it is nearly twenty-two years since the first atomic electricity was produced at the Arco Test Station, we can rightly say that nuclear power has come of age. The nuclear pacemaker, a miniature power plant of a sort, has been implanted in a number of cardiac patients just this week.

But the promise of nuclear power remains unfulfilled. Back in the late 1940s, glowing predictions about the peaceful atom were commonplace.

Robert M. Hutchins, then chancellor of the University of Chicago, where so much wartime atomic research had centered, boasted of the benefits:

> Heat will be so plentiful that it will even be used to melt snow as it falls.... A very few individuals working a few hours a day at very easy tasks in the central atomic power plant will provide all the heat, light and power required by the community, and these utilities will be so cheap that their cost can hardly be reckoned.

As the technical problems have been overcome, paradoxically, an array of delays, restrictions, uncertainties and opposition has prevented the grand vision of the late 1940s from reaching reality.

At the AEC we continue to believe that nuclear power will become the most important source of energy for the United States, especially for electricity. So we continue to develop old and new reactor systems and to pursue safety and regulatory programs. Accordingly, the AEC is not in the business of developing light-water reactors any more, but we are still in the business of assuring adequate safety of those already-existing power plants. In the same way that we provided the research and development for light-water reactors, we are now providing the research and development for another generation of nuclear plants.

Though central to the AEC program, research and development is only one aspect. In the liquid-metal fast-breeder reactor (LMFBR) project, for example, there are three phases, and the project is incomplete until all three are tried, tested and declared a triumph. (See Figure 19.)

It's comforting to work in materials technology, to develop fuels, or to provide the physics and engineering of a plant, without worrying about the problems from the abuse, misuse, or faulty application of the achievements of phase one. The real, exciting, and agonizing problems are in phases two and three, where the men are separated from the boys. Even when there is an overabundance of magnificent ideas in phase one, it is in phase two, where the hardware is constructed and the reactor is operated in a rather hostile environment, that difficulties often develop and components not built according to the rigorous specifications must be withdrawn from one contractor and given to another contractor. In phase three, the reactor finally enters the marketplace where it must achieve its ultimate success. It is not enough that an idea is good, a design perfectible, and a concept safe; the entire system, the whole reactor, must be assembled and operated efficiently, safely, and profitably.

Also of essential importance is the fuel cycle. Despite all the horror stories to the contrary, the AEC is profoundly concerned with the entire fuel

**Figure 19.**
**Phases in Achieving LMFBR Program Objectives**

*Overall Objective of LMFBR Program: Achieve early establishment of self-sustaining, competitive LMFBR industrial economy. Achievement of objective requires successful accomplishment of 3 phases.*

1. *R&D Phase—To Confirm Technical Aspects of Concept*
   *Develop fuels and materials technology*
   *Design control instrumentation*
   *Determine physics and heat transfer data*
   *Provide basic engineering data for component design*
   *Construct and operate facilities to provide design information*

2. *Engineering and Manufacturing Phase—To Provide Broad Industrial Base*
   *Manufacture and test fuel, clad, core hardware*
   *Design, build, and test components and systems*
   *Build and test reliable instrumentation*
   *Conduct overall prooftesting and quality assurance programs*
   *Develop and apply codes and standards*

3. *Utility Commitment Phase—To Purchase, Build and Operate Commercial LMFBR*
   *Take financial risks associated with demonstration plants and first-of-a-kind power plants*
      *uncertain costs*
      *uncertain schedules*
      *uncertain plant factors*
   *Purchase, manage construction, operation, and maintenance of commercial LMFBRs*

cycle, from mining to disposal. (See Figure 20.) There are risks and hazards in mining and handling the raw material (the Public Health Service recently published a report stating that 1 in 10 of the nation's 6,000 uranium miners will die prematurely of radiation exposure), as well as in its enrichment, fabrication, utilization, and disposal either as waste or by-products. The heart pacemaker that I mentioned before makes use of spent reactor fuel. By-products may be waste to some and beneficial to others. One by-product, cobalt, may be used as a source for radiography in applications such as cancer therapy.

**Figure 20.**
**Steps in the Supply of Atomic Fuel—Light Water Cycle**

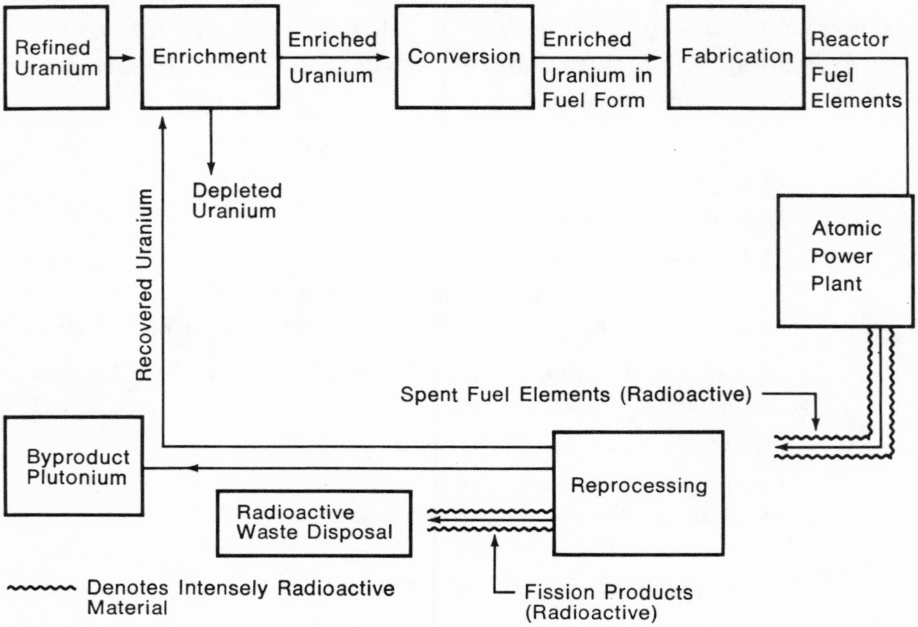

~~~~~ Denotes Intensely Radioactive
Material

## THE NUCLEAR ROLE

The urgent need for additional energy in the United States has clear implications for nuclear power. Back in 1962, in a report to President John F. Kennedy, the AEC "crudely estimated" that by the end of the twentieth century, nuclear installations would be generating 50% of the nation's total electric power. That same report, which, in the words of Chairman Glenn T. Seaborg, represented a "new and hard look at the role of nuclear power in our economy," urged the development of the LMFBR to exploit "the vast energy resources latent" in uranium 238 and thorium, the two most abundant atomic minerals. The AEC position and the energy prediction have not changed with the years. (See Figure 21.)

Now nobody, I think, and certainly not I, would buy a breeder reactor or even a more conventional light-water nuclear plant if there were adequate supplies of natural gas or oil for the nation. Still, nuclear power has a significant role because of its enormous potential for clean and sure energy.

**Figure 21.**
**U. S. Total Energy Requirements**

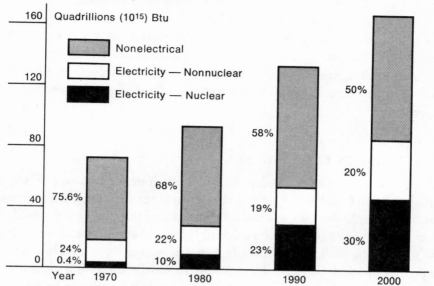

Sources: Bureau of Mines (through 1990); Atomic Energy Commission (for 2000).

Any nuclear reactor, whether it is the breeder or the propulsion systems for atomic submarines such as the Nautilus and the Seawolf, is a high-performance machine. It requires a degree of engineering competence and capability that exceeds all other energy systems.

I look at nuclear power in almost the same way that I view the supersonic passenger aircraft. There are pros and cons. If I could get from Washington to New York by train with greater speed, comfort and reliability than by plane, I would go by railroad every time. There would be no need to develop a big jet airplane. The safety of atomic units, which arouses so much controversy, must be discussed in a manner similar to the dangers of accidents with planes and trains.

Speaking as an engineer, I know that high-performance machines require high-performance workmen and operators. A nuclear power system, because of its complexities and workings, carries potential technical problems and economic risks. In the same way, an office on the fortieth floor always bears potentially unacceptable problems quite apart from safety. If the elevators or air conditioning go out, that lofty office takes on a different value. For a similar reason, I prefer trees around my home to provide shade and cool rather than an air-conditioning system inside. Of course, I would insulate my home with or without air conditioning, just as I would put brakes on an elevator whether it runs in a three-story or forty-story building.

A nuclear reactor is another kind of fire—a source of heat—attached to a generator. Instead of coal, oil, or gas, the reactor "burns" fuel, which, in the case of a light-water system, produces steam to run a turbine generator. There is nothing unique about nuclear power that enables it to make electricity without adverse environmental effects in any way different from coal, oil, or gas.

## SAFETY CONCERNS

One nuclear fuel element—three feet long, one-quarter of an inch in diameter, and clad in a steel sheath—is capable of equaling eighty tons of coal, for example. As long as the fuel element and the cladding material stay intact, there cannot be a safety problem. If these materials break or melt for any reason, the radioactivity would have to escape from the reactor core through additional barriers of containment. Furthermore, the radioactivity would need some force to free it outside the reactor. It will not be liberated, so to speak, without a positive pressure.

This is the philosophy of nuclear plant design. The cost of containment in one nuclear power plant runs to $25 million. In Britain and the Soviet Union, however, the public and the government have accepted nuclear power plants without the amount of containment that similar reactors are required to have in the United States—of course, the general public in these nations knows nothing about such details. Those who are wary of nuclear plants argue that the public demands containment, and we must assure their safety. But what is safe? Do 55,000 deaths each year make the automobile acceptable? Is zero adequate? In the sixteen years since the Shippingport plant went "on line," the record is zero deaths. Is it possible to continue that record in the future?

One safety issue which greatly concerns the public is the effect of low-level radiation on people living near a reactor. Biologists and other scientists who have studied low-level radiation have fairly well concluded, I think, that the amount of radiation people have been exposed to from nuclear reactors has been insignificant in comparison to their exposure in everyday life.

I live closely with nuclear power. I rode the first nuclear submarine to be sure that nobody would be exposed to any more risk than I would get myself. I have known many sailors who have been nuclear voyagers for years. Workers in nuclear power plants get no more radiation—in fact, less radiation—during their whole career on the job than pilots, stewardesses, and passengers receive flying between New York and Los Angeles in a high-altitude aircraft.

Now, I don't know if the effect will be significant. It may well be. All I can say is that the scientific talent working in this region to date has been unable to develop any information that substantiates the proposition that low-level radiation has had a significant effect on our well-being.

The AEC lowered its limits by 100 to do as much as it could to assure minimum radiation and to respond to the expressions of public concern. It is significant that the nuclear power reactor is an engineering machine that can accommodate the public. Before the new regulation was announced, by the way, we had already decided that we were not going to come even close to this radiation level on the breeder. What I am suggesting is that those of us concerned with reactor development are going to proceed as cautiously as possible because of the hostile environment.

The attitude of the workers and the public will change over a period of time. We know that the operation will become loose, and they will eventually accept casualties in reactor operation just as they accept the grim toll of automobile deaths. We don't want to end up with that number— and we won't, I assure you.

## DEVELOPMENT AND PRODUCTION

The first 1,000-Mw steam generating electricity plant didn't operate until 1965. The first 1,000-Mw nuclear plant is yet to operate. What happened is that people started worrying about the rising demand for electricity in the 1950s, and the industry began building larger and larger power plants. (See Figure 22.) As the size escalated, the engineering problems increased.

In contrast to the fossil fuel plants, the nuclear power plants had an enviable record in the 1950s. All those nuclear-powered submarines were operating beautifully. The name of the game was quality, reliability, and unlimited sources of power. The marketplace dictated large extrapolations in size, and there was no reason that they couldn't work. So, in the 1960s, a large number of sales occurred in the nuclear power business.

Large increases in the size of nuclear plants place large demands on engineering and technology. The engineering profession isn't that good. Just because I built a successful small pump does not mean I can build larger

184

**Figure 22.**
**Size Trend of U. S. Steam Electric Power Units**

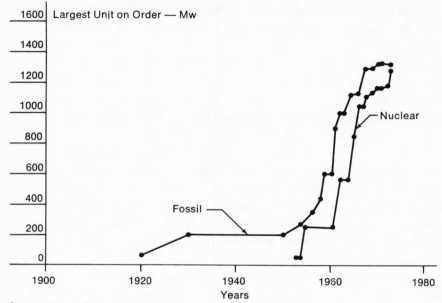

Source: Atomic Energy Commission.

ones and sell them like hotcakes. The important thing is that the nuclear plants were designed to compete with fossil fuel plants. The size of the plants was an economic trade-off. You can buy a 1,000-Mw plant more cheaply than you can buy two 500-Mw plants. In the same sense, it is cheaper to operate one large car than two small cars. It sounds good, but then you start figuring that you and your family want to go different places, and it doesn't work.

Now, the power plant itself, whether nuclear, oil or gas, does not insure the reliability of the whole system. Nevertheless, there was common consent among electric utilities in the 1960s that nuclear power provided inherent reliability. That idea has been dispelled these days. There is nothing in a nuclear plant that gives inherent reliability because it is an engineering machine that depends on many, many things working very well, none of which have anything to do with safety.

So when one considers the major causes of the energy crisis there are two aspects to be addressed—engineering and policy. In the first, we have to upgrade the engineering, quality, operability, and reliability of these plants. Until we do this, we are going to have an internal energy problem that is not going to be as fascinating and complicated to talk about as the "energy crisis." There has to be a capability to put these machines on the line in a reliable and predictable manner or we will not have the energy economy that we are counting on. This is important.

What I am pointing out is that our excellent record with the light-water nuclear reactor does not mean we will enjoy a similar success with the liquid-metal fast-breeder program. That is why we talk about a $2 billion to $3 billion program. That is why we talk about our concerns in developing pumps, valves, and heat exchangers. We are talking about a whole new research and development program.

I want to make clear that the AEC does not think nuclear power will solve all the nation's energy problems; nor do we think nuclear power should be used uniquely wherever we use energy. We believe the nation requires a mixture of various energy sources. We believe that there is a place for coal, oil, gas, nuclear and other sources of energy, depending on the use, availability, and projected need. We believe there will have to be trade-offs, with procedural determinations made on a case-by-case basis.

**Figure 23.**
**U. S. Central Station Nuclear Power Plants (orders by year)**

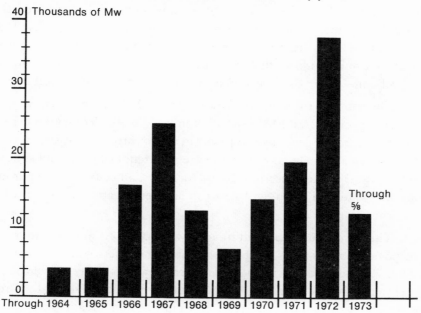

Source: Atomic Energy Commission.

We know that enough ideas now exist to convert coal to gas. Where one can transmit this synthetic gas, it would be wise to encourage that type of development to the same degree that we think we have encouraged nuclear power.

Sometimes I think the utilities have decided to go to nuclear power throughout the country at any cost. They are even putting reactors in Texas these days, right over the gas fields, because of the concern they have for the future. What's more, the orders are increasing rather rapidly. (See Figure 23.) In fact, the rate of sales raises serious doubts regarding our capabilities to produce these plants on a timely basis.

We had hoped, and I think this is borne out by our statements at congressional hearings, that the size of nuclear plants would have settled out at about the 10,000-Mw level in the period from 1969 to 1971, because there was a tremendously large backlog of plants already committed but not being brought in on time. It would be a great thing to have the industry get these plants under its belt.

However, the numbers of plants started increasing from 1970 to 1972. This came about, we believe, because of public concern for air quality and because of the increasing price and decreasing availability of fossil fuel. It seems that the utilities, looking at the various options, had decided that nuclear power plants, despite the problems they presented, were probably the best bet, and the sales record demonstrates this. Unfortunately, the delivery record doesn't quite endorse this approach, and that is a part of our present energy problem—a gap developed between commitment and capability.

The nation is running on a base of 300,000 Mw of installed capacity. Our nuclear capacity is 10,000 Mw, which is only 3% of the electricity generated today. But the percentage of nuclear plants in the country is increasing rapidly, and the chances are fairly good that the present trends of fossil fuel supplies and costs, as well as the concern of states, localities, and citizen action groups with air and water pollution, will result in an even greater swing to nuclear power in the future.

There's the rub. The lead time between purchase and operation of a nuclear power plant is from eight to ten years. Since the record of delivery is unimpressive so far, the effectiveness of nuclear power as a way of overcoming the energy crisis is long-term. In 1971 the nuclear industry claimed that from fifteen to eighteen atomic power reactors would be "on stream" in 1972. In reality, only eight were brought into operation. The fact remains clear: In terms of units and power capacity, nuclear plants are still far less productive than the hydropower and fossil fuel additions to the electric industry.

Nuclear technology is not at fault. The problem lies in engineering, quality assurance, workmanship, and licensing and regulatory delays. Our immediate nuclear future does not indicate a change of pace. In 1973 we will probably see ten more nuclear plants going into commercial operation, which means that they have been satisfactorily tested and found faultless. But it will be difficult to put more than ten into operation each year for the next few years, just as it was impossible to introduce two a year during the 1960s.

So, no matter what we do, it appears that electricity will be in short supply in the United States for a number of years. We are going to have to learn to turn out our lights, reduce our air-conditioning loads and that sort of thing. The handwriting is on the wall. It is easy to read that the nation is running short of reserve electrical capacity, and we will have to live by that message.

Part of the problem, as I have already observed, is engineering. The big utilities are confronted with the same problems that the public encounters in trying to get cars repaired and maintained properly or in obtaining adequate servicing for television sets and dishwashers. At my home, my services as an engineer-cum-handyman are what makes my wife keep me around.

# Discussion

Will there have to be some restrictions on industrial expansion because of the electricity shortage? *Newsweek* reported recently that Ford Motor Company has already found it could not immediately expand its plants because the utilities could not guarantee electricity. Is this going to become more widespread?

> *Yes. Just talk to some of the builders out in California constructing high-rise apartments entirely committed to electric power. The electricity shortage is bound to hit in the gut, so to speak; it is bound to.*

Is it going to restrict the growth of the economy and affect the employment rate?

> *I think it best to point to what happened in Britain when it was short of energy. It doesn't require much imagination to foresee the implications. Our way of life is dependent on electric growth.*
>
> *I described it once at a congressional hearing when I said it was like having a pet elephant die in your living room. I was trying to explain that owning a 1,000-Mw machine is fine as long as it is running, but when it craps out on you—well, what do you do with a dead elephant?*
>
> *So long as we are able to punch buttons and get things done, electricity is a great, lovable pet. But when we punch those buttons and nothing happens, then the unthinkable becomes thinkable. The dark reality hit us on November 9, 1965, when a "disturbance," as the power engineers call it, interrupted the operation of a backup relay at the Ontario hydroelectric facility, which is named for an obscure notable, Sir Adam Beck. This little disturbance caused an unexpected surge and shudder to flow through lines to the United States blacking out some 80,000 square miles and leaving 30 million people without electricity. The power failure had a sobering effect. The reliability of the utilities was in question.*
>
> *Reliability is essential. The industry needs reliable turbines, exchangers, switches, valves, pumps. The heat source can be coal, oil, gas, or uranium, but the rest of the system is the same for each. That's where reliability comes in.*

Whatever power source we happen to choose, whether it be coal or coal gas or oil or breeder reactors, some two kilowatts are wasted for every kilowatt produced. We might not need to invest millions of dollars in a breeder program if our fossil fuel plants were, say, 60% to 70% efficient.

*We have been looking for ways to achieve greater power plant efficiency for decades. Where can we get the 60% efficiency you are referring to? Not even fuel cells can reach that efficiency, and we have been working on fuel cells since 1888 or thereabouts. The higher efficiency of fuel cells depends on very clean fuel with no particulate matter—a virtually perfect fuel.*

*We have no other capability for large-scale production of power other than steam turbines. We can push up into the 40% range, which we do in modern fossil fuel plants with high-temperature machines. But we can't climb above 42% to 45%. We don't know how as long as we are dependent on steam.*

*Both the breeder and fusion reactors will still have the limitations associated with steam turbine generation, essentially throwing away 60%. In other words, we are replacing the heat source, that is all; cycle efficiency is still dictated by the steam turbine complex. (See Figure 24.)*

You don't see any technology coming in the next generation, or even next two generations, that gets around the steam turbine limitation?

*No, sir, not at all. Let me get even more specific. You hear all the talk about direct conversion—take the heat, run it into the wires, and generate electricity. That is the principle of the heart pacemaker that we have developed. But they never tell you about the cooling device that has to take away the other 80% or 90% of the heat that is thermionic and thermoelectric. This also happens in the fusion business. The heat source generates steam. What about that waste steam? Then there is solar energy. Solar energy will heat liquid metal, transfer it, store it in holders, store it in electric devices. It's great, practical, reliable—except for one major detail: It, too, uses steam for conversion, from 45% to 50%.*

*So you have to deal with the whole process, and that means engineering the whole process.*

**Figure 24.**
**Four Major Types of Reactors in U. S.**

Nuclear steam-supply components in a boiling-water reactor.

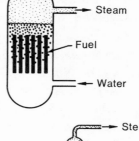

Nuclear steam-supply components in a pressurized-water reactor.

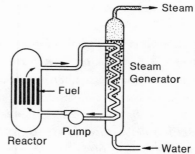

Nuclear steam-supply components in a gas-cooled reactor.

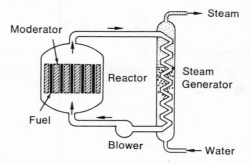

Nuclear steam-supply components in a liquid-metal fast-breeder reactor.

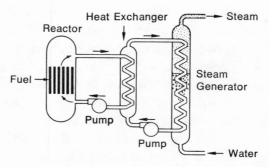

*Schematic drawings show the four major types of reactors in use or under development in the United States.*

*The power-generating portion of a nuclear power plant (below) is the same for each concept. Only in the boiling-water type (top left) does the steam pass directly from the reactor to the turbine. In a pressurized water reactor, the reactor-heated water is cycled through a steam generator to create the turbine-driving steam; the gas-cooled system is the same, except that helium instead of water passes through the reactor to be heated. In the liquid-metal fast-breeder concept, the molten sodium passes through the reactor and into an intermediate heat exchanger where, in turn, liquid sodium is heated and then cycled through the steam generator.*

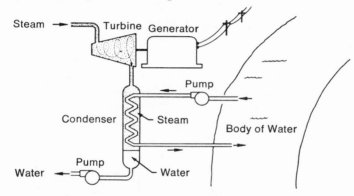

The power-generating portion of a nuclear power plant.

*Condenser cooling water does not touch the reactor in a nuclear power plant. The drawing illustrates that there is no physical contact between the coolant water and the steam generated by the heat of the reactor. The steam, having turned the electricity-producing turbine, condenses back into water as it passes around the coolant-water coils.*

Source: U. S. Atomic Energy Commission

**If the money going into the breeder power plant in the next twenty years would be used for fossil fuels or to develop fusion reactions, would we still need a breeder?**

*Personally, I think the answer is yes. Now, in addition to that, I must note that electricity isn't generated by money. It is generated by engineers and machines. We have worked on the breeder in this country for twenty years, and we have spent $800 million. Yet we didn't do very well by it. We have got to raise the capability of those* *working on it. When people offered more money for the breeder, I said, "Forget it!" I couldn't spend the money anyway, because we didn't have the capability.*

**What about the charges that you and your associates at the AEC are suppressing information warning that the various safety systems are not, in fact, as safe as you say they are?**

*Well, since Shippingport in 1957, we have accumulated 150 reactor years of operation without a death or an injury due to any nuclear cause. Besides this, there are more than 1,000 years of operation of Navy reactors; some 120 of those are now running with similarly good safety records.*

*The AEC's budget for fiscal 1974 calls for $66 million for research and development of nuclear safety. This is a $13 million increase over what we are spending in 1973. This project will analyze what happens if anything goes wrong in a reactor. We look at fuel failures, at cooling system failures; we rupture the blazes out of equipment that should never, never fail. (See Figure 25.) There is a*

**Figure 25.**
**Constituents of Nuclear Facility Safety, Economics, and Reliability**

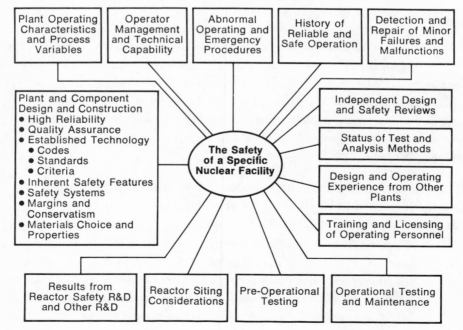

*test program at Oak Ridge, Tennessee, where we are breaking apart six-inch thick reactor grade materials that have been welded to the standards used in the industry. We are trying to find out what kinds of flaws could occur and how quickly they could fail.*

*We deliberately put reactor parts under stresses and strains, pressures and temperatures, and then analyzed the effects. We managed to get one vessel to fail at three times the maximum operating pressure. (See photo below.) We had to cut halfway into the vessel with a saw before we could get it to fail, even under these extreme conditions. The saw cut is clearly visible.*

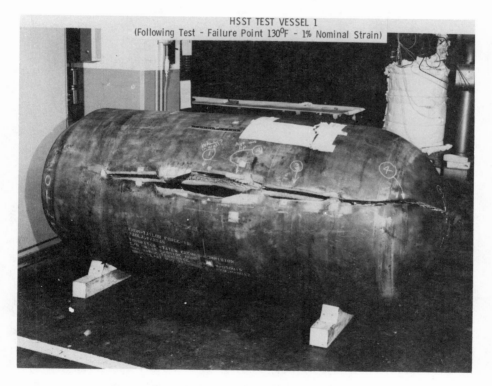

HSST TEST VESSEL 1
(Following Test - Failure Point 130°F - 1% Nominal Strain)

Could you address yourself to the meltdown of highly radioactive reactor cores and their cooling systems, the projects going on at the National Reactor Testing Station in Idaho.

*We run many simulation tests in this area. Through the testing program at Idaho on emergency core cooling, we can learn the slow-down characteristics in a reactor system. When a system operating at high pressure develops a leak, it will deflate in pressure very quickly, depending on the location of the leak. The fellows at NRTS decided to inject some water in one facility to try to understand what would happen, to discover if the water would cover the core and prevent a meltdown.*

*The main reason for running the test was to be able to start correlating some of these potential problems. (Don't forget, we supported this research in the first place, and we are continuing to support it.) I am concerned about the adequacy of emergency core cooling. Ruptures like this can occur. But discovering what you must do in a plant to prevent ruptures and to make sure that they don't occur is the first order of safety in this business as far as I am concerned.*

**I was worried about safety before your presentation, and now I am even more worried because your whole aim has been to emphasize the dangers of engineering complexities, incompetencies, and capabilities.**

*That is the gut issue right now. Let me not kid you. We must make sure that the engineering, construction, and maintenance of nuclear reactors are adequate to prevent accidents from occurring.*

*Of course, accidents are sometimes unpreventable. Now, as I observed at the outset, the Atomic Age began with the singular goal of building bombs, and, understandably, there remains a residual fear of the atom, even in peaceful uses like power reactors. Nuclear plants cannot explode like an atomic bomb. I have not met a single expert who entertains such a notion. A bomb requires a "critical mass" of weapon-grade fuel (nearly pure U-235) slammed together in a precise way that is just not possible in power plants where the chain reaction is carefully controlled and monitored by both men and computers, where comparatively low-grade fuel (only 3% U-235) is used, and where water or some other liquid circulates around the fuel core preventing the fuel elements from melting and moderating or slowing down the reaction.*

*There can be a "nuclear excursion," which is polite nuclearese for a runaway reaction. At NRTS we have deliberately simulated such accidents. In most, a cooling system failure results in a meltdown in the nuclear core, a rupture of the containment vessel, and the release of radioactive material into the atmosphere. This type of accident, unlikely though it is, sends shivers through many people and makes opponents more stubborn.*

*A meltdown of this type took place in 1966 in a nuclear plant at Lagoona Beach, Michigan, not far from Detroit. It was the Enrico Fermi plant, the world's first breeder reactor which was intended as a monument to the Italian Nobel Prize winner who had led the team at the University of Chicago in 1942. An accidental obstruction of the plumbing prevented the liquid sodium from cooling down the half ton of U-235 in the core. As the fuel elements heated up, parts of the core buckled and melted; the alarms sounded and the machine was shut down; but no radioactivity was released from the plant.*

*Since that agonizing fiasco, the experimental breeder reactors at NRTS near Idaho Falls have proved enormously successful.*

*But anxieties persist. It is appropriate, perhaps, to underline such anxieties with a statement by a leading and respected nuclear scientist, Alvin M. Weinberg, director of the Oak Ridge National Laboratory and winner of the Atoms for Peace Award in 1960. He has said:*

> There is the spectre of catastrophic failure of a large power reactor, of its engineered safeguard systems and of its containment vessel. If such ever happened, it would be a catastrophe indeed. Surely the chance that such an event will happen is very small. Yet one cannot prove negative propositions of this sort.... The best prospect of this never happening is the stake the whole nuclear community has in avoiding it.

*The point Mr. Weinberg is making in his remark is that the AEC and its scientists, reactor manufacturers, public utilities, and the government all realize, as he puts it, "that their futures, their aspirations—in a sense their whole lives—depend on avoiding such an incident. This is the best practical reason I can offer for believing that such a catastrophe is unlikely." Our research backs up this reasoning. (See Figure 26.)*

*Nevertheless, your question about our work on safeguards is valid. Let me relate it to a more familiar problem of automobile safety. If you have got poor tires on your car, is it safe? The answer is that it all depends—it depends on whether you are going to change those tires before setting out on a trip, on whether the car will be run no faster than 20 mph or, if the research shows it can be done, at 30 mph.*

---

**Figure 26.**
**Safety—Order of Approach**

*First Level—Accidents Can Be Prevented*

Design for maximum safety in normal operation and large tolerance for errors, defects, and system malfunctions

Employ design features inherently favorable to safe operation; emphasize quality, redundancy, testability, and inspectability

Assure continuing conformance to design objectives through rigorous programs of inspection and testing throughout plant life

*Second Level—Protective Systems Will Be Provided*

Assume incidents will occur—in spite of care taken in design, construction, and operation to prevent them

Provide reliable protection systems to assure such incidents are prevented, arrested, or safely accommodated

Design, test, and monitor these systems so that there is full assurance that they will operate when needed

*Third Level—Public Health and Safety Will Be Protected*

Test design against severe hypothetical accidents by assuming certain protective systems fail simultaneously with accident they are intended to control

Use analyses to indicate areas where improvements can be made

Carry out extensive testing and analytical programs to assure with confidence that adequate safety margins are provided

Provide an effective independent barrier for protection of the public

---

**Does your example of auto tires help to explain why nuclear reactors are being derated?**

*Yes, because there are questions asked by the community. But in my own mind I am more concerned about the integrity of the system than I am about its power level. In other words, I would get more comfort from being convinced of the reactor's structural soundness than in reducing the pressure. Now reducing the pressure may result in derating, but, if there is an area of concern, I want to know what it is from an engineering or technical standpoint.*

*I would not want to put out a press release saying nuclear power is OK. If we are worried about the whole operation, then it would be best to stop. If we are worried about the primary cooling system, it would be best to fix it. That is why I am saying that these are engineers' machines whose safety depends on more than just testing at Idaho. The real problem may depend on the choice of the material or the way the plant is operated or something like that. That is the issue that should be before the public.*

**The sum total of these issues seems to indicate that something is wrong. Therefore, don't build any more?**

*No, that is wrong. The point is, in fact, that you may want to build reactors more carefully and you may not mind holding them up to do this.*

**Are you opposed to the slowdown that the community, consumer groups, and environmental societies are forcing on you and the industry?**

*I, myself, have stopped more reactors than they will ever stop in the next five years. The way a plant is put together, the characteristics of that plant, may have absolutely nothing to do with testing in Idaho. One can be conservative in his engineering. One can design without knowledge just as well as one can design with knowledge.*

*You ride in cars and aircraft. How can you do that without knowing what research and development was done on those vehicles? The answer is relatively simple: The statistics and the information that is available to you relating to the safety of those vehicles have been developed in a manner to give you reasonable assurance that it is safe to ride in such vehicles.*

**Then why do you have an emergency core cooling system?**

*Because these plants, no matter how well we put them together today and no matter how well trained the people operating them are, have been designed for thirty years of life. Over this period there will be bum maintenance, there will be accidents occurring to them. I believe that our safety concerns are so great that we can well afford an emergency core cooling system on these machines—even though many people do disagree. Many other countries do not provide emergency core cooling systems for the same reason they do not provide containment.*

*Backup safety systems can, and should, be there even though they may never ever be used or may be used remotely for occurrences that they were designed to handle only in an extreme situation over the life of the system. The use of backup safety systems is prudent, and I would build plants with them.*

### Can you tell us, Mr. Shaw, about radioactive waste?

*At one time I had responsibility for the waste program. Then I ran into a Kansas Governor named Robert Docking on the controversial AEC decision to bury radioactive wastes, the so-called Project Salt Vault, in a deep salt mine at the city of Lyons (1971 population: 12,244). There is no question that the waste problem is one of the most difficult and intractable we must face. There is also no question that this is really reducible to the degree of assurance and how much one wants to pay for this degree of assurance.*

*I am willing, as an engineer, to take these fuel elements out of a reactor and store them in big concrete vaults that are encapsulated in domes similar to what we have in reactors, if people want that assurance regarding their safety. There is nothing wrong in doing that. It is a bit expensive. It ties up a lot of valuable material, and I don't think it is going to give an additional degree of safety that cannot be obtained by doing it other ways.*

### Shooting it to the sun, for instance?

*That is insane and unbelievable. Why mess up the sun?*

*There are a number of ways of handling these wastes. I would want to put them in a form that reduces their mobility. If you put waste in a can under pressure in a fluid or a gas and the container ruptures, the radioactive material escapes. The waste should be in such a form so that, if the can ruptures, the waste will not burst out. So the first criteria that we developed was to put the waste in a solid form with low stored energy. This criteria has been promulgated, and I think this is a tremendous gain because, until this policy was issued, wastes were stored in liquid form. There are wastes still stored in liquid form, under previous procedures.*

*The second step in storing solidified nuclear waste is to can the material, then recan it every fifty years so that radioactive material does not escape when the can deteriorates. This method costs money, though, and requires the handling of wastes, something that can cause accidents more frequently than leaving the material at a more permanent location.*

*Salt mines happen to be a pretty good location for storage and my personal feeling is that, over a period of time, we will be overjoyed to put the wastes in deep underground salt mines, which are the most stable of all geologic forms. I think there is ample capability, opportunity, and justification to put waste in salt mines.*

To avoid the greater risks that go with a large reactor, perhaps smaller ones with smaller risks would be better. Why not have three plants of 350-Mw capacity rather than one of 1,000-Mw capacity?

*Size may be an advantage in terms of fabrication, inspectability, monitoring, things like that. Don't rule it out. These are engineering judgments. I think from a reliability standpoint, the things that are going wrong in the big machines are amenable to correction. That is, we are having trouble because we are building them before we are designing them. This is not good, whether there are two 500-Mw machines or one 1,000-Mw machine.*

*So where we are short on resources, having two 500-Mw machines instead of one large one may leave you shorter yet in an area of bigger concern and may create even more problems of other types. We must demonstrate that we have a capability around the whole circuit to assure safety. Then we have got to look at what happens if any one of these goes wrong. We have got to provide for containment, for inspectability, for monitoring, and for what I refer to as hard-nosed surveillance that demands plants be shut down if there is even a doubt or a question.*

*Operate the plants in such a way that you can make sure they can be shut down. Take advantage of the fact that they are spread in single units throughout the country, so if incidents start occurring on one, similar models can be cleared, as in the aircraft business. If this requires shutting down ten plants, then you shut them down until you've solved the problem, rather than assume that they will all go at once like big bombs—which they will not.*

# Chapter 14

Richard Balzhiser

# Fuels for the Future

The federal energy strategy, as laid out in President Nixon's first energy message to Congress on June 4, 1971, called for both technological and nontechnological measures. Among the nontechnological ones was the accelerated leasing of offshore oil and gas tracts and of geothermal regions. On the technological side, the message identified the liquid-metal fast-breeder reactor, gasification of coal, and stack gas cleaning as high priority efforts.

This program has gone forward. But as the energy problems confronting the country continued to mount, President Nixon sent two more messages to Congress. (See Appendixes, pages 247–272.) The first message proposed gas-price deregulation to spur domestic exploration and eased oil import quotas to allow an adequate flow of foreign oil into the country. The second suggested ways the public and government could reduce energy consumption, called for a $10 billion research and development program for energy over the next five years, and proposed major changes in federal energy agencies.

The technical strategy, however, remains unchanged. In the short range there will be emphasis on coal and uranium; in the middle range (1980 to 2000), on breeder reactors; in the long range (after 2000), on fusion, solar, and geothermal sources of power.

Knowing the agenda for this symposium, I am sure that George Hill and Milton Shaw have dealt in depth with the revival of coal and the expansion of nuclear power. I will discuss here the fuels for the future.

The breeder program, as you well know, has had its share of problems, but we think it is now on the track. Certainly if one measures it in terms of the dollars committed to it, it ought to be on the track. The funding in the breeder is up to $323 million in the 1974 budget. With that kind of funding, money should not be a limitation to its progress.

Much of my research at the University of Michigan was in the area of liquid-metal technology, so I have some feel for the problems that have been solved and those that still remain unsolved. It is my own feeling that, while the liquid-metal breeder is certainly deserving of the priority treatment it is receiving, there are still potential difficulties in the peripheral parts of the system, such as heat exchangers and pumps. Instead of dealing with water, a fluid we can handle reasonably well, we are dealing with sodium, a far more aggressive fluid. If you follow the problems of the utility industries today, you know that they have their share of worries with the reliable performance of heat exchangers, among other things, on, among other things, many of their large nuclear plants. If you put in sodium, it is not going to be an easier problem to solve.

In addition to the liquid-metal breeder program, we should be carrying along some backup options in our research and development program. We are not advocating that these options receive the same emphasis as the liquid-metal breeder, but we think—at least for the next several years or until the Soviets, British, or French prove their systems to be technically and economically feasible—that we ought to keep alive programs like the gas-cooled breeder reactor, which builds on high temperature gas reactor technology. The gas breeder also builds on the liquid-metal breeder fuel technology. In that sense, if the liquid-metal breeder ran into trouble because of fuel, the gas breeder could very well fall victim to the same problem. But it provides a desirable backup. It is funded now at about $1 million dollars and is supported mainly by Gulf Atomic, the principal advocate of the system, and by some utilities.

The molten-salt breeder, which is zero in the 1974 budget, has been developed at the Oak Ridge National Laboratory. It is a radically different system and could, indeed, get around problems that might tie up both the liquid-metal breeder and gas-breeder reactors. However, the molten-salt breeder has serious problems of its own. If those problems are to be resolved, it is going to take a fair amount of funding.

If breeding is successful, we must recognize that we have energy resources that would be adequate for many, many, many years—though not without some concern. There are people who worry about plutonium handling—its safety aspects, transportation, hijacking, all of these things. I think some of those are red herrings.

Now let's go beyond the breeder and consider the other "limitless" sources of energy, fusion being the one that usually tops the list.

## FUSION RESEARCH

The fusion program is still at the stage in which we are trying to show its scientific feasibility. The problem of taming the reaction that makes possible hydrogen bombs—and putting it to work for peaceful purposes—has turned into one of the most difficult tasks of modern science. When this research was declassified in the mid-1950s, it seemed that it would soon be possible to tap a virtually inexhaustible source of power by achieving controlled fusion of heavy hydrogen. The difficulties arise because scientists are working with a relatively unexplored state of matter which must be heated to a temperature of between 50 and 100 million degrees Centigrade and maintained at this super-superheated level for about one second before the fusion or thermonuclear reaction takes place to release energy. The material itself is known as plasma—in this case, heavy hydrogen atoms that have dissociated into their constituents, charged negative electrons and positive nuclei. Vast amounts of energy will be released if and when these hydrogen particles can be fused to form heavier particles, which is just what happens inside the sun and other stars and in a hydrogen bomb.

Almost two and a half decades have been spent on this research, and the goal has eluded scientists with a nightmarish perversity. In that same period, man has broken the bonds of gravity and explored the moon. In those same years, man has made incredible strides toward understanding the mechanism of heredity. But the quest for controlling the fusion reaction goes on.

The AEC program to demonstrate that this technological peak will also be reached in the period between 1980 to 1982 is pretty much on schedule. The president's 1974 budget calls for a $46 million expenditure for the magnetic-confinement project, which is designed to hold the plasma steady so that it doesn't melt the container when superheated. The program has received substantial increases in funding in each of the last two years.

There is a second area of fusion research that I think is even more intriguing. This tantalizing area is laser fusion—a program that originated in weapons research. Much of the work is still classified, but it is being declassified at a faster rate these days.

Laser fusion holds out a promise of being a smaller and simpler system than the attempts to confine the plasma with strong magnetic fields. It requires a little pellet of hydrogen fuel dropped in a chamber, much as a quantity of gasoline is injected into an automobile engine. It is ignited with a high energy laser pulse that acts like a spark plug. The laser pulse hits the pellet and, if the theory is correct, creates enormous compressions and temperatures, both necessary conditions for starting the fusion reaction. The limiting factor in this particular technology appears to be the laser beam, just as confinement is the problem in the other approach.

Progress in both approaches has been very encouraging, but that doesn't mean that we can count on a commercial fusion power system before the year 2000. Clearly, we have a lot of problems in plasma physics and fusion technology that have to be resolved before that time.


## SOLAR POWER

Solar energy is exciting because it is unlimited as long as the sun continues to shine. It is also clean. But it has drawbacks as well, being diffuse and intermittent, which creates both technical and economic problems. The president's 1974 budget includes only $12 million for solar energy research. The National Science Foundation has been designated to allocate most of this for studies, and NASA undoubtedly will receive a small part. It is our feeling that the most immediate benefits of solar energy are for space conditioning and water heating, using something like rooftop photovoltaic cells having an efficiency of about 10%. More elaborate schemes for power stations seem further off.

One proposal by Aden and Marjorie Meinel of the University of Arizona would use the "greenhouse effect" by means of selective coatings on pipes carrying a molten mixture of sodium and potassium heated by solar radiation. By means of a heat exchanger, the heat is stored in an insulated chamber for at least one day and extracted from this chamber to run a conventional steam power plant at an efficiency of around 30%.

Another system, suggested by Alvin Hildebrandt and Gregory M. Haas of the University of Houston, requires reflecting the sun's rays accumulated from a square-mile area and focused into a solar furnace and boiler. Heat from the boiler at a temperature of 2,000 degrees Kelvin would be converted into electric power by a magnetohydrodynamic method at about 20% efficiency.

Solar energy seems to be marginally economic in some parts of the country. It has a high initial cost and is, therefore, something that people are reluctant to accept. In addition, it is laden with problems, not the least of which is the vast area needed to collect the sun's rays; M. King Hubbert, the expert geologist, has reckoned that an area about one-tenth the size of Arizona would be needed to yield the 350,000 Mw the United States consumed in

1970. Technology for solar power is now available, but the difficulties of putting it to use are great.

Still, the fuel is free, and we hope that the National Science Foundation will be able to enlist the support of various government departments and agencies to establish a market for solar energy—perhaps in defense facilities, in Washington buildings, on Navy surface ships. Acceptance in such places, we feel, would stimulate private companies, as well as the utilities, to look at the systems and perhaps improve them and reduce costs.

Some day we would expect to have solar-electrical panels that are part of a house or building roof. Space satellites are now powered by these panels of photovoltaic cells. But to make solar electricity both viable and economic for homes and power stations, the cost of these cells would have to be cut by several orders of magnitude and their durability would have to be clearly demonstrated. These are challenging tasks now being worked on by government and industry. When and if the needed breakthroughs will be achieved cannot be predicted. About all one can do is to make sure that investigation is not constrained by lack of funding.

## GEOTHERMAL ENERGY

Another futuristic possibility is geothermal power. Already available in California, with a capacity of 370 Mw, geothermal power is obtained by extracting heat stored in the earth by volcanoes and hot water in the sands of deep sedimentary basins. At the present time production is confined mainly to an area known as The Geysers in California, where geothermal power was developed in 1960. It is very attractive for electrical generating where it is available. As it turns out, a sort of 1970s gold rush fever is gripping the West, where the resource seems to be available. The federal government is considering the leasing of its land in areas where geothermal steam is believed to exist. As a supplemental power source, it would help California, but we don't see it as an important power source for most of the country.

There are other forms of geothermal energy. One that is beginning to look interesting is hot brines or hot water. These are available over a larger geographical region, presumably extending from the West Coast down through the Southwest and into the Gulf region. An important point to recognize here is that we are talking about hot water or brines that are only several hundred degrees. It is not much hotter than the energy we now throw away from our conventional generating plants. When dealing with energy sources at such low temperatures, there are some serious thermodynamic constraints in terms of how much of that energy can be converted to electrical energy. It means we have to develop a system to operate at those temperatures and operate efficiently enough so the power generated is competitive with what can be generated from conventional sources. What's more, once the heat has been recovered, a lot of dirty water or saline brines will have to be treated and then jettisoned.

The availability of water, I must emphasize, could well become an important constraint to the nation's energy supply. Until now we have been worried about the thermal effects associated with water used for cooling both conventional and nuclear power plants. In the future we will be using water to provide hydrogen for coal gasification and liquefaction as well as for treating oil shale and crude oil. Large quantities of water will also be required in the disposal of oil shale wastes and in the reclamation of strip-mined lands. When the water is needed in places like Colorado, Wyoming, and Utah, where it is already scarce, the political and economic problems are clear.

Even more widely available from a geographical point of view is the so-called hot-dry rock, which underlies most of the world at some depth. Here the problem is how to tap the energy. We are just beginning to look at the feasibility of drilling into these hot granite rocks, fracturing them in such a way that water could be pumped down, circulated through the fracture, and recovered through another well for use in much the same way as hot brines. This source of energy appears further off and more speculative, but it is certainly worthy of continued evaluation.

# Discussion

**Besides the work in solar research going on at the universities in Arizona and Houston, where else are studies being made?**

*There is one concept being investigated at the University of Delaware, another at the University of Minnesota in conjunction with Honeywell, and the government is supporting some small home solar units as demonstrations. It's technically possible, but economically unattractive so far.*

**To what extent is the government supporting the types of thermal power you described, Mr. Balzhiser?**

*I think it comes to $8 million or $9 million, with about $2.5 million going to the U. S. Geological Survey for resource assessment. About $3 million, I believe, will probably go into the hot rock fracturing experiments.*

**You have been quoted as saying that our weapons in the battle are something like "scientific roulette." The ideas are there, but nobody knows whether these ideas will work or, even if they do, whether they will prove adequate for our future needs needs and be economically possible. Is that your belief?**

*I think there is an element of truth in that — though I didn't know that "scientific roulette" was my phrase. I think you have to recognize that in research we are dealing with many unknowns, many imponderables, many frustrations. Some research ends in failure — though that, too, provides us with answers and insights. That's the nature of the scientific effort — experiment and trial, error and success.*

*The real uncertainty in much of energy research is one of economics. There are a lot of things that we can do technically today. We can generate electricity from the sun, from hot rock, from hot water. We can put a space station into stationary orbit and relay energy to the earth in the microwave form that Peter E. Glaser of Arthur D. Little, Inc. has proposed. The appealing thing about such schemes, far-fetched as they may seem today, is that they would add no heat load to the earth's biosphere.*

*The key question about all these possibilities, which in-
clude the breeder and fusion reactors, of course, is how reliably and
cheaply they are going to compete with the other energy options.
Much of our effort is directed at trying to refine the systems and
improve the technologies so that they will be useable.*

**But we don't know if it's economically feasible in the long run.**

*Take solar energy as an example. If the large collector arrays last
just two years or if the dirt and dust has to be swept off them after
every windstorm, they aren't going to be financially viable.*

**Do you feel any sense of urgency with regard to our present
energy resources and our needs for the near future, say, by 1985?
Are we running scared?**

*One could have predicted five years ago, by looking at demand and
supply, that the nation was going to have to do some things differently, that we had power problems on the horizon. The energy
crisis—if you want to call it that—has been precipitated by the
heightened environmental awareness and the social ethic that business as usual is no longer acceptable.*

*The delays in nuclear power, brought on in part by the
opposition of the environmentalists, made us more dependent on
oil, gas, and coal. But strip mining of coal is considered an ecological
obscenity; gas production is not keeping up with demand; oil which
meets the environmental standard of low sulfur content is coming
more and more from the Persian Gulf. What's more, the National
Environmental Policy Act of 1969, which requires impact statements,
has lengthened the decision-making process of the federal government; the Clean Air Act of 1970, affecting both power plants and
transportation vehicles, has perturbed the entire energy industry.*

*The United States doesn't really have a resource problem
since it possesses enough coal and uranium for centuries and probably
large amounts of still undiscovered oil and gas that, if developed,
could give us time to refine the coal and nuclear options to a point at
which they would be environmentally, economically, and ethically
acceptable for the future.*

*While it is inevitably going to cost consumers more as we
internalize the environmental costs, we are not talking about a
quantum jump in the price of energy. We will have to do things*

*differently, and we can't do it all overnight. This is the problem with installing stack gas cleaning, low emission engines, and many other pollution-reducing mechanisms. To expand on one of these, I think there is no way that we can meet the state implementation plans for clean air by 1975, not even by 1977; we are probably talking about 1980. If the states persist in moving quickly to secondary standards, it must result in a confrontation with industries because it is beyond their capabilities. Unless large amounts of low-sulfur oil are readily available on the world market, which seems unlikely, there will not be enough clean fuel around in the next few years. Certainly, coal cannot meet the standards.*

*Let me say this differently. I think we could meet the Clean Air Act standards, because the legislation gives the administrator the discretion of a two-year delay. I think we could meet, or come very close to meeting, the primary standards nationwide by 1977 if we went at it in a more meticulous manner rather than trying to roll things back everywhere, if we targeted what clean fuels and what stack gas cleaning technology would then be available in those areas where they are really needed, if we permitted the use of high-sulfur fuel in places where it does not contribute to primary standard problems, if we allowed the construction of high stacks to adequately disseminate the pollutants without creating a health hazard. As interim solutions, these would do a pretty good job of approaching primary standards by 1977, perhaps even by 1975.*

*It is technically possible to provide stack gas cleaning now, but I don't consider it economically or commercially viable. We can build a system that will extract the sulfur compounds from the stack gas, but the system doesn't yet operate as reliably as it should. What's more, it may mean an investment of $25 million to $50 million, while we are still moving along the learning curve.*

*I think within the next year we will have solved some of those problems, at least in the first generation of systems. A utility should be able to order a system and have the vendor guarantee performance. Even at the time it is ordered, you must bear in mind, that it may take thirty to thirty-six months to get the thing designed, constructed, and inserted into the system. So it may be mid-1974 before the stack gas cleaning units can be ordered with some confidence, and it may be 1977 before the first ones are in stock. Further-*

*more, there is a limit to the construction capacity, for one of the important constraints in the whole energy area is manpower—engineering manpower and construction manpower. The people trying to make stack gas cleaning systems will be competing for the skilled workers building nuclear reactors, oil refineries, naptha gasifiers, petrochemical plants, and so on. All of these draw on the same manpower pool. So it's not likely that the objectives of the Clean Air Act will be met according to the present timetable.*

Are you talking about not being able to meet the sulfur dioxide standards?

*Primarily sulfur dioxide.*

Are the particulate standards achievable?

*Well, we get into some interesting problems with particulates. As you may know, the better the job we do removing sulfur from the stack gas, the tougher it is getting the particulates out. Not only is there a synergistic effect in terms of what it does in your lungs, but there is an interrelationship between sulfur and particulates in electrostatic precipitators. So the combination of particulates of just the right size and sulfur dioxide is a much more serious health hazard than either is alone. We have much to learn about this matter.*

*Precipitators operate more efficiently and get more of the particulates out if the gas contains sulfur dioxide. So if you clean it up too well, the particulates, for some reason, don't come out as well. In some cases sulfur has been injected to reduce the particulates. A similar problem has occurred when low-sulfur coal has been burned.*

*There is another perplexing problem: Stack gas cleaning systems produce a sludge which must be stored and turns out to be almost as bad a problem as the one we set out to solve. Trying to close the loop by processing the sludge, so that there is a reasonable waste product, adds tremendously to the cost. Many will probably try to pond this waste and, in doing so, will create another environmental horror.*

Several of the speakers have hinted very strongly that the secondary standards may be postponed. You seem to think that even the primary standards will be moved from 1975 to 1977. Is that what you are saying?

*I think a lot depends on just how the states go about setting up their plans. Now, keep in mind that the legislation simply says you have to meet federal standards in primary ambient air quality. It doesn't say that you can't go further, and it doesn't say how you should meet these standards.*

*There is a second part of the legislation relating to new source performance standards. We have had a continuing disagreement with EPA on new source performance standards. Over a year ago EPA said stack gas cleaning technology was available and new source performance standards were initially based on a plant in Lawrence, Kansas, that has since been shut down. More recently EPA has pointed to units operating on Japanese aluminum and rubber plants. A few stack gas cleaning units have operated rather well in Japan but under conditions different from those in utilities in the United States. EPA claims that, even if the units were not demonstrated in Lawrence, Kansas, they have now been proved feasible. Therefore, EPA refuses to change the standard. So, as it now stands, there is a new performance standard which says that every new plant has to meet emission standards commensurate with the technology that EPA contends is available.*

*As to the ambient standard, the regulation requires each state to formulate a plan that will meet at least the primary standard. The regulation doesn't prohibit industries from using high stacks; it doesn't prohibit industries from continuing to burn high-sulfur coal; it doesn't require industries to switch to oil or some other low-sulfur fuel. The regulation leaves it to each state to determine the specific air quality within its borders.*

*The states, it turns out, aren't all that well equipped to handle the problem. It is much easier for the states to simply require every industry or every plant to burn clean fuel or, as an alternative, clean up the emissions. The states just don't see the problem of the utilities, for instance, in obtaining all the clean fuel they need or all the stack gas cleaning capacity they require.*

**What do you think the possibilities are of delaying primary standards to 1977, as provided by the National Environmental Policy Act?**

*My guess is that the EPA administrator is going to have to do it. The*

212

*option is to make a more massive switch to oil than is underway at the present time. There is already a trend among power plants to change to oil. This simply creates other problems.*

When you spoke of nuclear power, you suggested that some problems are red herrings. Which problems are these?

*The real red herring is the fear that plutonium will be stolen or hijacked for a foreign power or a terrorist gang or a blackmailer. It would be difficult to pull off, considering both the security precautions and the handling dangers. Then, too, any country or institution is vulnerable in a lot of other ways. The Munich Olympic Games in 1972 proved that. Moreover, there are easier, more subtle, and more insidious ways that are just as deadly and bear less risk. There are biological routes, such as water systems, that do not involve the complexities of making a weapon.*

With the increasing cost, complexity, and danger involved in all of these systems, do you see some point at which government will have to assume control of the utility industries—either in terms of ownership or direction or by some sort of control whereby final decisions would be made in Washington?

*That could happen, but not necessarily for those reasons. I think the utility industries have some real problems ahead. Let me try to spell them out: They have operated for the last few years with very marginal reserve capacity, particularly in the Midwest, Northeast, and Southeast. They have "lucked out" because the weather has not been as bad as it could have been. Chicago experienced a voltage reduction for the first time last year. Before the Democratic convention in Miami in 1972, the city was threatened by a blackout. In August 1972 the Northeast came within an eyelash of having a blackout. The reserve capacity is very low; dirty, old, polluting units are still in use because of the delay in bringing new capacity on line.*

*Some power stations are undermaintained. Peaking equipment is being used to meet baseload at certain periods. The system is overstrained.*

*Once there are some major power failures, there will be an outcry of rage from the public. The congressional reaction may be that the private sector can't handle it, so maybe the government should take over. That would be a serious mistake, but I think it could happen.*

*The utilities face still another problem: They have been operating for quite a period of time with essentially constant rates— even reduced rates— because over the lifetime of the industry (which means the past seventy or eighty years), operating efficiency has improved fast enough so that, although other costs may have risen, the companies have managed to keep their rates fairly stable or even reduce them relatively. Now that is changing, and it is changing very rapidly. Costs are going up as the companies have to address the problems of thermal pollution, particulate removal, and sulfur oxide cleanup. Delays in building nuclear plants are raising the costs of those plants. I don't think they are going to get the kind of response from the rate commissions which would enable them to maintain the good financial base they must have in order to compete for investment dollars in the markets. The bond ratings of some utilities have already dropped a notch or two. If that continues, it feeds back into the system and costs will go up even faster.*

When we embark on crash programs like the moon odyssey, we think little about allocating $40 billion to the task. Is the collision course of energy and environment just a technical problem or are there political pressures and economic interests that prevent just and lasting solutions?

*Some people contrast our ability to go to the moon or concoct an anti-polio vaccine with our inability to solve our energy and environment problems. But you have to realize the size and complexity of the energy industry in comparison with the space effort.*

*NASA had a specific mission once President Kennedy directed in 1962 that the United States would land a man on the moon within the same decade. Once defined, the moon landing was amply financed. Penny pinching was never mentioned. The military devoted its resources to it; the private sector developed most of the hardware. In contrast, the energy industry is on its own. It consists of thousands of electric and gas utilities, oil and coal companies, plus suppliers and manufacturers, all operating in a competitive free enterprise system. In the delivery of energy under conditions where economics are vital and many options exist, the precise definition of research and development programs and responsibilities are fuzzy, complex, defensive, and diffuse.*

**Are you saying that we're at the mercy of the energy industry?**

*No, I think much can be done. But one needs to set some ground rules so that the thousands of different and competing corporate command centers can function in ways that provide incentives to pursue the goals that are consistent with the national interest.*

*Put yourself in the position of the corporate executive trying to make decisions that will satisfy his major shareholders in the face of rapidly changing ground rules such as oil import quotas, environmental standards, dollar devaluations, scientific innovations, and so forth. I question whether industry is capable of perpetuating the type of conspiratorial actions in terms of a manufactured energy crisis that some critics have suggested. The complex and diffuse nature of the whole industry makes it difficult to manage the development of technology or the implementation of technology on a centralized or monolithic structure similar to the space program.*

**Has President Nixon committed the nation's resources to meeting a technological deadline for, say, coal gasification or breeder reactors comparable to President Kennedy's challenge to hit the moon?**

*A target date of 1980 has been put on the breeder. Coal gasification is a different thing. It can be achieved today, but the experimental programs are being conducted to make it cheaper.*

*Still, the energy situation is not comparable to the moon landing. In our competitive laissez-faire economy, the market is the regulator. Economists say that market forces should operate, and, once that happens, the supply-demand problem will take care of itself, with the cost of energy rising and consumers buying less of it at the higher price. I don't begrudge the economists their solution, but I believe that research and development on the new energy frontiers must be supported by the government. And the government is not now organized to meet our energy needs in a coherent and comprehensive way.*

# Chapter 15

**Stephen J. Gage**

# Who Should Pay for Clean Energy Research?

I would like to say something about the energy resource base and about the industry structure that has developed that base, then move into the research and development which might be applicable for different types of fuels.

So, to begin, I will discuss coal, the nation's most abundant fossil fuel resource. For convenience I will define $10^{18}$ Btu's as a Q—or a unit roughly equal to a quintillion. Using this measurement, coal represents 32Q, assuming a 50% recovery rate which is the average for coal extraction by deep mining and surface mining. At our current level of consumption, there is *enough coal to see the United States through its decacentennial*—the 1,000th anniversary of the American Revolution.

### MINING RESEARCH

There are today about ten fairly large coal mining operations in the country and nearly 1,000 small operations, many of which are strip mines because underground mining has become so capital intensive, so expensive, and so hazardous. Most of the small operators rarely file permits, even in states where they are required to file, rarely belong to any coal mining federation or association, and just as rarely articulate their particular views on public policies.

Now the strip-mining industry is beset by a large number of problems, best epitomized by the dialogue taking place on Capitol Hill right now to hammer out a coal mining regulation. The deep mining industry is also wracked by problems. The Coal Mine Health and Safety Act is forcing changes in a number of mines and forcing a number of the smaller mines out of operation—not that this isn't necessarily desirable as far as achieving the social purposes embodied in that act.

There are other problems, too. There is the problem in getting enough miners to work underground. Moreover, the coal mining industry is very fragmented, and this has resulted in very low levels of research and development. About the only research and development which, even by a stretch of the imagination, can be defined as real contributions has been done by the large equipment manufacturers who are interested in selling another expensive piece of equipment. It is research and development that comes up with a big-volume item like the front-end loaders or designs large-size buckets so that their moving capacity is increased from six cubic feet to fifteen cubic yards.

So the coal industry, particularly on the recovery end, is very, very low in technology intensiveness. Indeed, throughout the fuel supply chain, technology doesn't improve much. There have been instrumental improvements in coal fire boilers over the years, but the same ones were being used in the 1920s and 1930s. The major problem facing the coal industry today is the sulfur content of its product, which intensifies the need for research and development and for advanced technology in extraction.

In the eastern part of the United States, most of the low-sulfur coal (below 1% sulfur) lies in forty to fifty counties in southern Appalachia, eastern Kentucky, southern West Virginia, eastern Virginia and northeastern Tennessee. About half of that coal is extracted by underground mining, half by surface mining. Surface mining in that area is almost entirely contour mining—that is, cutting a bench around the edge of the mountains. Most of the slopes in the area, as stated in a report recently sent to the Senate Interior Committee, lie above twenty degrees. In fact, a good number of the slopes lie above twenty-five and thirty degrees. These are very steep slopes, and, frankly, the environmental damage usually goes up considerably with the angle of the slope. The miners push the spoil out over the bench and dump it down the mountainside, and the steeper the slope, the more dispersed the spoils, the more destruction from runoff and drainage. The environmental ravages from surface mining are awful.

There appear to be technological innovations with which coal mining would cause only minimal damages. That is an area which will be under increasing pressure. Unfortunately, there is no single body within the coal industry or within the federal government that can take the lead in doing the kinds of things that need to be done.

## DRILLING IMPROVEMENTS

The oil industry, which has been a potent force in the United States economy from John Rockefeller to John Connally and now, I guess, to John Ehrlichman, reached a major turning point in January 1972 when the Texas Railway Commission quietly killed the prorationing policy which it had in operation since the 1930s. What the commission did in the 1930s was to allow the Texas producers to go to 100% of maximum efficiency recovery (MER) so that, essentially, the wells in Texas were going at full bore. Since then, wells in Louisiana have moved up towards 100% MER. It happens that the nation is now operating pretty much at full bore with domestic oil production.

With the demand for crude oil continuing to grow, and with no likely substitute available for the next five to ten years, there is an increasing shortfall between domestic production and demand. This is going to be largely satisfied, it appears, with foreign imports. Not even the Alaska finds at Prudhoe Bay or other discoveries in the West or offshore in the Gulf of Mexico and elsewhere on the Outer Continental Shelf will make the United States self-sufficient.

Now the petroleum industry prides itself on having done what they consider a fair amount of research and development—mostly development, and this has concentrated on more efficient drill bits to dig more deeply at cheaper costs with each successive generation of bits. By using tougher steel and other more exotic materials, they no longer have to pull out the drill mechanism every 100 feet to replace the drill bit.

More recently, as they started to advance into the Gulf and elsewhere in the seas, the oil operators began building platforms. This was a major development throughout the better part of the 1950s and well into the 1960s. During that time, they moved out farther and farther, in many cases up to 400 and 500 feet. And because of the storms that hit the Gulf, the platforms had to be designed to withstand considerable stress without collapsing. Not that they are as worried about the platform itself collapsing, as they were about losing the oil and gas production during the exploration because that would represent an economic loss to them.

More recently, oilmen have begun exploring and exploiting the resources farther out beyond the so-called technological limit of 200 meters. That is not a technological limit now. We are drilling beyond 200 meters with standing platforms, and operators can see oil and gas reserves even well beyond that. So the industry started developing a potential for subsea drilling, completion, and production.

This has brought a whole new dimension—a much more expensive dimension—into its research and development efforts, because it has to take a systems approach to that kind of an operation. Since the drill rigs would be largely unmanned, they have to have a degree of redundancy in design that begins to approach that of a modern jet aircraft or, for more exotic designs, that of a space capsule.

This has resulted in a considerable change in attitude, at least among the research people in the oil and gas industry. For the first time, they have run into a discontinuity; they must now have a new systems approach.

Frankly, they have not spent a lot of money on it; in fact, no one except the oil companies knows how much money they are spending on it. The industry has been very hostile toward government participation in almost any research and development activities which would encroach upon the proprietary rights of the companies to patents, as well as to tools and technology.

## EXPLORATION AND RECOVERY

By contrast, the gas industry has had to coexist with government. Historically, oil producers have controlled the production of natural gas. Gas is usually discovered in tandem with oil, but, unlike oil, the production of gas is regulated by the Federal Power Commission. Now, the oil companies have blamed the arguable shortage of natural gas on the FPC for being ungenerous about price increases, and, not surprisingly, talk of a gas shortage—like talk of an impending shortage of any commodity—drove prices upward. According to the geologists, however, there are vast untapped gas fields out West.

To determine the extent of these fields, and perhaps to liberate the natural gas deposits trapped deep underground in tight rocks and sands, the AEC has justified some of its underground testing. The gas industry sees the possibility of stimulating gas flow in the sedimentary basin beneath the Rocky Mountains. At the end of the 1960s, the Bureau of Mines estimated that the rocky reservoirs held 317 trillion cubic feet of gas.

Accordingly, the AEC proposed that, by breaking up the rocks with a nuclear device or bomb, the gas could be freed. Of the 317 trillion cubic feet of gas thought to lie like Montezuma's treasure out West, about 199 trillion cubic feet is believed to be located in the Green River Basin of Wyoming, and 118 trillion cubic feet distributed among the Uinta Basin of Utah, the Piceance Basin of Colorado, and the San Juan Basin of New Mexico. In 1965 the El Paso Natural Gas Company submitted a proposal to the AEC and the Department of the Interior for a test of a 20- to 30-kiloton nuclear "shot" in the San Juan Basin to stimulate a gas flow. On December 10, 1967, a 26-kiloton nuclear explosive was set off 4,240 feet underground in an experiment bearing the catchy title "Gasbuggy." It did indeed stimulate production—so far there has been a sixfold increase over the output of conventional wells in the area—but the gas could not be distributed commercially. It contained radioactive tritium.

The AEC has been spending between $5 million and $10 million in the last decade on this kind of research—a relatively small investment when compared with other lines of development in the federal budget. But this is quite a bit larger than the amount given to the Bureau of Mines for oil and gas exploration and recovery. The latest estimate puts these western gas deposits at some 600 trillion cubic feet, which would represent maybe a thirty-year supply at the rate we are now using natural gas. If these deposits could be developed, it is possible that between 1 trillion and 3 trillion cubic feet would be available per year. This would be a welcome supplement to the present natural gas supply.

On oil shale, which happens to coexist in the same area, we have now embarked on another attempt, after some fifty years of false starts, at using those considerable resources under the Rockies. Sometime this year, it appears, the Department of the Interior will accept bonus bids on six tracts in the Piceance Basin, the Uinta Basin, and the Green River Basin. At least two companies, Tosco and Superior Oil, have processes which they think will produce oil at competitive prices.

There appears to have been similar progress in ameliorating the environmental impacts of oil shale production. But there are many questions remaining. What small amount of money the federal government is spending in this area has been used by the Bureau of Mines in trying to grow scrub brush on spent oil shale and on a retort process that the bureau has operated at Anvil Points, Colorado.

Now, the internalization of the environmental cost of oil shale mining and retorting will probably be very critical to the economic viability of the venture. Among the techniques to encourage oil shale development—and somewhat of a new approach—are the terms written into the contracts which will probably be signed between the Department of the Interior and the oil shale developers. These terms would allow the developers to hold back a certain fraction of the royalty payments if they run into expenses which are extraordinary—extraordinary in terms of meeting environmental requirements for the area. So, in a sense, that will be a subsidy of oil shale development.

For the sake of comparisons with the quantity of coal remaining, which I gave as 32Q, oil appears to be limited to less than 1Q and natural gas, including the gas still locked in those tight rocks and sands, also seems to be under 1Q. There may be several Q of oil shale that could possibly be recovered economically and efficiently. The very rich oil shales tend to be pretty sparse.

## REACTOR FUELS

Milton Shaw has already gone over the nuclear potentials of light-water reactors and breeder reactors, and Richard Balzhiser has spoken of fusion research. A number of people are pointing out that uranium resources are fairly well confined to probably less than 1Q. With the breeder, it is a different story, because the breeder produces more fuel in the form of plutonium 239 than you burn up with U-235 or recycled Pu-239. The fuel cycle in the breeder becomes relatively independent of the costs and availability of the feed materials. So, if the breeder is successfully developed and implemented, the uranium resource base then goes to about 150Q. This gives you an idea of the impetus for developing the breeder.

To finish this part of the nuclear scenario, the limiting feed stock for the fusion reactor appears to be the lithium which is mixed with neutrons. It appears that we have considerable deposits of lithium. If it is used efficiently in fusion reactors, it provides an energy resource of probably 1,000Q, which gives you an idea of the almost unlimited nature of that resource. But to use it for power, the fusion reactor would have to be operating commercially.

Another feed material for fusion reactors is deuterium, which we can extract from both fresh water and ocean water. I think 1 part in 5,000 of the sea is deuterium oxide, rather than water, so there is no resource limitation for a deuterium-deuterium reaction and only a slight limitation for a deuterium-lithium reaction. The uranium and lithium would be used primarily in central electric generating stations.

The electric power industry is probably much more highly rationalized than any of the other industries. There has been fairly tight interutility cooperation by way of the Edison Electric Institute for quite a number of years. In the last few years, they have begun to organize seriously to form the Electric Power Research Institute which, it is claimed, will be supported by voluntary taxes on each consumer's bill. The institute will be funded at the level of about $120 million to $150 million within the next three or four years. The utilities will participate voluntarily in this program, but once a utility elects to join the program, it will have to get approval from its rate commission before placing a research and development surcharge on each consumer's bill. This turns out to be, I believe, .05 mills per kilowatt hour, which should amount to only a few cents per month for the customer. In the aggregate, however, it can mean as much as $150 million a year.

There are around 80 to 100 fairly large utilities across the country, and the institute seems to have pretty good backing from most. There are closer to 3,200 utilities in all, many of which are small municipalities and units operated by the Rural Electrification Administration (REA). Of the big investor-owned utilities, though, the institute claims 75% support.

## FUNDING AND ALLOCATION

The federal government is now spending about $650 million a year for all energy research and development. (See Figure 27.) Others may cite the figure $3 billion a year, but that would be true only if the cost of equipping, operating, and maintaining the Tennessee Valley and Bonneville authorities was included, a figure which adds more than $2 billion right away. There is also the amount being spent by the AEC (the biggest spender), the Department of the Interior, and a number of other agencies that are far less involved. This totals about $650 million in 1973. It will rise to $772 million in 1974. Many claim that this is wholly inadequate.

The Senate Commerce Committee, under the leadership of Senator Warren Magnuson, has been pushing the last several years toward passing a bill that would significantly expand federal energy research and development efforts. Last year Senator Magnuson held hearings on the bill, which proposed a $1 billion fund. Senator Henry M. Jackson and several others supporters have joined him this year on a bill that seeks $20 billion for ten years of energy research. That would, in effect, triple the federal research and development budget. It probably would be much more effective than a simple tripling would indicate, because about 70% of the federal energy research and development budget is now going toward the development of only nuclear energy. In the 1973 budget, the liquid-metal fast-breeder reactor (LMFBR) got around $350 million out of $642 million. Nuclear fusion research got another $65 million on top of that. So, those two shared a fairly large piece of the action.

Let me reiterate that nuclear power is used almost exclusively for electric power generation, not for operating automobiles, trucks, aircraft, or any other uses. Yet, about 70% of the federal budget for clean energy research and development goes to nuclear power. Nuclear hardware is dear. As the AEC ends the test phase of the LMFBR and starts the construction phase for the

222

## Figure 27.
## Federal Funds for Pollution Control and Abatement
## (summary: 1970–1972)

| Medium or Pollutant | Obligations | | | Agency | Outlays | | |
|---|---|---|---|---|---|---|---|
| | 1970 | 1971 | 1972 est. | | 1970 | 1971 | 1972 est. |
| Total[a] | 1,071 | 2,017 | 3,288 | Total | 751 | 1,149 | 1,975 |
| Water | 677 | 1,533 | 2,539 | Environmental Protection Agency[c] | 388 | 718 | 1,287 |
| Air | 189 | 245 | 433 | Atomic Energy Commission | 116 | 122 | 136 |
| Land | 35 | 49 | 60 | Dept. of Defense | 42 | 89 | 180 |
| Living things, materials, etc. | 100 | 136 | 194 | Dept. of Agriculture | 91 | 67 | 107 |
| Multi-media[b] | 69 | 53 | 63 | Dept. of Interior | 37 | 45 | 87 |
| Selected pollutants[a] | | | | Dept. of Commerce | 22 | 20 | 26 |
| Radiation | 116 | 46 | 61 | Dept. of Transportation | 11 | 22 | 56 |
| Noise | 36 | 36 | 48 | National Aero. and Space Admin. | 15 | 25 | 30 |
| Pesticides | 30 | 137 | 144 | National Science Foundation | 7 | 9 | 11 |
| Solid wastes | 20 | 41 | 57 | Other | 23 | 33 | 55 |

Source: U. S. Office of Management and Budget, *Special Analyses, Budget of the United States Government.*

Note: In millions of dollars. For years ending June 30. Obligations refer to liabilities, contracts, and other commitments entered into requiring the payment of money by the government. Outlays refer to the issuance of checks or disbursements of cash by the government to liquidate obligations. (Outlays during any fiscal year may be payments of obligations incurred in prior years or in the same year.) For complete definitions, see *The Budget of the United States Government, 1973,* part 6, The Budget System and Concepts, pp. 482–492.

[a]Funds for "Selected pollutants" included in "medium" breakdown above. Excludes $85 million in 1972 for Environmental Protection Agency.
[b]More than one of media shown above.
[c]Includes funds for activities carried out by U. S. Departments of Health, Education, and Welfare; Agriculture, Interior; and by Atomic Energy Commission and Federal Radiation Council prior to Dec. 2, 1970.

demonstration reactor, costs mount. The AEC is still finishing the fast-flux test facility (FFTF), which is a mini-demonstration reactor. The demonstration breeder will cost $500 million and up. The cost of the FFTF was estimated at $100 million, but it now looks as if it is going to cost $200 million by the time it is completed.

I would be surprised if the industry is spending much more than one-tenth of that in similar activities. The electric power industry, through the Edison Electric Institute, spent about $8 million to $10 million on seventy-five or eighty projects that it was funding. The utilities claim they have been spending many millions of dollars on other things, mostly—at least by my understanding—engineering operations and maintenance programs.

The Edison Electric Institute, the American Public Power Association, and the Tennessee Valley Authority have come up with a pot of about $250 million to be ladled out for building a big demonstration breeder reactor in Tennessee. That will be one-third or one-fourth of the total cost, depending on how the cost of the beast escalates. The TVA money, of course, will be levied against its customers. This will be, essentially, a surcharge on their wholesale electric bill; it won't be coming out of the federal budget itself. They do have some money in the federal budget, though—a matter of a few million dollars—for the engineering work that will be required to site the breeder at Clinch River.

For a proposed coal gasification project, there is talk of $20 million from the federal government and $10 million from the companies which make up the American Gas Association. There are a number of smaller projects which involved federal-industry cooperation. The Bonneville Power Administration and the Department of the Interior have put up money along with the industry to do quite a bit of work on the ultra-high voltage transmission and superconducting underground transmission.

Besides direct federal research and joint federal-industry research and development, the industry can do its own work. Industry certainly should be doing its own development work in areas where the development costs can be recaptured and profits realized in a reasonable period of time.

I think industry tends to be quite conservative, and necessarily so. The companies have to show a return on their investments in a certain period of time or they are not going to take a particularly risky route. They have to make decisions quite early in the research and development stream on whether to conduct fairly inexpensive benchtop or small pilot-plant experiments rather than expensive, scaled-up projects which would get them into much higher investments.

So industry has probably ruled out a good number of ideas which have later turned out to be very sound in economics. At the time they had made their decision on a particular scheme it did not appear favorable.

# Discussion

**Could you give me an example of the techniques developed to minimize the damage from strip mining?**

*Due to pressure from regulatory bodies, techniques have become available in the last few years that can minimize the damage from strip mining on steep slopes. Except in the West, where there are real questions about the suitability of mining in arid areas, or in areas where there are very fragile ecosystems, we are now able to return the land to its original condition. I am talking essentially about the central parts of the country—the big coal fields in southern Illinois, southern Indiana, western Kentucky, and the Appalachian flatland of Ohio. In these places, it is a matter of money and adequate enforcement. It is a matter of having a solid enough law behind the enforcement agencies to get the job done.*

*But there are very serious concerns about strip mining in steep areas, such as Montana and Wyoming. In Pennsylvania, eastern Kentucky, and northern West Virginia, the industries have demonstrated a process which is called by a number of names, depending on which part of the woods you are in. One is called "modified block cut," another "cut and fill," a third "cut and haul back." The salient point of the modified block is that the spoils are not spilled down the bank. There is no way you can contour mine and not damage the surrounding environment irretrievably if you allow the mining companies to throw the spoils down the bench. And the companies have maintained, up until the last few years, that there was no way to mine coal economically unless this was done. So they have been allowed to do it.*

*Pennsylvania has a law against mining a slope over twenty degrees unless it can be demonstrated that the mining can be done with an equal amount of environmental protection. So, just as an example, an operator in Indiana County, Pennsylvania, mining 90,000 tons a year, decided he would use a few caterpillar front-end loaders and four or five trucks to pick up the overburden, put it in the trucks, drive right up the hill, dump the spoils down, and pick up the coal that had been exposed in the process. He was able to get the coal out of a three-foot thick seam, which is sort of marginally economic anyway. He got the coal out and he restored the land in a pleasant slope of about twenty-three degrees. He demonstrated that he could do it.*

*The modified block cut will cost the mining company more once it engages in contour backfilling—maybe twice or three times what the terrible old method cost.*

*Suppose the operator can't stabilize on the downslope. Our basic conclusion, after studying the situation, was that widespread use of the modified block cut would allow continued mining in fairly steep areas except where there are wrong soil conditions, so that the soil cannot be stabilized when it is put back on the bench.*

*Some of the big, more progressive coal companies would do it right away if they had to. Most of them are not in contour areas. Most of them are area mining. They have big machines producing coal at $2.50 or $3.00 a ton and selling it for $7.00 or $8.00 a ton. They really take advantage of the economies of scale.*

*Most of the companies, though, that are mining these very steep places are small operations. The main problem, as I see it, is communicating what we want those operators to do and following up, because there are literally hundreds of strip miners.*

**Is it your conclusion that steep slope mining be outlawed?**

*I will let you make your own conclusion.*

**Is there any agency in the federal government that looks at both the resource base and the energy needs of tomorrow, and then decides how much should be spent on research in a particular area?**

*Well, I believe it was in 1967 that the energy policy staff was set up in the Office of Science and Technology (OST) by President Johnson. The idea was to have David Freeman head up an office which could look largely at the research and development sector, and also at some of these broader questions of resources, and then make some sense out of it all. At that time, the AEC was hellbent for nuclear power and the Department of the Interior was interested only in coal, oil, and gas.*

*Two things have happened since then. First, there is President Nixon's proposal for a new Department of Energy and Natural Resources. Under this reorganization, both the Atomic Energy Commission and the Department of the Interior would simultaneously*

226

*begin developing into energy agencies. If you look at the environmental impact statements which those departments have prepared on their projects and look also at the alternative sections of those statements, you would realize that both of those agencies have come a long way in the last year or year and a half in becoming truly conscious of energy resources, energy conversion, and energy use.*

*I think documents from the Department of the Interior in the last year have reflected much more consciousness of the fact that nuclear energy is here to stay.*

*United States Energy Through the Year 2000, prepared for the Interior by Walter G. Dupree, Jr. and James A. West, is a far different document than those that came out of the department two years ago because it gives nuclear energy its proper due.*

*Now OST is gone, and energy is being considered in many places—in the White House, the AEC, Interior, EPA, FPC, the Geological Survey, even in the Department of Commerce through its National Oceanic and Atmospheric Administration.*

*I think an agency for energy activities would make a lot of sense, although a little healthy competition is a good thing as long as it is not really squandering our resources because of duplication or trying to find favor with the president or the general public. I think that the threat of the Advanced Technology Division in the Atomic Energy Commission, which is doing the nonnuclear work, has made the Bureau of Mines and the Office of Coal Research sit up and take note.*

*Even the talked-about threat of making reactor development move over from AEC into the Department of the Interior has put the reactor development group in much more of a defensive posture and has made Milton Shaw talk about the breeder and lightwater reactors in terms of national priorities rather than in terms of the AEC's priorities.*

*What worries me about all this is that under a single department there will be a tendency to keep the dirty linen out of sight, to keep things quiet. As a citizen, I would prefer more open debate in the public forum.*

*Let's say that the technocrats in the Atomic Energy Commission are successful in capturing control of the bureaucracy in a De-*

*partment of Energy and Natural Resources (DENR). They will be fighting for the buck, and, if there is $1 billion in the pot, the AEC people are going to want essentially the same proportion that they are now getting. They will be competing, therefore, with, say, coal gasification. On the other hand, if the coal interests and the petroleum interests capture control of the DENR bureaucracy, they may seriously impede the progress toward reactor research or geothermal steam.*

**Who will pay for clean energy research?**

*The consumer will pay. It is how they pay and how much return they get for their dollars that is important.*

# Chapter 16
**Charles J. DiBona**

# Reconciling Our Energy
# and Environmental Demands

Our concern
with energy and environment is intertwined inevitably today with our concern
for the bounty and the beauty of America. It is ironic that a nation possessing
such natural abundance and beauty now finds that energy production is in
conflict with environmental protection. There is obviously a compelling need
to figure out a way or many different ways of bringing both into some sort of
balance or harmony.

There are three principal reasons, I think, why energy and environment are on a collision course.

## MINING AND COMBUSTION

Coal represents the most serious confrontation. We have one-third of
the total world's supply, but we rely on it for less than one-fifth of our energy
needs. Historically, one of the reasons we use less coal than other fossil fuels is
the low cost and relative cleanliness of natural gas and oil. There is also the
difficulty of transporting coal. The environmental inhibitions have to do with
its mining and its burning.

With regard to the combustion of coal, the 1970 Clean Air Act sets
standards for sulphur oxides in the air, the ambient air standards. There are
two standards: One is the primary standard, which affects human health; the
other, the secondary standard, concerns the general welfare.

The primary standards have to be met by July 1975. The secondary
standards were, according to the law, to be met in some reasonable time. They
were to be set by the states and approved by the Environmental Protection
Agency. The secondary standards are obviously more strict with regard to the
amount of sulphur oxide that can be spewed into the air than are the primary
standards. Many of the states have set secondary standards which are very strict

and which apply uniformly throughout the state without discriminating between urban areas and rural areas. Furthermore, the states propose to implement the secondary standards at the same time that the primary standards have to be implemented. The net effect of this is that, if the secondary standards are applied in 1975 at the levels that they presently have been submitted, we'll have a very sharp reduction in the amount of coal we can burn after July 1975.

Even if it were possible to move coal very freely in the United States with a very efficient transportation system and without worrying about the cost, and even if the stack gas scrubbers were actually working effectively in 1975, there would still be a reduction in the amount of coal consumed in the United States by 100 million tons per year. But assuming it is hard to move the coal around, and assuming the calculations are based simply on the percentage of power plants presently using high-sulfur coal and then relating that to the standards, you will find that the reduction in coal consumption will be around 300 million tons per year.

Both of these are strained assumptions, and the cut in coal use is probably in between—perhaps a reduction of 150 million to 200 million tons a year. Translate that into other terms, and it might be a little easier to understand what the consequences are.

Let's assume that we didn't reduce the amount of electricity to offset the reduction in coal, but had to provide energy from another source. The most available source would be imported oil. If 200 million tons of coal were eliminated in a year, we would have to import 2.4 million barrels of oil a day in order to provide the same number of Btu's. Depending on the price of oil at the time, that would cost us anywhere between $2 billion and $4 billion a year in foreign exchange. Indeed, it would be $4 billion if the price of oil hit around $5 a barrel in 1975. To put this in perspective: We had problems meeting all of our fuel needs last year, and we imported 4.7 million barrels a day.

Now, we have large deposits of low-sulfur coal. In Appalachia there are deposits of low-sulfur coal, and about 40% of the coal there is surface-mined. However, in central and northern Appalachia, most of the very low-sulfur coal that is surface-mined is mined on very steep slopes, slopes well in excess of fifteen degrees.

So it is moot whether that coal would be available under new strip-mining regulations. It seems to me that there is a likelihood that these two factors could be additive in 1975. The high-sulfur coal which would be available can't be burned because of the clean air standards, and the low-sulfur coal which could be burned under the clean air standards can't be mined.

There is some coal mined—either deep-mined or surface-mined on the flat spots where the landscape and its vegetation can be replaced or restored. So, coal is in serious conflict with our concern for the environment and our demands for energy.

Consider the environmental standards for automobiles, which have raised problems with regard to our fuel consumption. On one hand, you hear about the increase of gasoline consumed per mile brought about as a consequence of pollution control devices that are put on automobiles. It also happens to be the case that the new gasolines used in the more advanced systems for automobiles require special cracking processes, and this, I am told, reduces the number of gallons of gasoline you can get out of a barrel of oil. You get other products out of it, but not as much gasoline. The net result is a reduction in the total efficiency of the system by something on the order of 25%.

## CONSERVATION PRACTICES

Another reason that energy and environment are in conflict has to do with the whole question of energy conservation. There are a number of steps that the consumer can take—and the government can help—to bring about a reduction in the amount of energy we consume, increase the efficiency with which we use it, reduce the demand for energy, and also help with our environmental problems.

One method which has been discussed, is simply to provide the consumer with more information through labeling of energy-consuming devices like air conditioners and refrigerators, so that the person buying one of these appliances can also determine how efficient the appliance is and have some notion of what his expenditures on fuel are going to be.

The second thing the government can do is provide demonstration projects and make the data available. For example, right now the General Services Administration is building an office building in Manchester, New Hampshire, specifically designed to minimize the amount of energy used. It will serve as an experiment from which information can be provided to architects.

A third, and more direct step, would be for the government to change the standards on insulation for houses financed under FHA loans—and that could be extended to mobile homes, as well.

To the extent that world prices and other factors will raise the price of energy, the average consumer is going to be looking at his energy consumption as never before, in this country at least. That should lead to changes in attitudes toward the size of automobiles and a number of other energy-gulping devices. The rising rate of energy demand in the United States is not inevitable. In the past, it has not been as high as it has been in the last few years. We had long periods in which the increase in demand for energy was small—between 2% and 3%, not 5% as it is now.

Demand will make a big difference in how much energy we will need in 1980 or 1985. It makes a difference, therefore, in the real options that are available.

# Discussion

Do you see any likelihood of the federal government's mandating some changes in energy demand or consumption? You mentioned, for example, the requirement of higher insulation standards.

*I can imagine that happening without much trouble.*

**What about smaller cars? Do you envision a tax on horsepower, for instance?**

*I don't see that happening right now—though there are many factors that would tend to drive people toward smaller automobiles. The insurance rates on large automobiles are considerably higher than on small automobiles. Gasoline isn't as cheap as it was three or four years ago, or even three or four months ago. But I don't foresee a horsepower tax.*

How do we reconcile the energy and environmental demands?

*One of the ways I have suggested here is energy conservation. That is obviously the simplest way, because it involves reducing the amount of energy that you consume and that, of course, makes it easier to meet energy demands.*

*With regard to the coal problem, a decision to delay meeting the secondary standards would go a long way toward reconciling both of those problems. Incidentally, a delay would require no change in the law; that is, it is a question of what is meant by the definition of reasonable time or reasonable period. We are going to have some difficulties meeting the primary standard in urban areas. It might make a lot of sense to put all of our efforts into insuring that primary standards in those areas are met. That means insuring that stack gas cleaning devices are targeted for places which have, or tend to have, higher levels of pollution, and that stocks of low-sulfur oil, gas, and coal go to places which presently have the highest pollution levels. So there is a real way in which we can reconcile our interests in improving the quality of the environment.*

Do you think the goal of national self-sufficiency in energy is realistic?

*I don't think there is any possibility of being self-sufficient in the next few years.*

Is it possible to foresee this in the next two decades?

> *It is conceivable, but highly unlikely. If you mean that we would have no inputs of oil at all, that is highly unlikely in the next two decades.*

There are those who argue that both the present environmental standards and those called for in the Clean Air Act are not really adequate when one projects the growth in energy consumption. Yet you seem to suggest a rather serious compromise with the Clean Air Act.

> *There is no compromise with the Act. What I have suggested is within the limits of the act. It is also true that rather than having a degredation of the environment over the last few years there is positive evidence of improvement.*

There are those who say that particulate matter is being taken out, but other matter, like photochemical oxidants, are still a problem, and that the health problem of the air has not improved but has, in fact, deteriorated.

> *There is always going to be some dispute. I think you can make the statement that the air is cleaner and defend it, which suggests we are moving in the right direction.*

What happens when a state passes legislation banning offshore drilling and super ports, but the federal government initiates these developments in the national interest?

> *I don't think you could build those facilities without agreement by the states. Any state can prevent these facilities if it chooses to do so. So, even if the federal government were inclined—and as far as I know, it is not—it couldn't preempt the states.*

The reports are that the administration prefers to "drain America first."

> *We must look at this in terms of alternatives for the future. Research and development will permit us to have more alternatives twenty or thirty years from now than we presently have.*

Does it appear, then, that we will be producing fossil fuel at a greater rate now in hopes that research and development in the future years will provide an alternative?

> *Part of the thrust of research and development is to increase the*

*ability to get clean fossil fuels. You state a rather simple dichotomy that our alternatives are to either import more or "drain America first." The first alternative will preserve our resources in precisely the state they are today. The second will use up our resources so that at some point in the not too distant future, we will run out. The facts of the matter are that the problem is a great deal more complex—in ways that such a simple dichotomy misses.*

*Our reserves are a function of how much we pay to extract them. In a normal oil well, we take out about 31% of the oil today, a much larger percentage than we used to remove. So every oil well where we stop production still contains 69% of the oil that was there originally. As time passes, we are going to develop ways of getting more and more of the oil out.*

*Similarly, our alternative with regard to high-sulfur coal is to burn it in its present state, which is rather dirty, or not to use it. But there are other alternatives—coal gasification, low-Btu gasification, which radically increases the cost of the coal for consumption, and we are also spending money heavily in research and development to solvent-refine coal, or to convert coal to high-Btu gas. What this does, essentially, is take out the sulfur, turn it into a convenient, clean form for burning. It is a resource that we should be very reluctant to either neglect or exhaust.*

*The question of how we can extract oil from shale is a question which may be solved rather soon. It is an operation that would make most mines look like sandpile operations, but there is the possibility of in situ extraction of the oil. We have simply got to work on ways of making use of that fossil resource. There is more oil in shale than there is in the Persian Gulf.*

There are those that say the large-scale production of oil shale will be over the dead bodies of all those in the Sierra Club, Friends of the Earth, and the state of Colorado.

*It depends on what methods are used and what success we can have in research and development. Difficult problems can rarely be solved by simplistic answers.*

What kinds of proposals do you have for cutting in half the rate of energy growth? In addition to voluntary measures, do

**you foresee any action by the government?**

*It is true that energy conservation is going to come about largely because of the choices of individual consumers. That raises questions about the role of the government. It seems to me that it is appropriate for the government to provide information so that people can make choices. It seems to me that it is important for the government to make people aware of the implications of those choices—that is, to report that there is a real problem and to explain what the consequences of that problem are, then to suggest solutions and to explain what effects they are likely to have.*

*It is clear that the government, in its own operations, can be aware of the costs and consequences of energy and do something about curbing its use. Controls on things that are normally regulated by the government, such as insulation standards in homes, are activities that the government can carry out.*

*Going beyond that raises some complex issues: To simply require that no automobile may be built with an engine of more than 200 horsepower, for instance, is not something that I would be inclined to recommend. To encourage the development of urban mass transportation, the administration proposed using the Highway Trust Fund, but the idea had trouble getting out of committee and into Congress.*

# Chapter 17

Henry M. Jackson

# Is a National Energy-Environment Policy Possible?

Why weren't there some early warning signals of the impending collision between energy and environment? As the number of brownouts, fishkills, smog alerts and oil spills increased intolerably, *why didn't we realize it was time for action?*

Some of us—too few of us—became aware of the threat to our "quality of life" five or six years ago, before the first Earth Day of April 22, 1970. Having spent my entire public career in one aspect or another of conservation in both houses of Congress, I began to understand, particularly as chairman of the Senate Interior Committee, that traditional conservation measures were not enough to preserve our environmental heritage; establishing the Redwood National Park, national seashores, and wilderness areas, significant though these actions were, would be insufficient. We needed a national showdown to deal with a national problem.

In the summer of 1968, Laurence Rockefeller and I co-sponsored a colloquium on the environment in the Old Supreme Court Chamber of the nation's Capitol. The discussion attracted some of our leading conservationists and principal academics. Its coverage by the press and in the media was exactly zilch.

When I inquired why there had been no coverage, I was informed that a matter like the environment was so broad, so complex, so esoteric, and so metaphysical that reporters and editors were reluctant to deal with it— anyway, there was no "hard news" in it.

Similarly, congressmen themselves didn't grasp the implications right away. I was able to steer the National Environmental Policy Act through the Senate without much debate. It didn't take very long because few members really knew what was going on. The same thing happened in the House of Representatives. There had been more internecine conflict over our committee's

238

jurisdiction than concern with the substance of the problem. The energy problem is a victim of the same malaise. Both problems are interrelated at many points, just as the great web of life is interrelated.

## UNPLANNED GROWTH PATTERNS

If there is anything that has characterized the post-World War II period, it has been the pace of change in our national life. At the core of it is the gross national product. It took 200 years to reach a $1 trillion gross national product, which, as I recall, occurred in December 1970. It took about 185 years to get the first $500 million gross national product and only fifteen years to get the second $500 million. That Herculean rate of growth has brought to the fore the environmental problem—that is, the corruption of the air, the water, and everything around us—because of the pace of scientific and technological developments without any planning, without any programming, without any consideration as to their impact.

It is equally true of energy. Only three or four years ago we were talking about a goal of nine million automobiles. Last year we produced twelve million cars. The demand for energy has been insatiable on the part of industry, government, and all the people. Last year, for example, petroleum industry estimates and government estimates called for a 3.75% increase in oil and oil products. It leaped to almost 8%.

In Europe and in the developing Third World, demands are soaring as well. Europe's consumption rate has been double that of ours in the postwar period. So we are confronted with a situation in which the pace of change has been so rapid that we have completely ignored the impact, direct and collaterally, on our society and its most civilizing amenities.

Is there an energy crisis? The answer is obvious. I don't care how you look at it, unless you are going to make Spartans of all Americans, we do not have within the United States at this point in time sufficient traditional sources of energy—I am referring to petroleum and natural gas—to meet our demands.

In 1948 we were a net exporter of petroleum products. Last year we imported 27% of our oil supply. This year the import estimate is 35%. By 1980 some predict that 50% —I predict 60% —of our petroleum will be imported.

## BUILDING UP RESERVES

So, no matter what happens, we are going to be importing petroleum over the next ten or twelve years. This raises an obvious question for the long term: How reliable is the source of all this petroleum? Until this year only 3% came from the Persian Gulf; the bulk of it came from our own Western Hemisphere, meaning Venezuela and Canada. Indochina has provided a new source, as has Africa. But the staggering statistic is that 80% of the world's known oil reserves, excluding the Soviet Union and China, is in the Persian Gulf. Think about that a bit.

Currently Europe gets 80% of all of its petroleum products from the Middle East, and Japan gets 90% of its oil from that region. This poses a serious problem, because we are just now moving into the Persian Gulf and the Middle East. There is also the problem of the OPEC cartel and how we will cope with it.

I think it is obvious that we have to join together in a consumers consortium and work with our allies. We can't go off unilaterally, otherwise we are going to upset the market. I think there needs to be a pulling together of Canada, North America, Western Europe and Japan to bargain collectively in dealing with that aspect of the problem. For the near term, most Americans are shocked to find that we do not have a strategic reserve of oil. Our reserve is practically zero. If you pump out the tanks and the pipelines, there may be as much as a 5-day reserve in the United States. So our first near-term objective, it seems to me, must be to build up a 90-day reserve. By contrast, Great Britain has an oil reserve of 105 days at the present time. Sweden has a 120-day reserve, and the Common Market countries of Europe average a 60-day supply and are working to hoard a 90-day reserve.

Another immediate requirement is to move the petroleum that we have in Alaska, which represents one-fourth of our known reserves. Our total reserve last year was 40 billion barrels in the United States, and 10 billion barrels of that was in Alaska. Accordingly, my committee is now amending the bill to solve the right-of-way issue, which affects the movement of all energy in the United States.

What's more, the Senate Interior Committee that I chair is working with the Public Works Committee, the Commerce Committee, and the Atomic Energy Committee to put together all the pieces of a national energy policy. We have introduced the major legislation to provide alternative sources of supply—gasification and liquefaction of coal, conversion of oil shale, geo-thermal heat, and the far-out and far-off solutions, such as solar energy, fusion power, and others.

I believe that there has never been a time when there was a greater need for an honest evaluation of our economic requirements, our industrial growth, and our environmental heritage, because they are on course for a "crunch." The truth is that we, as a people, tend to look for scapegoats. We like the "Devil theory" of history. When we don't have solutions to a problem, we seek out a devil and start beating it.

I find that my job is—or at least should be—to proceed as an honest and vigilant judge trying to find ways in which we can have a compatible program for achieving sensible goals and objectives of growth, while, at the same time, *preventing an energy crisis from spoiling the environment and an environmental crisis from spoiling our energy-based economy.*

I don't think environmentalists can go around saying, "This is your problem, brother," refusing to accept the need, for example, of the petroleum in Alaska. That is irresponsible and irredeemable. My objection holds true for the oil industry as well. Our job—the job of all of us together—is to work out and come up with a strategy of responsibility that we can all accept and on which we will all act.

# Discussion

Why, after fourteen or fifteen years of oil import quotas, imposed because of national security needs and costing the American public from $3 billion to $5 billion more for petroleum products, do we now discover that we have no strategic reserves in the United States?

> *From the very beginning, I personally opposed oil import quotas as a national security measure. The honest answer is that it was a device to fix the price of oil high enough so that there would be, ostensibly, greater exploration in our own country. The reason, in my judgment, that we are confronting this current problem of oil and gasoline shortages is that last summer the oil industry tried to fine-tune supply and demand by failing to properly recognize the demand requirements for what we call No. 2 fuel oil—that is diesel oil and gasoline. I don't think there is any doubt about it—the oil companies did not want any surplus because that would depress prices.*
>
> > *When you attempt to fine-tune the economy and behavior of a nation as big and complex as the United States, you are inevitably in trouble. The oil companies miscalculated. The problem is not that there is an inadequate supply of petroleum in the world. There is an adequate amount. I opposed the quota concept because it was a "fix" in the name of trying to regulate prices.*

I would gather on the basis of the argument for your legislation that we have to develop self-sufficiency?

> *From every standpoint, we need to develop indigenous alternative sources. Our balance of payments deficit was more than $3 billion this past year, just in petroleum. By 1980 it will be, at the minimum, around $21 billion in petroleum imports alone. The need to be able to bargain, if you will pardon the expression, with OPEC, would be enhanced, first, by possessing a 90-day reserve and second, by possessing an indigenous production program. Doing this will make a tremendous difference in the reliability of our supply and in the expense to the consumer. One friend of mine who knows the industry pretty well has said we would save $1 a barrel. Well, importing billions of barrels of oil translates to billions of dollars to the American consumer. This would certainly help pay the cost of my proposal*

*for a $20 billion Manhattan-type project to put America's scientific and technological competence on the energy problem.*

We accept the axiom that energy fuels the growth of the country. Is it part of the equation that the gross national product will have to increase at the same rate or even faster than it has in the past?

> *If you are going to achieve full employment, if you are going to make it possible for minorities to be fully employed, you can't avoid the need to increase our output of goods and services at a time when so many are not enjoying the benefits of our economic system. It depends on what kind of growth we want. Growth is directly related to jobs and to revenue. Every time you increase the gross national product by $1 billion, you have a potential for $350 million in federal revenue. In the recession of 1969–1970 we lost $100 billion in revenues because of the slowdown in the gross national product rate; the states, counties, and municipalities lost $5 billion that year. So the answer is that we have to direct ourselves to the means by which we have this growth so we can avoid a corruption of the air, the water, and the land. I am confident that we have the capacity—scientifically and technologically—to do it.*

There seems to be in this symposium a consensus that the government would like to act but feels it cannot act boldly until the public fully realizes what is happening. Will we have to wait for public awareness to demand some action?

> *I believe there is an opportunity for conservation. One of the things that I have suggested, which, of course, would make many people unhappy, is a tax on horsepower. But I think we are going to have to come to that. Then people who use a larger amount of petroleum products would pay for it.*
>
> *We could well find ourselves wearing a little heavier clothing and pushing the thermostat back. Northern Europe does this out of habit and custom. I have an ongoing argument in my own family. I like the house temperature at about 65 degrees and the rest of them want it at 75. I am outvoted.*
>
> *Now, we have got to use balance and sense in this. We are not going to solve the whole energy problem merely by putting a tax on horsepower and by cutting back on the amount of energy used in*

*heating homes. But we can make a substantial difference in the problem. It will help to stop the use of natural gas on such an enormous scale to fire the boilers for the utility industry and for industry as a whole. One-half of all our natural gas is being used now for that purpose because it is cheaper and cleaner and because it enables the utilities and industries to immediately meet environmental standards.*

*As for air pollution, there are many aspects, all of which must be examined. The effect of the new auto emission controls has been to increase the consumption of gasoline and, thereby, aggravate the energy crisis. That aspect wasn't given one iota of consideration.*

*This, again, points up the fact that energy and environment are interwoven almost everywhere. Unless we look at the whole picture, we will solve part of one problem only to create several more.*

What are the chances of getting legislation that sees far enough in advance so that the impact five or ten years down the pike is a favorable one, even though the policies may be out of favor among the public?

*It will be tough. We have been working on bills for two years. Every time I made a statement warning about what is now happening, I was fortunate to have it in the financial page. I could never get it on the front page or the nighttime television news.*

*The public wakes up when it feels the bite, and they are going to feel it this year. I will tell you very bluntly that I am going to time certain bills to the situation, because I am a realist and want to get the legislation passed.*

Would zero population growth help?

*Well, we almost have that now. Population growth has leveled off; there is virtually no growth. But I don't think that is our problem in the United States at all. I think the real population problem is where people are going to live.*

*We are being dishonest by not facing up to our own urban problems. A census was taken in 1790, a year after this republic was founded, and at that time 95% of the people lived in rural areas. Today 70% of our people live on 1% of the land. This is the problem, and this is why I am working on another bill, the National Land Use Planning Act.*

*This is a rough issue, because the states have failed to zone. We are not doing the job of looking ahead and deciding where people are going to live and where they should live in relation to their jobs. We are not pinpointing what land ought to be developed and what ought to be conserved or where our transportation corridors should be. We have to identify the routes for cars and buses as well as the channels for waste, slurry, electricity. Nobody is doing this. And some day we will pay the price of our present neglect or indifference or stupidity.*

You mentioned the mismanagement aspect of the fuel shortage. What can be done to make the oil companies respond and react responsibly to the public need?

*Your questions are excellent, and they point up the magnitude of the problem. As reporters, you will find that one of the hardest things is to get the facts. You can't go to any one agency or department in the government and obtain the facts on the energy situation, because they get all their data from industry.*

*One of the many bills that we are proposing would empower the General Accounting Office to collect the data and to be able to provide the accurate information regarding supplies of petroleum products and other energy products. It would be a project comparable to the Bureau of Labor Statistics, so that there would be some integrity behind the energy industry figures, not just self-serving statements and findings. After all, this information gives us an analysis of the nation's lifeblood. Energy touches on everything. Can you think of any aspect of our national life it does not touch?*

*We can't just decree environmental standards. We have to have the kind of scientific data to back up what we propose to do.*

*I am concerned to find out whether the Japanese are really meeting car emission standards. If they can meet them, why can't Detroit? I think this is an important issue and we ought to investigate. Now maybe the Japanese claim is not a valid one. I can't answer responsibly because I don't have impartial information on automobile emissions.*

Who is protecting the public interest in the energy crisis?

*Well, we are trying to do it in our committee in connection with our study of the problems. I think the administration has not attacked the problems. It has not recognized that what is needed is one person really in charge of dealing with the energy-environment problems. If you try to find out who is really in charge, you will find it very difficult. Various aspects are under the Secretary of the Treasury, George Shultz; some issues are handled by Charles DiBona, who is the representative of John Erlichman, the action officer at the White House; Henry Kissinger manages the national security aspects; and there are aides, assistants and consultants for all of these people, as well. In sum, I think there has been a failure to attempt, with seriousness, honesty, and responsibility, to get to the heart of the matter.*

# Appendix A

# Text of President Nixon's Special Message to Congress on Energy and Resources April 18, 1973

# THE WHITE HOUSE

TO THE CONGRESS OF THE UNITED STATES:

At home and abroad, America is in a time of transition. Old problems are yielding to new initiatives, but in their place new problems are arising which once again challenge our ingenuity and require vigorous action. Nowhere is this more clearly true than in the field of energy.

As America has become more prosperous and more heavily industrialized, our demands for energy have soared. Today, with 6 percent of the world's population, we consume almost a third of all the energy used in the world. Our energy demands have grown so rapidly that they now outstrip our available supplies, and at our present rate of growth, our energy needs a dozen years from now will be nearly double what they were in 1970.

In the years immediately ahead, we must face up to the possibility of occasional energy shortages and some increase in energy prices.

Clearly, we are facing a vitally important energy challenge. If present trends continue unchecked, we could face a genuine energy crisis. But that crisis can and should be averted, for we have the capacity and the resources to meet our energy needs if only we take the proper steps—and take them now.

More than half the world's total reserves of coal are located within the United States. This resource alone would be enough to provide for our energy needs for well over a century. We have potential resources of billions of barrels of recoverable oil, similar quantities of shale oil and more than 2,000 trillion cubic feet of natural gas. Properly managed, and with more attention on the part of consumers to the conservation of energy, these supplies can last for as long as our economy depends on conventional fuels.

In addition to natural fuels, we can draw upon hydroelectric plants and increasing numbers of nuclear powered facilities. Moreover, long before our present energy sources are exhausted, America's vast capabilities in research and development can provide us with new, clean and virtually unlimited sources of power.

Thus we should not be misled into pessimistic predictions of an energy disaster. But neither should we be lulled into a false sense of security. We must examine our circumstances realistically, carefully weigh the alternatives—and then move forward decisively.

## WEIGHING THE ALTERNATIVES

Over 90 percent of the energy we consume today in the United States comes from three sources: natural gas, coal and petroleum. Each source presents us with a different set of problems.

Natural gas is our cleanest fuel and is most preferred in order to protect our environment, but ill-considered regulations of natural gas prices by the Federal Government have produced a serious and increasing scarcity of this fuel.

We have vast quantities of coal, but the extraction and use of coal have presented such persistent environmental problems that, today, less than 20 percent of our energy needs are met by coal and the health of the entire coal industry is seriously threatened.

Our third conventional resource is oil, but domestic production of available oil is no longer able to keep pace with demands.

In determining how we should expand and develop these resources, along with others such as nuclear power, we must take into account not only our economic goals, but also our environmental goals and our national security goals. Each of these areas is profoundly affected by our decisions concerning energy.

If we are to maintain the vigor of our economy, the health of our environment, and the security of our energy resources, it is essential that we strike the right balance among these priorities.

The choices are difficult, but we cannot refuse to act because of this. We cannot stand still simply because it is difficult to go forward. That is the one choice Americans must never make.

The energy challenge is one of the great opportunities of our time. We have already begun to meet that challenge, and realize its opportunities.

## NATIONAL ENERGY POLICY

In 1971, I sent to the Congress the first message on energy policies ever submitted by an American President. In that message I proposed a number of specific steps to meet our projected needs by increasing our supply of clean energy in America.

Those steps included expanded research and development to obtain more clean energy, increased availability of energy resources located on Federal lands, increased efforts in the development of nuclear power, and a new Federal organization to plan and manage our energy programs.

In the twenty-two months since I submitted that message, America's energy research and development efforts have been expanded by 50 percent.

In order to increase domestic production of conventional fuels, sales of oil and gas leases on the Outer Continental Shelf have been increased. Federal and State standards to protect the marine environment in which these leases are located are being tightened. We have developed a more rigorous surveillance capability and an improved ability to prevent and clean up oil spills.

We are planning to proceed with the development of oil shale and geothermal energy sources on Federal lands, so long as an evaluation now underway shows that our environment can be adequately protected.

We have also taken new steps to expand our uranium enrichment capacity for the production of fuels for nuclear power plants, to standardize nuclear power plant designs, and to ensure the continuation of an already enviable safety record.

We have issued new standards and guidelines, and have taken other actions to increase and encourage better conservation of energy.

In short, we have made a strong beginning in our effort to ensure that America will always have the power needed to fuel its prosperity. But what we have accomplished is only a beginning.

Now we must build on our increased knowledge, and on the accomplishments of the past twenty-two months, to develop a more comprehensive, integrated national energy policy. To carry out this policy we must:

—increase domestic production of all forms of energy;

—act to conserve energy more effectively;

—strive to meet our energy needs at the lowest cost consistent with the protection of both our national security and our natural environment;

—reduce excessive regulatory and administrative impediments which have delayed or prevented construction of energy-producing facilities;

—act in concert with other nations to conduct research in the energy field and to find ways to prevent serious shortages; and

—apply our vast scientific and technological capacities—both public and private—so we can utilize our current energy resources more wisely and develop new sources and new forms of energy.

The actions I am announcing today and the proposals I am submitting to the Congress are designed to achieve these objectives. They reflect the fact that we are in a period of transition, in which we must work to avoid or at least minimize short-term supply shortages, while we act to expand and develop our domestic supplies in order to meet long-term energy needs.

We should not suppose this transition period will be easy. The task ahead will require the concerted and cooperative efforts of consumers, industry, and government.

## DEVELOPING OUR DOMESTIC ENERGY RESOURCES

The effort to increase domestic energy production in a manner consistent with our economic, environmental and security interests should focus on the following areas:

*Natural Gas*

Natural gas is America's premium fuel. It is clean-burning and thus has the least detrimental effect on our environment.

Since 1966, our consumption of natural gas has increased by over one-third, so that today natural gas comprises 32 percent of the total energy we consume from all sources. During this same period, our proven and available reserves of natural gas have decreased by a fifth. Unless we act responsibly, we will soon encounter increasing shortages of this vital fuel.

Yet the problem of shortages results less from inadequate resources than from ill-conceived regulation. Natural gas is the fuel most heavily regulated by the Federal Government—through the Federal Power Commission. Not only are the operations of interstate natural gas pipelines regulated, as was originally and properly intended by the Congress, but the price of the natural gas supplied to these pipelines by thousands of independent producers has also been regulated.

For more than a decade the prices of natural gas supplied to pipelines under this extended regulation have been kept artificially low. As a result, demand has been artificially stimulated, but the exploration and development required to provide new supplies to satisfy this increasing demand have been allowed to wither. This form of government regulation has contributed heavily to the shortages we have experienced, and to the greater scarcity we now anticipate.

As a result of its low regulated price, more than 50 percent of our natural gas is consumed by industrial users and utilities, many of which might otherwise be using coal or oil. While homeowners are being forced to turn away from natural gas and toward more expensive fuels, unnecessarily large quantities of natural gas are being used by industry.

Furthermore, because prices within producing States are often higher than the interstate prices established by the Federal Power Commission, most newly discovered and newly produced natural gas does not enter interstate pipelines. Potential consumers in non-producing States thus suffer the worst shortages. While the Federal Power Commission has tried to alleviate these problems, the regulatory framework and attendant judicial constraints inhibit the ability of the Commission to respond adequately.

It is clear that the price paid to producers for natural gas in interstate trade must increase if there is to be the needed incentive for increasing supply and reducing inefficient usage. Some have suggested additional regulation to provide new incentives, but we have already seen the pitfalls in this approach. We must regulate less, not more. At the same time, we cannot remove all natural gas regulations without greatly inflating the price of gas currently in production and generating windfall profits.

To resolve this issue, I am proposing that gas from new wells, gas newly-dedicated to interstate markets, and the continuing production of natural gas from expired contracts should no longer be subject to price regulation at the wellhead. Enactment of this legislation should stimulate new exploration and development. At the same time, because increased prices on new unregulated gas would be averaged in with the prices for gas that is still regulated, the consumer should be protected against precipitous cost increases.

To add further consumer protection against unjustified price increases, I propose that the Secretary of the Interior be given authority to impose a ceiling on the price of new natural gas when circumstances warrant. Before exercising this power, the Secretary would consider the cost of alternative domestic fuels, taking into account the superiority of natural gas from an environmental standpoint. He would also consider the importance of encouraging production and more efficient use of natural gas.

## Outer Continental Shelf

Approximately half of the oil and gas resources in this country are located on public lands, primarily on the Outer Continental Shelf (OCS). The speed at which we can increase our domestic energy production will depend in large measure on how rapidly these resources can be developed.

Since 1954, the Department of the Interior has leased to private developers almost 8 million acres on the Outer Continental Shelf. But this is only a small percentage of these potentially productive areas. At a time when we are being forced to obtain almost 30 percent of our oil from foreign sources, this level of development is not adequate.

I am therefore directing the Secretary of the Interior to take steps which would triple the annual acreage leased on the Outer Continental Shelf by 1979, beginning with expanded sales in 1974 in the Gulf of Mexico and including areas beyond 200 meters in depth under conditions consistent with my oceans policy statement of May, 1970. By 1985, this accelerated leasing rate could increase annual energy production by an estimated 1.5 billion barrels of oil (approximately 16 percent of our projected oil requirements in that year), and 5 trillion cubic feet of natural gas (approximately 20 percent of expected demand for natural gas that year).

In the past, a central concern in bringing these particular resources into production has been the threat of environmental damage. Today, new techniques, new regulations and standards, and new surveillance capabilities enable us to reduce and control environmental dangers substantially. We should now take advantage of this progress. The resources under the Shelf, and on all our public lands, belong to all Americans, and the critical needs of all Americans for new energy supplies require that we develop them.

If at any time it is determined that exploration and development of a specific shelf area can only proceed with inadequate protection of the environment, we will not commence or continue operations. This policy was reflected in the suspension of 35 leases in the Santa Barbara Channel in 1971. We are continuing the Santa Barbara suspensions, and I again request that the Congress pass legislation that would provide for appropriate settlement for those who are forced to relinquish their leases in the area.

At the same time, I am directing the Secretary of the Interior to proceed with leasing the Outer Continental Shelf beyond the Channel Islands of California if the reviews now underway show that the environmental risks are acceptable.

I am also asking the Chairman of the Council on Environmental Quality to work with the Environmental Protection Agency, in consultation with the National Academy of Sciences and appropriate Federal agencies, to study the environmental impact of oil and gas production on the Atlantic Outer Continental Shelf and in the Gulf of Alaska. No drilling will be undertaken in these areas until its environmental impact is determined. Governors, legislators and citizens of these areas will be consulted in this process.

Finally, I am asking the Secretary of the Interior to develop a long-term leasing program for *all* energy resources on public lands, based on a thorough analysis of the Nation's energy, environmental, and economic objectives.

*Alaskan Pipeline*

Another important source of domestic oil exists on the North Slope of Alaska. Although private industry stands ready to develop these reserves and the Federal Government has spent large sums on environmental analyses, this project is still being delayed. This delay is not related to any adverse judicial findings concerning environmental impact, but rather to an outmoded legal restriction regarding the width of the right of way for the proposed pipeline.

At a time when we are importing growing quantities of oil at great detriment to our balance of payments, and at a time when we are also experiencing significant oil shortages, we clearly need the two million barrels a day which the North Slope could provide—a supply equal to fully one-third of our present import levels.

In recent weeks I have proposed legislation to the Congress which would remove the present restriction on the pipeline. I appeal to the Congress to act swiftly on this matter so that we can begin construction of the pipeline with all possible speed.

I oppose any further delay in order to restudy the advisability of building the pipeline through Canada. Our interest in rapidly increasing our supply of oil is best served by an Alaskan pipeline. It could be completed much more quickly than a Canadian pipeline; its entire capacity would be used to carry domestically owned oil to American markets where it is needed; and construction of an Alaskan pipeline would create a significant number of American jobs both in Alaska and in the maritime industry.

## Shale Oil

Recoverable deposits of shale oil in the continental United States are estimated at some 600 billion barrels, 80 billion of which are considered easily accessible.

At the time of my Energy Message of 1971, I requested the Secretary of the Interior to develop an oil shale leasing program on a pilot basis and to provide me with a thorough evaluation of the environmental impact of such a program. The Secretary has prepared this pilot project and expects to have a final environmental impact statement soon. If the environmental risks are acceptable, we will proceed with the program.

To date there has been no commercial production of shale oil in the United States. Our pilot program will provide us with valuable experience in using various operational techniques and acting under various environmental conditions. Under the proposed program, the costs both of development and environmental protection would be borne by the private lessee.

## Geothermal Leases

At the time of my earlier Energy Message, I also directed the Department of the Interior to prepare a leasing program for the development of geothermal energy on Federal lands. The regulations and final environmental analysis for such a program should be completed by late spring of this year.

If the analysis indicates that we can proceed in an environmentally acceptable manner, I expect leasing of geothermal fields on Federal lands to begin soon thereafter.

The use of geothermal energy could be of significant importance to many of our western areas, and by supplying a part of the western energy demand, could release other energy resources that would otherwise have to be used. Today, for instance, power from the Geysers geothermal field in California furnishes about one-third of the electric power of the city of San Francisco.

New technologies in locating and producing geothermal energy are now under development. During the coming fiscal year, the National Science Foundation and the Geological Survey will intensify their research and development efforts in this field.

## Coal

Coal is our most abundant and least costly domestic source of energy. Nevertheless, at a time when energy shortages loom on the horizon, coal provides less than 20 percent of our energy demands, and there is serious danger that its use will be reduced even further. If this reduction occurs, we would have to increase our oil imports rapidly, with all the trade and security problems this would entail.

Production of coal has been limited not only by competition from natural gas— a competition which has been artificially induced by Federal price regulation—but also by emerging environmental concerns and mine health and safety requirements. In order to meet environmental standards, utilities have shifted to natural gas and imported low-sulphur fuel oil. The problem is compounded by the fact that some low-sulphur coal resources are not being developed because of uncertainty about Federal and State mining regulations.

I urge that highest national priority be given to expanded development and utilization of our coal resources. Present and potential users who are able to choose among energy sources should consider the national interest as they make their choice. Each decision against coal increases petroleum or gas consumption, compromising our national self-sufficiency and raising the cost of meeting our energy needs.

In my State of the Union Message on Natural Resources and the Environment earlier this year, I called for strong legislation to protect the environment from abuse caused by mining. I now repeat that call. Until the coal industry knows the mining rules under which it will have to operate, our vast reserves of low-sulphur coal will not be developed as rapidly as they should be and the under-utilization of such coal will persist.

The Clean Air Act of 1970, as amended, requires that primary air quality standards—those related to health—must be met by 1975, while more stringent secondary standards—those related to the "general welfare"—must be met within a reasonable period. The States are moving very effectively to meet primary standards established by the Clean Air Act, and I am encouraged by their efforts.

At the same time, our concern for the "general welfare" or national interest should take into account considerations of national security and economic prosperity, as well as our environment.

If we insisted upon meeting both primary and secondary clean air standards by 1975, we could prevent the use of up to 155 million tons of coal per year. This would force an increase in demand for oil of 1.6 million barrels per day. This oil would have to be imported, with an adverse effect on our balance of payments of some $1.5 billion or more a year. Such a development would also threaten the loss of an estimated 26,000 coal mining jobs.

If, on the other hand, we carry out the provisions of the Clean Air Act in a judicious manner, carefully meeting the primary, health-related standards, but not moving in a precipitous way toward meeting the secondary standards, then we should be able to use virtually all of that coal which would otherwise go unused.

The Environmental Protection Agency has indicated that the reasonable time allowed by the Clean Air Act for meeting secondary standards could extend beyond 1975. Last year, the Administrator of the Environmental Protection Agency sent to all State governors a letter explaining that during the current period of shortages in low-sulphur fuel, the States should not require the burning of such fuels except where necessary to meet the primary standards for the protection of health. This action by the States should permit the desirable substitution of coal for low-sulphur fuel in many instances. I strongly support this policy.

Many State regulatory commissions permit their State utilities to pass on increased fuel costs to the consumer in the form of higher rates, but there are sometimes lags in allowing the costs of environmental control equipment to be passed on in a similar way. Such lags discourage the use of environmental control technology and encourage the use of low-sulphur fuels, most of which are imported.

To increase the incentive for using new environmental technology, I urge all State utility commissions to ensure that utilities receive a rapid and fair return on pollution control equipment, including stack gas cleaning devices and coal gasification processes.

As an additional measure to increase the production and use of coal, I am directing that a new reporting system on national coal production be instituted within the Department of the Interior, and I am asking the Federal Power Commission for regular reports on the use of coal by utilities.

I am also stepping up our spending for research and development in coal, with special emphasis on technology for sulphur removal and the development of low-cost, clean-burning forms of coal.

*Nuclear Energy*

Although our greatest dependence for energy until now has been on fossil fuels such as coal and oil, we must not and we need not continue this heavy reliance in the future. The major alternative to fossil fuel energy for the remainder of this century is nuclear energy.

Our well-established nuclear technology already represents an indispensable source of energy for meeting present needs. At present there are 30 nuclear power plants in operation in the United States; of the new electrical generator capacity contracted for during 1972, 70 percent will be nuclear powered. By 1980, the amount of electricity generated by nuclear reactors will be equivalent to 1.25 billion barrels of oil, or 8 trillion cubic feet of gas. It is estimated that nuclear power will provide more than one-quarter of this country's electrical production by 1985, and over half by the year 2000.

Most nuclear power plants now in operation utilize light water reactors. In the near future, some will use high temperature gas-cooled reactors. These techniques will be supplemented during the next decade by the fast breeder reactor, which will bring about a 30-fold increase in the efficiency with which we utilize our domestic uranium resources. At present, development of the liquid metal fast breeder reactor is our highest priority target for nuclear research and development.

Nuclear power generation has an extraordinary safety record. There has never been a nuclear-related fatality in our civilian atomic energy program. We intend to maintain that record by increasing research and development in reactor safety.

The process of determining the safety and environmental acceptability of nuclear power plants is more vigorous and more open to public participation than for any comparable industrial enterprise. Every effort must be made by the Government and industry to protect public health and safety and to provide satisfactory answers to those with honest concerns about this source of power.

At the same time, we must seek to avoid unreasonable delays in developing nuclear power. They serve only to impose unnecessary costs and aggravate our energy shortages. It is discouraging to know that nuclear facilities capable of generating 27,000 megawatts of electric power which were expected to be operational by 1972 were not completed. To replace that generating capacity we would have to use the equivalent of one-third of the natural gas the country used for generating electricity in 1972. This situation must not continue.

In my first Energy Special Message in 1971, I proposed that utilities prepare and publish long-range plans for the siting of nuclear power plants and transmission lines. This legislation would provide a Federal-State framework for licensing individual plants on the basis of a full and balanced consideration of both environmental and energy needs. The Congress has not acted on that proposal. I am resubmitting that legislation this year with a number of new provisions to simplify licensing, including one to require that the Government act on all completed license applications within 18 months after they are received.

I would also emphasize that the private sector's role in future nuclear development must continue to grow. The Atomic Energy Commission is presently taking steps to provide greater amounts of enriched uranium fuel for the Nation's nuclear power plants. However, this expansion will not fully meet our needs in the 1980's; the Government now looks to private industry to provide the additional capacity that will be required.

Our nuclear technology is a national asset of inestimable value. It is essential that we press forward with its development.

The increasing occurrence of unnecessary delays in the development of energy facilities must be ended if we are to meet our energy needs. To be sure, reasonable safeguards must be vigorously maintained for protection of the public and of our environment. Full public participation and questioning must also be allowed as we decide where new energy facilities are to be built. We need to streamline our governmental procedures for licensing and inspections, reduce overlapping jurisdictions and eliminate confusion generated by the government.

To achieve these ends I am taking several steps. During the coming year we will examine various possibilities to assure that all public and private interests are impartially and expeditiously weighed in all government proceedings for permits, licensing and inspections.

I am again proposing siting legislation to the Congress for electric facilities and for the first time, for deepwater ports. All of my new siting legislation includes provision for simplified licensing at both Federal and State levels. It is vital that the Congress take prompt and favorable action on these proposals.

*Encouraging Domestic Exploration*

Our tax system now provides needed incentives for mineral exploration in the form of percentage depletion allowances and deductions for certain drilling expenses. These provisions do not, however, distinguish between exploration for new reserves and development of existing reserves.

In order to encourage increased exploration, I ask the Congress to extend the investment credit provisions of our present tax law so that a credit will be provided for all exploratory drilling for new oil and gas fields. Under this proposal, a somewhat higher credit would apply for successful exploratory wells than for unsuccessful ones, in order to put an additional premium on results.

The investment credit has proven itself a powerful stimulus to industrial activity. I expect it to be equally effective in the search for new reserves.

## IMPORTING TO MEET OUR ENERGY NEEDS

*Oil Imports*

In order to avert a short-term fuel shortage and to keep fuel costs as low as possible, it will be necessary for us to increase fuel imports. At the same time, in order to reduce our long-term reliance on imports, we must encourage the exploration and development of our domestic oil and the construction of refineries to process it.

The present quota system for oil imports—the Mandatory Oil Import Program—was established at a time when we could produce more oil at home than we were using. By imposing quantitative restrictions on imports, the quota system restricted imports of foreign oil. It also encouraged the development of our domestic petroleum industry in the interest of national security.

Today, however, we are not producing as much oil as we are using, and we must import ever larger amounts to meet our needs.

As a result, the current Mandatory Oil Import Program is of virtually no benefit any longer. Instead, it has the very real potential of aggravating our supply problems, and it denies us the flexibility we need to deal quickly and efficiently with our import requirements. General dissatisfaction with the program and the apparent need for change has led to uncertainty. Under these conditions, there can be little long-range investment planning for new drilling and refinery construction.

Effective today, I am removing by proclamation all existing tariffs on imported crude oil and products. Holders of import licenses will be able to import petroleum duty free. This action will help hold down the cost of energy to the American consumer.

Effective today, I am also suspending direct control over the quantity of crude oil and refined products which can be imported. In place of these controls, I am substituting a license-fee quota system.

Under the new system, present holders of import licenses may import petroleum exempt from fees up to the level of their 1973 quota allocations. For imports in excess of the 1973 level, a fee must be paid by the importer.

This system should achieve several objectives.

First, it should help to meet our immediate energy needs by encouraging importation of foreign oil at the lowest cost to consumers, while also providing incentives for exploration and development of our domestic resources to meet our long-term needs. There will be little paid in fees this year, although all exemptions from fees will be phased out over several years. By gradually increasing fees over the next two and one-half years to a maximum level of one-half cent per gallon for crude oil and one and one-half cents per gallon for all refined products, we should continue to meet our energy needs while encouraging industry to increase its domestic production.

Second, this system should encourage refinery construction in the United States, because the fees are higher for refined products than for crude oil. As an added incentive, crude oil in amounts up to three-fourths of new refining capacity may be imported without being subject to any fees. This special allowance will be available to an oil company during the first five years after it builds or expands its refining capacity.

Third, this system should provide the flexibility we must have to meet short and long-term needs efficiently. We will review the fee level periodically to ensure that we are imposing the lowest fees consistent with our intention to increase domestic production while keeping costs to the consumer at the lowest possible level. We will also make full use of the Oil Import Appeals Board to ensure that the needs of all elements of the petroleum industry are met, particularly those of independent operators who help to maintain market competition.

Fourth, the new system should contribute to our national security. Increased domestic production will leave us less dependent on foreign supplies. At the same time, we will adjust the fees in a manner designed to encourage, to the extent possible, the security of our foreign supplies. Finally, I am directing the Oil Policy Committee to examine incentives aimed at increasing our domestic storage capacity or shut-in production. In this way we will provide buffer stocks to insulate ourselves against a temporary loss of foreign supplies.

*Deepwater Ports*

It is clear that in the foreseeable future, we will have to import oil in large quantities. We should do this as cheaply as we can with minimal damage to the environment. Unfortunately, our present capabilities are inadequate for these purposes.

The answer to this problem lies in deepwater ports which can accommodate those larger ships, providing important economic advantages while reducing the risks of collision and grounding. Recent studies by the Council on Environmental Quality demonstrate that we can expect considerably less pollution if we use fewer but larger tankers and deepwater facilities, as opposed to the many small tankers and conventional facilities which we would otherwise need.

If we do not enlarge our deepwater port capacity, it is clear that both American and foreign companies will expand oil transshipment terminals in the Bahamas and the Canadian Maritime Provinces. From these terminals, oil will be brought to our conventional ports by growing numbers of small and medium size transshipment vessels, thereby increasing the risks of pollution from shipping operations and accidents. At the same time, the United States will lose the jobs and capital that those foreign facilities provide.

Given these considerations, I believe we must move forward with an ambitious program to create new deepwater ports for receiving petroleum imports.

The development of ports has usually been a responsibility of State and local governments and the private sector. However, States cannot issue licenses beyond the three-mile limit. I am therefore proposing legislation to permit the Department of the Interior to issue such licenses. Licensing would be contingent upon full and proper evaluation of environmental impact, and would provide for strict navigation and safety, as well as proper land use requirements. The proposed legislation specifically provides for Federal cooperation with State and local authorities.

## CONSERVING ENERGY

The abundance of America's natural resources has been one of our greatest advantages in the past. But if this abundance encourages us to take our resources for granted, then it may well be a detriment to our future.

Common sense clearly dictates that as we expand the types and sources of energy available to us for the future, we must direct equal attention to conserving the energy available to us today, and we must explore means to limit future growth in energy demand.

We as a nation must develop a national energy conservation ethic. Industry can help by designing products which conserve energy and by using energy more efficiently. All workers and consumers can help by continually saving energy in their day-to-day activities: by turning out lights, tuning up automobiles, reducing the use of air conditioning and heating, and purchasing products which use energy efficiently.

Government at all levels also has an important role to play, both by conserving energy directly, and by providing leadership in energy conservation efforts.

I am directing today that an Office of Energy Conservation be established in the Department of the Interior to coordinate the energy conservation programs which are presently scattered throughout the Federal establishment. This office will conduct research and work with consumer and environmental groups in their efforts to educate consumers on ways to get the greatest return on their energy dollar.

To provide consumers with further information, I am directing the Department of Commerce, working with the Council on Environmental Quality and the Environmental Protection Agency, to develop a voluntary system of energy efficiency labels for major home appliances. These labels should provide data on energy use as well as a rating comparing the product's efficiency to other similar products. In addition, the Environmental Protection Agency will soon release the results of its tests of fuel efficiency in automobiles.

There are other ways, too, in which government can exercise leadership in this field. I urge again, for example, that we allow local officials to use money from Highway Trust Fund for mass transit purposes. Greater reliance on mass transit can do a great deal to help us conserve gasoline.

The Federal Government can also lead by example. The General Services Administration, for instance, is constructing a new Federal office building using advanced energy conservation techniques, with a goal of reducing energy use by 20 percent over typical buildings of the same size. At the same time, the National Bureau of Standards is evaluating energy use in a full-size house within its laboratories. When this evaluation is complete, analytical techniques will be available to help predict energy use for new dwellings. This information, together with the experience gained in the construction and operation of the demonstration Federal building, will assist architects and contractors to design and construct energy-efficient buildings.

Significant steps to upgrade insulation standards on single and multi-family dwellings were taken at my direction in 1971 and 1972, helping to reduce heat loss and otherwise conserve energy in the residential sector. As soon as the results of these important demonstration projects are available, I will direct the Federal Housing Administration to update its insulation standards in light of what we have learned and to consider their possible extension to mobile homes.

Finally, we should recognize that the single most effective means of encouraging energy conservation is to ensure that energy prices reflect their true costs. By eliminating regulations such as the current ceiling on natural gas prices and by ensuring that the costs of adequate environmental controls are equitably allocated, we can move toward more efficient distribution of our resources.

Energy conservation is a national necessity, but I believe that it can be undertaken most effectively on a voluntary basis. If the challenge is ignored, the result will be a danger of increased shortages, increased prices, damage to the environment and the increased possibility that conservation will have to be undertaken by compulsory means in the future. There should be no need for a nation which has always been rich in energy to have to turn to energy rationing. This is a part of the energy challenge which every American can help to meet, and I call upon every American to do his or her part.

## RESEARCH AND DEVELOPMENT

If we are to be certain that the forward thrust of our economy will not be hampered by insufficient energy supplies or by energy supplies that are prohibitively expensive, then we must not continue to be dependent on conventional forms of energy. We must instead make every useful effort through research and development to provide both alternative sources of energy and new technologies for producing and utilizing this energy.

For the short-term future, our research and development strategy will provide technologies to extract and utilize our existing fossil fuels in a manner most compatible with a healthy environment.

In the longer run, from 1985 to the beginning of the next century, we will have more sophisticated development of our fossil fuel resources and on the full development of the Liquid Metal Fast Breeder Reactor. Our efforts for the distant future center on the development of technologies—such as nuclear fusion and solar power—that can provide us with a virtually limitless supply of clean energy.

In my 1971 Energy Special Message to the Congress I outlined a broadly based research and development program. I proposed the expansion of cooperative Government-industry efforts to develop the Liquid Metal Fast Breeder Reactor, coal gasification, and stack gas cleaning systems at the demonstration level. These programs are all progressing well.

My budget for fiscal year 1974 provides for an increase in energy research and development funding of 20 percent over the level of 1973.

My 1974 budget provides for creation of a new central energy fund in the Interior Department to provide additional money for non-nuclear research and development, with the greatest part designated for coal research. This central fund is designed to give us the flexibility we need for rapid exploitation of new, especially promising energy technologies with near-term payoffs.

One of the most promising programs that will be receiving increased funding in fiscal year 1974 is the solvent refined coal process which will produce low-ash, low-sulphur fuels from coal. Altogether, coal research and development and proposed funding is increased by 27 percent.

In addition to increased funding for the Liquid Metal Fast Breeder Reactor, I am asking for greater research and development on reactor safety and radioactive waste disposal, and the production of nuclear fuel.

The waters of the world contain potential fuel—in the form of a special isotope of hydrogen—sufficient to power fusion reactors for thousands of years. Scientists at the Atomic Energy Commission now predict with increasing confidence that we can demonstrate laboratory feasibility of controlled thermonuclear fusion by magnetic confinement in the near future. We have also advanced to the point where some scientists believe the feasibility of laser fusion could be demonstrated within the next several years. I have proposed in my 1974 budget a 35 percent increase in funding for our total fusion research and development effort to accelerate experimental programs and to initiate preliminary reactor design studies.

While we look to breeder reactors to meet our mid-term energy needs, today's commercial power reactors will continue to provide most of our nuclear generating capacity for the balance of this century. Although nuclear reactors have had a remarkable safety record, my 1974 budget provides additional funds to assure that our rapidly growing reliance on nuclear power will not compromise public health and safety. This includes work on systems for safe storage of the radioactive waste which nuclear reactors produce. The Atomic Energy Commission is working on additional improvements in surface storage and will continue to explore the possibility of underground burial for long-term containment of these wastes.

Solar energy holds great promise as a potentially limitless source of clean energy. My new budget triples our solar energy research and development effort to a level of $12 million. A major portion of these funds would be devoted to accelerating the development of commercial systems for heating and cooling buildings.

Research and development funds relating to environmental control technologies would be increased 24 percent in my 1974 budget. This research includes a variety of projects related to stack gas cleaning and includes the construction of a demonstration sulphur dioxide removal plant. In addition, the Atomic Energy Commission and the Environmental Protection Agency will continue to conduct research on the thermal effects of power plants.

While the Federal Government is significantly increasing its commitment to energy research and development, a large share of such research is and should be conducted by the private sector.

I am especially pleased that the electric utilities have recognized the importance of research in meeting the rapidly escalating demand for electrical energy. The recent establishment of the Electric Power Research Institute, which will have a budget in 1974 in excess of $100 million, can help develop technology to meet both load demands and environmental regulations currently challenging the industry.

Historically the electric power industry has allocated a smaller portion of its revenues to research than have most other technology-dependent industries. This pattern has been partly attributable to the reluctance of some State utility commissions to include increased research and development expenditures in utility rate bases. Recently the Federal Power Commission instituted a national rule to allow the recovery of research and development expenditures in rates. State regulatory agencies have followed the FPC's lead and are liberalizing their treatment of research and development expenditures consistent with our changing national energy demands.

I am hopeful that this trend will continue and I urge all State utility commissions to review their regulations regarding research and development expenditures to ensure that the electric utility industry can fully cooperate in a national energy research and development effort.

It is foolish and self-defeating to allocate funds more rapidly than they can be effectively spent. At the same time, we must carefully monitor our progress and our needs to ensure that our funding is adequate. When additional funds are found to be essential, I shall do everything I can to see that they are provided.


## INTERNATIONAL COOPERATION

The energy challenge confronts every nation. Where there is such a community of interest, there is both a cause and a basis for cooperative action.

Today, the United States is involved in a number of cooperative, international efforts. We have joined with the other 22 member-nations of the Organization for Economic Cooperation and Development to produce a comprehensive report on long-term problems and to develop an agreement for sharing oil in times of acute shortages. The European Economic Community has already discussed the need for cooperative efforts and is preparing recommendations for a Community energy policy. We have expressed a desire to work together with them in this effort.

We have also agreed with the Soviet Union to pursue joint research in magnetohydrodynamics (MHD), a highly efficient process for generating electricity, and to exchange information on fusion, fission, the generation of electricity, transmission and pollution control technology. These efforts should be a model for joint research efforts with other countries. Additionally, American companies are looking into the possibility of joint projects with the Soviet Union to develop natural resources for the benefit of both nations.

I have also instructed the Department of State, in coordination with the Atomic Energy Commission, other appropriate Government agencies, and the Congress to move rapidly in developing a program of international cooperation in research and development on new forms of energy and in developing international mechanisms for dealing with energy questions in times of critical shortages.

I believe the energy challenge provides an important opportunity for nations to pursue vital objectives through peaceful cooperation. No chance should be lost to strengthen the structure of peace we are seeking to build in the world, and few issues provide us with as good an opportunity to demonstrate that there is more to be gained in pursuing our national interests through mutual cooperation than through destructive competition or dangerous confrontation.

*Federal Energy Organization*

If we are to meet the energy challenge, the current fragmented organization of energy-related activities in the executive branch of the Government must be overhauled.

In 1971, I proposed legislation to consolidate Federal energy-related activities within a new Department of Natural Resources. The 92nd Congress did not act on this proposal. In the interim I have created a new post of Counsellor to the President on Natural Resources to assist in the policy coordination in the natural resources field.

Today I am taking executive action specifically to improve the Federal organization of energy activities.

I have directed the Secretary of the Interior to strengthen his Department's organization of energy activities in several ways.

— The responsibilities of the new Assistant Secretary for Energy and Minerals will be expanded to incorporate all departmental energy activities;
— The Department is to develop a capacity for gathering and analysis of energy data;
— An Office of Energy Conservation is being created to seek means for reducing demands for energy;
— The Department of the Interior has also strengthened its capabilities for overseeing and coordinating a broader range of energy research and development.

By Executive order, I have placed authority in the Department of the Treasury for directing the Oil Policy Committee. That Committee coordinates the oil import program and makes recommendations to me for changes in that program. The Deputy Secretary of the Treasury has been designated Chairman of that Committee.

Through a second Executive order, effective today, I am strengthening the capabilities of the Executive Office of the President to deal with top level energy policy matters by establishing a special energy committee composed of three of my principal advisors. The order also reaffirms the appointment of a Special Consultant, who heads an energy staff in the Office of the President.

Additionally, a new division of Energy and Science is being established within the Office of Management and Budget.

While these executive actions will help, more fundamental reorganization is needed. To meet this need, I shall propose legislation to establish a Department of Energy and Natural Resources (DENR) building on the legislation I submitted in 1971, with heightened emphasis on energy programs.

This new Department would provide leadership across the entire range of national energy. It would, in short, be responsible for administering the national energy policy detailed in this message.

## CONCLUSION

Nations succeed only as they are able to respond to challenge, and to change when circumstances and opportunities require change.

When the first settlers came to America, they found a land of untold natural wealth, and this became the cornerstone of the most prosperous nation in the world. As we have grown in population, in prosperity, in industrial capacity, in all those indices that reflect the constant upward thrust in the American standard of living, the demands on our natural resources have also grown.

Today, the energy resources which have fueled so much of our national growth are not sufficiently developed to meet the constantly increasing demands which have been placed upon them. The time has come to change the way we meet these demands. The challenge facing us represents one of the great opportunities of our time—an opportunity to create an even stronger domestic economy, a cleaner environment, and a better life for all our people.

The proposals I am submitting and the actions I will take can give us the tools to do this important job.

The need for action is urgent. I hope the Congress will act with dispatch on the proposals I am submitting. But in the final analysis, the ultimate responsibility does not rest merely with the Congress or with this Administration. It rests with all of us— with government, with industry and with the individual citizen.

Whenever we have been confronted with great national challenges in the past, the American people have done their duty. I am confident we shall do so now.

RICHARD NIXON

THE WHITE HOUSE,
April 18, 1973.

# Appendix B

# Text of President Nixon's Statement on Energy June 29, 1973

One of the most critical problems on America's agenda today is to meet our vital energy needs.

Two months ago I announced a comprehensive program to move us forward in that effort. Today I am taking the following additional measures:

First, I am appointing John A. Love, Governor of Colorado, to direct a new energy office that will be responsible for formulating and coordinating energy policies at the Presidential level.

Second, I am asking the Congress to create a new Cabinet-level department devoted to energy and natural resources and a new independent Energy Research and Development Administration.

Third, I am initiating a $10 billion program for research and development in the energy field, which will extend over the next five years.

Finally, I am launching a conservation drive to reduce anticipated personal consumption of energy resources across the Nation by 5 percent over the next twelve months. The Federal Government will take the lead in this effort, by reducing its anticipated consumption by 7 percent during this same period.

America faces a serious energy problem. While we have only 6 percent of the world's population, we consume one-third of the world's energy output. The supply of domestic energy resources available to us is not keeping pace with our ever-growing demand, and unless we act swiftly and effectively, we could face a genuine energy crisis in the foreseeable future.

*Progress Since April*

On April 18, I submitted a message to the Congress discussing the energy challenge and the steps necessary to meet it. That message emphasized that as we work to conserve our energy demands, we must also undertake an intensive effort to expand our energy supplies. I am happy to report that many of these steps are already underway, and that they are proving effective.

— At least eight oil companies have made firm decisions to undertake significant refinery construction projects. Within the next three years these projects will increase refinery capacity by more than 1.5 million barrels daily—a 10 percent increase over existing capacity.

— We have announced and carried out a voluntary oil allocation program to help provide farmers and essential government and health services, as well as independent refiners and marketers, with an equitable share of available petroleum.

— A great deal of oil from the Outer Continental Shelf and other Federal lands, which has traditionally been retained by the producers, has been allocated to small independent refiners to augment their present supplies. That figure has already reached 100 thousand barrels of oil per day and will increase to 160 thousand by mid-August.

— The Council on Environmental Quality has begun a study of the environmental impact of drilling on the Atlantic Outer Continental Shelf and in the Gulf of Alaska. The study is scheduled for completion by next spring.

—The Senate Committee on Interior and Insular Affairs has reported out legislation which would finally permit the construction of an Alaskan pipeline. Legislation will shortly be reported out in the House of Representatives. Since construction of that pipeline would provide two million barrels of domestic oil a day, I again urge that the Congress give swift approval to this legislation.

—The Office of Energy Conservation and the Office of Energy Data and Analysis have been established at the Department of the Interior. Although not yet fully staffed, they are now beginning to provide information we must have to proceed with our developing energy policy.

—The Commerce Department has proposed regulations covering the labeling of household appliances so that consumers can make comparisons of the efficiency with which the appliances consume energy.

—The Environmental Protection Agency has published information on gasoline mileage for 1973 automobiles.

—The Department of State is taking steps to consult with the major oil-producing nations to develop the cooperative arrangements needed to ensure adequate and stable sources of oil in the future. We are also working closely with the other major oil-consuming nations in studying ways of meeting growing world demand for energy supplies. These include emergency sharing arrangements, as well as stockpile and rationing programs which might lead to more coordinated policies for meeting oil supply shortages should they occur in the future.

Several of the steps which I announced in April were in the form of legislative proposals which will help to increase energy supplies. They called for the Alaskan pipeline, competitive pricing of natural gas, licensing of deepwater ports, streamlining of powerplant siting, and a rational framework for controls over surface mining. Only the pipeline request has been finally acted on in committee. I hope the Congress will now act quickly and favorably on my other requests.

These steps are a beginning. But they are only a beginning.

## REORGANIZATION

The acquisition, distribution, and consumption of energy resources have become increasingly complex and increasingly critical to the functioning of our economy and our society. But the organization of the Federal Government to meet its responsibilities for energy and other natural resource policies has not changed to meet the new demands. The Federal Government cannot effectively meet its obligations in these areas under the present organizational structures, and the time has come to change them.

### Energy Policy Office

Effective immediately, the duties of the Special Energy Committee and National Energy Office which I set up 2 months ago to advise and assist in the preliminary organizational phases of the Federal response to the energy challenge will be combined in an expanded Energy Policy Office within the Executive Office of the President. This office will be responsible for the formulation and coordination of energy policies at the Presidential level.

This office will be headed by Governor Love, who will be an Assistant to the President as well as Director of the Energy Policy Office. He will spend full time on this assignment and will report directly to me. My Special Consultant on energy matters, Charles DiBona, will continue in his present advisory capacity, working within the new office.

## Department of Energy and Natural Resources

Two years ago I sent to the Congress my proposals for a sweeping reorganization of executive departments and independent agencies to provide an executive branch structure more responsive to the basic goals of public policy. One of those proposals called for a Department of Natural Resources.

During the time these proposals have been receiving the consideration of the Congress, my Administration has continued to refine and improve them. It has become increasingly obvious that reorganization is imperative, and nowhere more clearly so than in the areas of natural resources and related energy matters.

I am therefore proposing today the establishment of a new Cabinet-level Department of Energy and Natural Resources, responsible for the balanced utilization and conservation of America's energy and natural resources.

The Department of Energy and Natural Resources would take charge of all of the present activities of the Department of the Interior, except the Office of Coal Research and certain other energy research and development programs, which would be transferred to a new Energy Research and Development Administration. It would also assume the responsibilities of the Forest Service and certain water resources activities of the Soil Conservation Service from the Department of Agriculture; the planning and funding of the civil functions of the Army Corps of Engineers; the duties of the National Oceanic and Atmospheric Administration of the Department of Commerce, the uranium and thorium assessment functions of the Atomic Energy Commission, the functions of the Interagency Water Resources Council, and gas pipeline safety functions of the Department of Transportation.

## Energy Research and Development Administration

I am further proposing to the Congress that we create an Energy Research and Development Administration.

The new Administration would have central responsibility for the planning, management and conduct of the Government's energy research and development and for working with industry so that promising new technologies can be developed and put promptly to work. The new Administration would be organized to give significant new emphasis to fossil fuels and potential new forms of energy, while also assuring continued progress in developing nuclear power.

In order to create the new Administration, the present functions of the Atomic Energy Commission, except those pertaining to licensing and related regulatory responsibilities, would be transferred to it as would most of the energy research and development programs of the Department of Interior. The scientific and technological resources of the AEC should provide a solid foundation for building a well-conceived and well-executed effort.

Under my proposal, the five-member organization of the AEC would be retained to provide direction for a separate and renamed Nuclear Energy Commission which would carry on the important licensing and regulatory activities now within the AEC. In addition, I have asked that a comprehensive study be undertaken, in full consultation with the Congress, to determine the best way to organize all energy-related regulatory activities of the Government.

## RESEARCH AND DEVELOPMENT

While we must rely on conventional forms of fuel to meet our immediate energy needs, it is clear that the answer to our long-term needs lies in developing new forms of energy.

With this necessity in mind, I am taking three steps immediately to enlarge our Federal energy research and development efforts.

First, I am initiating a Federal energy research and development effort of $10 billion over a five-year period, beginning in fiscal year 1975. To give impetus to this drive, I am directing that an additional $100 million in fiscal year 1974 be devoted to the acceleration of certain existing projects and the initiation of new projects in a number of critical research and development areas. At least one-half of the funding for the new initiatives for this coming fiscal year will be devoted to coal research and development with emphasis on producing clean liquid fuels from coal, improving mining techniques to increase coal mining safety and productivity, accelerating our coal gasification program and developing improved combustion systems. The remainder of the $100 million will be for research and development projects on advanced energy conversion systems, environmental control, geothermal steam, conservation, and gas-cooled nuclear reactors. While it is essential that we maintain the present budget ceiling for fiscal year 1974, these vital programs must and can be funded within that ceiling.

Second, I am directing the Chairman of the Atomic Energy Commission to undertake an immediate review of Federal and private energy research and development activities, under the general direction of the Energy Policy Office, and to recommend an integrated energy research and development program for the Nation. This program should encourage and actively involve industry in cooperative efforts to develop and demonstrate new technologies that will permit better use of our energy resources. I am also directing the Chairman, in consultation with the Department of the Interior and other agencies, to recommend by September 1 of this year specific projects to which the additional $100 million would be allocated during fiscal year 1974. By December 1 of this year, I am asking for her recommendations for energy research and development programs which should be included in my fiscal year 1975 budget.

Third, I am establishing an Energy Research and Development Advisory Council reporting to the Energy Policy Office, to be composed of leading experts in various areas of energy research and development from outside the Government.

I feel that these steps will greatly improve and expand our current energy research and development effort and will ensure the development of technologies vital to meeting our future energy needs.

## CONSERVATION

### The Federal Effort

In my Energy Message of April 18, I announced preliminary steps to conserve America's fuel supplies. I said at that time that while energy conservation is a national necessity, conservation efforts could be undertaken on a voluntary basis. I still believe this.

However, public persuasion alone is not sufficient to the challenge confronting us. The Federal Government is the largest consumer of energy in the country and, as such, it has its own unique role to play in reducing energy consumption and thus setting an example for all consumers.

Effective today, I am therefore ordering the Federal Government to achieve a seven percent reduction in its anticipated energy consumption over the next 12 months.

I have directed the heads of all Cabinet departments and other Federal agencies to report by July 31 on the specific steps they will take to meet this target. Secretary Morton will be responsible for monitoring agency efforts and reporting their progress to me.

These conservation measures are to be designed to ensure that no vital services are impaired nor the proper functioning of these departments and agencies curtailed. Exceptions will be permitted only in unique circumstances, such as the program of uranium enrichment at the AEC where a substantial reduction in energy consumption would have a detrimental effect on our efforts to provide new forms of energy.

While the precise means of conserving energy will be left to the discretion of Cabinet and agency heads, I am directing that conservation efforts include the following measures:

—Reduction in the level of air conditioning of all Federal office buildings throughout the summer.

—Reduction in the number of official trips taken by Federal employees.

—Purchase or leasing of automobiles and other vehicles which provide good gasoline mileage.

Each department and agency is expected to review all of its activities to determine how its own demands might be reduced. The Department of Defense, the largest single consumer of energy within the executive branch, has already examined its activities and has taken steps to reduce its energy demands by 10 percent over last year—steps which will in no way jeopardize our military preparedness.

### Conservation in the Private Sector

I am also directing all departments and agencies to work closely with Secretary Morton and the Office of Energy Conservation in the development of long-term energy conservation plans and recommendations for both the private and the public sector.

At my request, the Secretary of the Interior, the Secretary of Commerce and Governor Love are to meet with representatives of American industry to discuss ways of cutting back on unnecessary consumption of energy and to urge their active participation in the conservation effort.

Further, I have directed the Secretary of Transportation to work with the Nation's airlines, the Civil Aeronautics Board, and the Federal Aviation Administration to reduce flight speeds, and, where possible, the frequency of commercial airline flights. This effort is now underway. By effecting only a small reduction in speeds and flights, it is possible to achieve significant reductions in energy consumption.

*Placing the Challenge in Perspective*

As these measures cover a broad range of activities in the public and private sectors, I want to put both the problem and the proposed conservation measures into perspective. We all need to understand the dimensions of the challenge, as well as the significance of the role every single American has to play in meeting it.

The Department of the Interior estimates that under the conditions of current usage, our available supply of gasoline this summer could fall short of demand by one or two percent and possibly as much as five percent should the most adverse conditions prevail. To overcome this potential shortage, and to reduce pressure on supplies of other energy resources, I am suggesting that a reasonable and attainable national goal is to reduce anticipated energy use by individual consumers by five percent.

We can achieve this goal by making very small alterations in our present living habits, for steps such as those we are taking at the Federal level can be taken with equal effectiveness by private individuals. We need not sacrifice any activities vital to our economy or to our well-being as a people.

Raising the thermostat of an air conditioner by just 4 degrees, for instance, will result in a saving of an estimated 15-20 percent in its use of electricity.

Just as the Government can obtain energy efficient automobiles, private citizens can do the same. Nearly three-quarters of the gasoline used in America is consumed by automobiles.

Those who drive automobiles can also assist by driving more slowly. A car travelling 50 miles per hour uses 20 to 25 percent less gasoline per mile than the same car travelling 70 miles per hour. Carpooling and using public transportation will result in further fuel savings.

In order to help reduce driving speeds, I am today taking the additional step of writing to each of the Nation's Governors, asking them to work with their State legislatures to reduce highway speed limits in a manner consistent with safety and efficiency, as well as with energy needs.

I also continue to urge the Congress to pass highway-mass transit legislation which would provide States and localities flexibility to choose between capital investment in highways or mass transit. Diversion of some commuter traffic from single occupant automobiles to mass transit will result in significant energy and environmental benefits, and at the same time, permit the highways to be operated in the efficient manner for which they were designed.

Energy conservation is not just sound policy for the country, it is also good economics for the consumer.

Changing to a more efficient automobile, for example, could produce savings of as much as one thousand gallons of gas in the course of a year. A savings of one thousand gallons of gas equals a personal savings of approximately $400.

Cutting down on air conditioning and heating, of course, also cuts down on the family gas or electric or oil bill.

Actions to reduce the rate of growth in energy demands will also improve our ability to protect and improve the quality of our environment.

The conservation of existing energy resources is not a proposal; it is a necessity. It is a requirement that will remain with us indefinitely, and it is for this reason that I believe that the American people must develop an energy conservation ethic.

As a matter of simple prudence and common sense, we must not waste our resources, however abundant they may seem. To do otherwise, in a world of finite resources, reflects adversely upon what we are as a people and a Nation.

## CONCLUSION

We face a challenge in meeting our energy needs. In the past, the American people have viewed challenges as an opportunity to improve our Nation, and to move forward. The steps I have outlined above are not meant to be conclusive. They are part of the ongoing process.

I urge the Congress to act with due concern for our energy needs by rapid consideration of all of my legislative proposals in this field, especially my request to clear the way for the Alaskan pipeline.

Over the coming years it is essential that we increase our supplies of energy.

I urge the members of the Federal Government to play their role in meeting the spirit and the letter of my energy-conservation directives.

I urge private industry to respond with all the imagination and resourcefulness that has made this Nation the richest on earth.

But the final question of whether we can avoid an energy crisis will be determined by the response of the American people to their country's needs. In the past, whenever we have been faced with real challenges, the American people have joined together to share in the common interest.

I am confident we will do so now.